Exploring Grief

As modern society's routine sequestration of death and grief is increasingly replaced by late-modern society's growing concern with existential issues and emotionality, this book explores grief as a social emotion, bringing together contributions from scholars across the social sciences and humanities to examine its social and cultural aspects. Thematically organized in order to consider the historical changes in our understanding of grief, literary treatments of grief, contemporary forms of grief and grief as a perspective from which to engage in critique of society, it provides insights into the sociality of grief and will appeal to scholars of sociology, social theory and cultural studies with interests in the emotions and social pathologies.

Michael Hviid Jacobsen is Professor of Sociology at Aalborg University, Denmark. He is the editor of *The Poetics of Crime* and *Postmortal Society* and *Critical and Cultural Interactionism* and coeditor of *The Sociology of Zygmunt Bauman, Encountering the Everyday, The Transformation of Modernity, Utopia: Social Theory and the Future, Liquid Criminology, Imaginative Methodologies: The Poetic Imagination in the Social Sciences* and *Towards a Criminology of Emotions.*

Anders Petersen is Associate Professor of Sociology at Aalborg University, Denmark. He is the coauthor of *Late Modern Subjectivity and its Discontents* and the coeditor of *The Social Pathologies of Contemporary Civilization, Imaginative Methodologies: The Poetic Imagination in the Social Sciences* and *Critical Happiness Studies.*

Exploring Grief

Towards a Sociology of Sorrow

Edited by
Michael Hviid Jacobsen and
Anders Petersen

Routledge
Taylor & Francis Group

LONDON AND NEW YORK

First published 2020 by Routledge

2 Park Square, Milton Park, Abingdon, Oxon, OX14 4RN
605 Third Avenue, New York, NY 10017

Routledge is an imprint of the Taylor & Francis Group, an informa business

First issued in paperback 2020

British Library Cataloguing-in-Publication Data
A catalogue record for this book is available from the British Library

Library of Congress Cataloging-in-Publication Data
A catalog record for this book has been requested

ISBN: 978-0-367-19246-4 (hbk)
ISBN: 978-0-367-77680-0 (pbk)

Typeset in Times New Roman
by Apex CoVantage, LLC

In immortal friendship and loving memory of Keith Tester
(1960–2019) – you are missed!

Contents

Contributors

Fiona A. Anderau is an undergraduate student at the University of Zürich, Switzerland, studying sociology as her major and English as her minor. Her research interests include English literature, popular culture, digital sociology, sociology of emotions, gender and sexuality.

Kjersti Bale is Professor of comparative literature at the University of Oslo, Norway. Her research interests include melancholy, literature and emotion, literary theory, aesthetics, the essay, literature and ethics.

Hilde Bondevik is Professor of medical humanities at the University of Oslo, Norway. Her research interests include history of diagnosis, medicalization, literature and medicine, gender and health and critical studies of cancer survivorship.

Tashel C. Bordere is Assistant Professor of human development and family science at the University of Missouri-Columbia, United States. Her research interests include African American youth and young adult bereavement and adjustment to loss, social justice issues in loss, qualitative methods and culturally responsive programming.

Douglas J. Davies is Fellow of The British Academy and Professor in the study of religion and Director of The Centre for Death and Life Studies at Durham University, United Kingdom. He has published widely on matters of funerary ritual, emotions, Mormonism and relations between anthropology and theology.

Allan V. Horwitz is Board of Governors Distinguished Professor Emeritus of sociology at Rutgers University, United States. Most of his recent research examines the historical portrayal of various mental illnesses including depression, anxiety and PTSD.

Michael Hviid Jacobsen is Professor of sociology at Aalborg University, Denmark. He has published extensively on topics such as death and dying, palliative care, emotions, utopia, critique, deviance, interactionism, ethics, criminology, qualitative research and social theory.

Nina R. Jakoby is PhD and *Privatdozentin* (PD) at the Institute of Sociology at the University of Zurich, Switzerland, and also a project manager at the Office for Gender Equality (University of Zurich). Her research interests include sociology of emotions, death and bereavement, gender and organizations.

Patricia Jalland is Professor Emeritus of history at the Australian National University, Canberra, Australia. Her research interests include social and cultural history of death, grief and mourning in Britain and Australia, social history of old age in Australia and history of women and the family in Britain and Australia.

Mary Ellen Macdonald is a medical anthropologist and is Associate Professor at McGill University, Montreal, Canada. Her research interests focus on how social, cultural and political forces intersect to both produce and respond to forms of vulnerability within Canadian society.

Anders Petersen is Associate Professor of sociology at Aalborg University, Denmark. He has published extensively on topics such as diagnostic culture, social pathologies, social critique, qualitative research and social theory.

Christian Riegel is Professor of English at Campion College, University of Regina, and Director of the Interactive Media, Poetics, Aesthetics, Cognition, and Technology Lab. His research interests include the literary work of mourning, textuality and memorializing, disability studies and technology development, Canadian literature and writing in English post-1970.

Paul C. Rosenblatt is Professor Emeritus of family social science at the University of Minnesota, United States. His research interests include couple and family systems, qualitative research, individual and family grief, cultural influences on families and researchers, the impact of oppressive systems on families and family theory.

Jack Santino is Professor in the department of popular culture at Bowling Green State University, United States. His research interests include the intersection of politics and protest with carnival, ritual and demonstrations; the public memorialization of death; and traditional and emergent celebrations.

Peter N. Stearns is University Professor of history at George Mason University, United States. He works extensively on the modern history of emotions and also on broader cultural changes associated with death and dying.

Preface and acknowledgements

In many ways, life can be described as tragedy waiting to happen. Even though this may sound excessively gloomy, no life can be lived without the experience of loss and, at times, the traumatizing emotional impact of such losses. Grief is one of the emotions that most people will eventually come to experience – when a loved one dies or when they have to deal with the so-called 'anticipatory grief' associated with their own imminent death or the passing of others. A life without grief is almost unimaginable. Grief is an integral part of life – and life is a lesson in learning to live with and cope with grief. Despite the fact that we often seem to think that grief is something that internally (and thus invisibly) affects the grieving individual, grief is for all practical intents and purposes a social and cultural phenomenon shaped by the many different historical and cultural ways in which we conduct, evaluate and understand our lives. This book is therefore a contribution to an understanding of grief as a historically, culturally and socially complex and diversified emotion.

This book is the outcome of many years of dealing with research topics that in different ways relate to the topic of grief such as death, palliative care, diagnostic cultures, emotions, psychiatric illness and deviance. This book is also a joint venture between academics from somewhat different cultural backgrounds and neighbouring academic disciplines. Therefore, we would, first and foremost, like to extend our gratitude to the many contributors to this volume. Each in their way, with their individual insights and experiences, they have given voice to the multifaceted nature of grief. Moreover, we also want to thank our two editors at Routledge, Neil Jordan and Alice Salt, for their always accommodating, friendly and supportive approach to their editorial responsibilities. Finally, it is our hope with this book to promote some of the more historical, social and cultural perspectives on grief as a human emotion that – perhaps especially in these years – often seems to drown in discussions about symptoms, trajectories, diagnoses and treatment regimes.

Aalborg University, spring 2019
Michael Hviid Jacobsen and Anders Petersen

Introduction

Towards a sociology of grief – historical, cultural and social explorations of grief as an emotion

Michael Hviid Jacobsen and Anders Petersen

Introduction

There is nothing as unfathomable and painful as the loss of a loved one, another irreplaceable human being, leaving an unfillable void in one's life. No life can be fully lived that does not – at some point and in some shape or form – need to come to terms with the experience of loss and even the loss of another loved human being. In this way, life can be defined as loss waiting to happen. Although this might sound excessively dramatic and depressing, this is nevertheless the way of all life. Since death is and in all probability remains an integral part of human life, grief is and remains an inescapable response to loss. Grief is thus something that we will sooner or later have to expect and accept as becoming a part of our emotional experiences. It is almost like a non-negotiable clause inscribed in life from the very beginning that we will eventually have to experience grief.

Grief is an emotion that is first and foremost associated with the experience of loss, and even though one can semantically discuss the intricate differences between commonly used and seemingly synonymous words such as 'grief', 'mourning', 'bereavement' and 'sorrow' (in Danish, for example, we only use *sorg* to cover all these closely associated terms), they all in each their way relate to the experience of loss. Whereas 'sorrow' is a general word covering experiences of loss or sadness that may or may not relate specifically to death, 'grief' is often used to describe the emotional reactions following or at times occurring prior to death (as in 'anticipatory grief'), 'mourning' is used to characterize the behavioural aspects of experiencing grief (such as performing rituals and mourning practices) and finally 'bereavement' – a term often used more in clinical-academic contexts – refers to the objective/formal state of having experienced loss (e.g., being 'recently bereaved'). Obviously, there are many different ways to conceptualize and use these terms in ordinary language as well as in academic contexts, and their interrelationships and conceptual boundaries are often framed in a variety of specific and indeed also different ways (see, e.g., Sprang and McNeil 1995:5; Walter 1999:xv; Jakoby 2012:680–681). We already here need to stress that in this book we will be using all of these words, at times even interchangeably, because they each in their way can help us to understand different historical, cultural and social aspects and dimensions of experiencing death and loss.

We may grieve the loss of many different things in life – the experience of a romantic breakup, the bankruptcy of a family business, the dream of a career that never came true, a favourite football team losing an important cup final and so on. However, grief is most commonly perceived as a uniquely human response that is related specifically to the permanent and irretrievable loss of another human being (Petersen and Jacobsen 2018). However, as this book also covers, the concept of grief can also relate to the loss of non-human companions. Hence, loss is a very diversified and multifaceted human experience (Jakoby 2015) of which death, and the grieving after a death, is but one specific case. Research has been conducted showing that animals such as elephants, dolphins and a number of other species may behave in manners following the death of a fellow creature that in many ways seem to resemble the human response to death. We do not wish here to venture into a detailed debate or provide an in-depth comparison of the differences and similarities between animal and human ways of reacting to loss. However, we do believe that grief as an emotional response – as the chapters in this book will also show – is a historically, culturally and socially inscribed emotion. Even though grief is a universal human experience, since all known cultures and societies have mourned the passing of people, *the way* we grieve differs quite considerably. Hence history, culture, society – and perhaps even the economy – are all important factors in understanding the why, how, when, where, how long and about whom we grieve. There are therefore certain socially and culturally sanctioned 'feeling rules' at work regarding how and whom we grieve (see, e.g., Hochschild 1983; Butler 2016). Moreover, we do think it important to propose that grief is an emotion that relates specifically to the experience of death. There is no doubt that it can indeed be pretty painful to see one's favourite team lose a cup final or to experience the breakup of one's longtime sweetheart; however, it is difficult to meaningfully compare the emotional intensity, duration and depths of such events to the irredeemable loss of a loved one – a loved one who has been a more or less indispensable and irreplaceable part of one's life – through death. The cup final may perhaps be won next season and the once so beloved girlfriend may in time be substituted by another. In this way, death and grief are interlocked in an eternal embrace. Even though it is almost impossible, no matter how hard one tries (and perhaps also in the end undesirable), to escape the experience of grief, we may all – as individuals, families, social, national and cultural groups – try to discover our own ways of learning how to deal with it. As the Chinese proverb goes: 'You cannot prevent the birds of sorrow from flying over your head, but you can prevent them from building a nest in your hair'. Grief is thus an inherent part of the human condition and of the hopes and expectations that each of us must hold to our future experiences. Life *is* grief waiting to happen. But how we understand grief, how we comprehend the norms and social rules surrounding grief, how we display it, how we sanction it and how we deal with it differs quite considerably from historical epoch to epoch, from culture to culture and from society to society. This is exactly the reason why we need a sociology of sorrow, a sociology that specifically – without neglecting the individual aspects – emphasizes the historical, social, cultural and societal dimensions of grief.

In the remainder of this Introduction, we want to provide an initial and admittedly rather general framework allowing us to decipher, analyze and discuss the many different and specific facets of grief as a historical, cultural and social emotion in the chapters to come.

Grief in history – grief as history

Life has a history. Even death has a history. Obviously, grief also has a history. In fact, all emotions have histories. Hence our conception of grief does not stand still. In the lives of individuals as well as in the history of society and culture, our understanding of grief changes over time. We therefore need to understand grief as a historical phenomenon. As English writer C. S. Lewis – in an ill-concealed critique of the, at the time, prevalent psychoanalytical theories of stages in grief – observed in the autobiographical reflections on his experience with grief: 'I thought I could describe a *state*; make a map of sorrow. Sorrow, however, turns out to be not a state but a process. It needs not a map but a history' (Lewis 1961/1984:55, original emphasis). Grief has a personal as well as a social history. The personal history of grief has to do with the way the emotional turbulence of loss of a loved one reverberates throughout an individual's life with fluctuating waves of intensity. The social history of grief has to do with how society – with its traditions, norms, values and feeling rules – shapes the way the experience and expression of grief is made possible. Presumably, philosopher G.W.F. Hegel once insisted that world history is the record of what man does with death (Whaley 1981:1). Since death and grief are so closely interconnected, one might therefore also claim that world history is the record of what man does with grief. Since people have been dying since the beginning of time, their deaths have also been mourned and commemorated in ways that were rooted in and characteristic of the society and culture in which they took place. Looking at the development of death and mourning rituals throughout history and across cultures, one will discover that it has been bountifully diversified, yet there are also some common developmental traits allowing for comparison (see, e.g., Ariès 1981, 1985; Davey 1890/2013; Kellehear 2007; Kerrigan 2007; Stearns 2007).

A useful place to start out when considering at least the most recent history of grief is in the work by Geoffrey Gorer. Gorer, who was trained as an anthropologist and amongst other topics wrote about cultural anthropology, American national character and the Marquis de Sade (and who was a friend of George Orwell), in his pioneering book *Death, Grief and Mourning*, from 1965 – based on recollections of some of his own childhood experiences with death and mourning – provided some important insights into the transformation of grief from the 19th century and onwards. It was Gorer's contention that grief had gradually replaced sex as the major taboo in the 20th-century Western world. Taking us back to the beginning of the 20th century, Gorer's first vivid memory of observing grief was from when he was 5 years old and Edward VII died. At the time it was customary for mourners to wear black clothes, and Gorer recalled how 'this mass of black-garbed humanity struck me as a most depressing sight' (Gorer 1965:xv).

This was a period when grief took time and when widows and widowers were expected to follow the etiquette of quite comprehensive and time-consuming mourning rituals.

Gorer's second childhood recollection of death and grief was of a more personal nature. His father had gone missing when the Lusitania was sunk in 1915, and after several days of anxious waiting, it was finally confirmed that his father had not survived. He had died heroically, given up his seat in a lifeboat and his life belt to two women who both survived. Gorer remembered that in the time following the confirmation of his father's death, he would wear black ties and have bands of crêpe sown on the sleeves of his suits in order publicly to show his loss. During World War I, the public display of grief persisted with the all too familiar sight of widows dressed in full black garments and veils parading the streets. However, it was Gorer's contention that in the aftermath of World War I, these traditional and extensive mourning rituals and customs, rooted as they were in a Victorian and Romantic culture celebrating death and cultivating mourning, gradually began to disappear and were replaced by more subdued and less publicly visible expressions of grief (Jalland 1999). With the unimaginable mass deaths of World War II, the topics of death and mourning slowly but surely became something not talked about and certainly not displayed in public. Hence in a much-cited article from 1955 featured in *Encounter*, Gorer provocatively claimed that a certain prudery had begun to surround the topic of death, and he insisted that death had thus become pornographic (Gorer 1955). So, whereas the taboo on sex had gradually been lifted, a new taboo on death and dying had been imposed. As a consequence of this development, grief was also seen as something inappropriate to share openly with others, because it was regarded as a sort of emotional masturbation that should for all practical purposes be kept behind closed doors. The social ban on and social isolation associated with death and grief began to sneak in.

The last piece of personal experience with grief provided by Gorer relates to the early 1960s when his younger brother Peter – who had himself lost his first wife to tuberculosis towards the end of the war and had suffered from a deep sense of loss – passed away. He was diagnosed with advanced and incurable cancer but was until the very end kept in the dark about the severity of his situation. Gorer discussed his brother's situation with a friend and doctor, and they decided that only Peter's wife, Elizabeth, was to be informed about her husband's predicament. In a memoir written about Peter's life and career (he was in fact a brilliant and internationally renowned immunologist and pathologist), it was – perhaps quite fitting for the time – observed how the deep secrecy surrounding his imminent death was 'wisely and skilfully withheld from him' (Medawar 1961:106). After Gorer's brother died, his sister-in-law suffered from social isolation, despair and depression, and even though she did not publicly show off her status as recently bereaved, she was nevertheless treated by those around her as if she were a social leper. Gorer remarked that 'only if she [Elizabeth] acted as though nothing of consequence had happened was she again socially acceptable' (Gorer 1965:xxxii), and as he thus noted in his conclusion, summarizing the status of grief and mourning rituals in modern society, 'giving way to grief is stigmatized as morbid, unhealthy, demoralizing' (Gorer 1965:130). Obviously, one should always be wary of taking such personal or private experience as historical evidence. However, many other scholars and researchers testifying to the tabooed, denied, sequestered and repressed fate of death and grief in the latter part of the 20th century have since corroborated what Gorer described.

When death during the age of modernity increasingly became, in the apt words of Polish sociologist Zygmunt Bauman (1992), the 'scandal of reason', it is therefore perhaps unsurprising that grief simultaneously became an embarrassment and something to be shunned. This view of death and grief has also been corroborated by French historian Philippe Ariès, who described the emotional state of affairs regarding death and grief in the mid-20th century in the following powerful and provocative way:

> One must avoid – no longer for the sake of the dying person, but for society's sake, for the sake of those close to the dying person – the disturbance and the overly strong and unbearable emotion caused by the ugliness of dying and by the very presence of death in the midst of a happy life, for it is henceforth given that life is always happy or should always seem to be so.
>
> (Ariès 1974a:87)

Grief (also the so-called anticipatory grief) was thus seen as an offence to the idea (or illusion) of a happy and carefree life and as a party pooper. All in all, Gorer provided useful insight into the way in which our understanding of and approach to death and grief has changed quite dramatically throughout the past century – a view that has since been empirically corroborated by many historians, sociologists, psychologists and journalists (see, e.g., Ariès 1974a; Stannard 1977; Lifton and Olson 1974; Mitford 1963).

Like Gorer, we all have our deeply personal recollections of loss and grief. Such memories in many ways play an important part in defining who we have become and how we feel. They also tell us something important about the time – in our own lives as well as in the historical time – when we experienced grief. Obviously, one needs to be wary of using the highly autobiographical nature of Gorer's observations of and experiences with grief as 'evidence' to extrapolate uncritically to wider historical, cultural and social contexts without due certain reservations and qualifications. The history of death and grief and their historical convulsions is far from unilinear or one-dimensional as it often appears in historical documents or personal recollections. Moreover, many of Gorer's observations related specifically to either the death of royalties or to death and mourning relating to extraordinary circumstances such as war or disaster. The vast majority of deaths – and the grief that follows – are not the outcome of such dramatic circumstances, and this also needs to be taken into consideration. Finally, Gorer's contention of the gradual disappearance of public mourning rituals after World War I has been contested (see, e.g., Cannadine 1981) as is the general notion of the denial and taboo on death in the 20th century (see, e.g., Kellehear 1984; Tradii and Robert 2017; Robert and Tradii 2017; Zimmermann and Rodin 2004; Walter 1991). However, Gorer's memoirs and insights do inform us about some of the important changes that the experience of grief and the accompanying mourning rituals have undergone during the past one hundred years as a backdrop against which to understand what is currently taking place in contemporary society.

Spectacular death – spectacular grief

It seems that we are now in the process of leaving the age of so-called 'forbidden death' (Ariès 1974a) and the accompanying hidden grief of modern society behind. There are many indicators and signs showing us that the grip of the impenetrable death taboo and the prudery surrounding grief described by Gorer and a host of colleagues in the middle and latter part of the 20th century is gradually loosened, leaving room for a more open and indeed realistic confrontation with our mortal condition. Already some decades ago, social scientists thus began to speak of a 'revival of death' (Walter 1994) consisting of a new openness – public as well as private – towards talking about death (for example, at 'dining with death' events or in designated 'death cafés', see Fong 2017) and an awareness of the importance of taking a personal stance and developing a reflexive responsibility for one's own death instead of leaving it to either tradition or institutional or professional discretion.

It has also been observed how we have now moved from a 'modern grief' perspective – looking at grief as a private phenomenon that is firmly locating the grieving process within the closed circles of individual and nuclear family and is based on expert knowledge often expressed in unilinear stage models of the grieving process – to an apparently more 'postmodern grief' experience that opens up for new forms of grief, new theories on how to understand it, new networks and social groups within which to cope with and share it, and not least new ways of expressing it (Walter 2007, 2008). This 'revival thesis' – which has been conceptualized in a variety of different versions – also suggests that many of the rituals, customs and practices regarding dying, death and mourning of earlier times, and perhaps especially those from the 18th century when death and mourning were prominent features of everyday life, are now in the process of being reinvented and are increasingly coupled with the demands of individual choice and consumer culture. We now want to invent our own personally meaningful rituals, rediscover the rituals and traditions of the past and create our life and death as pieces of artwork that bear witness to who we are and what we were. In this way, we are hoping that death can truly become a 'death of one's own' (Beck 2002), just as life is also seen as a project for which the individual is personally responsible. Whether the death taboo, as some seem to claim (e.g., Berridge 2002), is now in fact a thing of the past is obviously difficult to determine (not least because taboos are difficult to measure and document), but there is no doubt that death and grief in many ways today are more openly discussed in the media than was the case just a few decades ago. This interest in discussing, preplanning and making important decisions (ceremonial, judicial and ethical) about death and dying is matched by the rise of a 'new pornography of death' (Berridge 2002) that celebrates death and inaugurates a kind of death voyeurism evident, for example, in the huge popularity of the constantly touring Body World exhibitions, 'dark tourism', the transgressive artistic display of and playing with human mortality, the uses of death symbolism in contemporary advertising and the television and Internet cornucopia of violent death, which allows us to experience death vicariously (see, e.g., Gilbert 2007; McIlwain 2005; Noys 2005; Stone 2018). More recently, it has thus been proposed that we have entered the age of so-called 'spectacular death', which refers to a time when death – previously hidden, forbidden and denied – is increasingly becoming a phenomenon embraced (if not even appropriated) by mass media, popular culture and not least professional and scientific arenas. Some of the main characteristics of this spectacular death are: *the new mediated visibility of death, the commercialization of death, the re-ritualization of death, the palliative care revolution* and finally *death as a topic of academic attention and specialization* (Jacobsen 2016). The 'forbidden death' of the 20th century – itself in many respects a reversal of the 'tamed death' of the Middle Ages (Ariès 1974b) – is now seemingly in the process of being re-reversed into a spectacular death in which death is something we not only have to but also want to confront if we want to live authentic and subjectively meaningful lives.

In this time and age (call it 'postmodern', 'late-modern', 'reflexive-modern', 'liquid-modern' or something less sociologistic), it seems that not only death but also grief in many respects is becoming spectacular – something to be observed, discussed, dissected, politicized and made part of public debates. The era of 'spectacular grief' inaugurates a time when it becomes not only interesting but also opportune (for 'grief researchers', 'grief therapists' and 'grief counsellors') to rediscover, reconceptualize, investigate, appropriate and attempt to monopolize the agenda dealing with the social, emotional, medical and psychological dimensions of grief. Grief, which a few decades ago was regarded as a niche reserved for the few, is now the talk of the town in many scientific circles: research networks, research grants, research centres and research seminars. Additionally, torrents of scientific literature dealing with many different aspects of grief are being published. Obviously, this interest in grief also expands beyond the realm of academia and into the worlds of artistic and creative expression. The fiction and nonfiction literature on death, dying and grief is booming, and nowadays you will even find critically acclaimed titles reflecting on death, dying and grief on the shelves of airport bookshops (e.g., Gawande 2015; O'Mahony 2016; Schillace 2015), something that was almost unimaginable during the age of forbidden death. Today, books about grief become bestsellers, especially those that are autobiographical and deeply personal and that feature accessible depictions of how grief feels or what it does to people. For example, Max Porter's award-winning book *Grief is the Thing with Feathers* (2015) or Julia Samuel's *Grief Works* (2017) are but a few examples of this quite widespread interest in reading about grief in fiction and nonfiction genres. One could also mention Megan Devine's *It's OK that You're Not OK* (2017) or Joanne Cacciatore's *Bearing the Unbearable* (2017); these combine personal stories of loss with spiritual and therapeutic advice. In a

Danish context, from which we write, the personal portrayals by bereaved parents of the loss of a child have received a lot of attention and critical acclaim (Kjær 2016; Aidt 2017). Books like these can help their readers understand that loss and grief – even the grief that is rife with outrage, pain and despair – are quite natural and normal, perhaps especially following the tragic death of a child. So in contemporary society grief is far from invisible or hidden, and popular cultural depictions of grief abound in contemporary fiction and nonfiction, television and cinema (see, e.g., Almeida 2004; Armstrong 2012; Morse 2017; Stroebe 2018).

Moreover, the interest in grief is also burgeoning in the world outside of academia and the media as people strive to create meaning and discover new ways of dealing with and displaying grief. Grief has now, once again, gone public, which is evident in, for instance, Grief Awareness Day, memorial walks, the Good Death Week (promoting 'good life, good death and good grief'), the inventing and reinventing of mortuary and mourning rituals – what Erika Doss (2010) has called contemporary society's 'memorial mania' – and the spectacular 'grief gatherings' in the wake of terrorist attacks or tragic accidents (what is at times in the research literature described as 'spontaneous grief' and 'spontaneous memorials'). These are all part and parcel to the contemporary 'carnival of grief', where everybody – but perhaps especially researchers, healthcare professionals and media producers – now seems to swell in the selfsame grief that was previously a no-go topic. Today, grief is no longer shrouded in squeamishness and silence – if it ever actually was; it is instead exposed, shared, celebrated and made the object of an almost unprecedented curiosity. Whether this tendency, to rephrase Gorer's classic thesis on the status of death in the mid-20th century, could be captured by the notion of the 'pornography of grief' is a matter of conjecture, but it certainly shows how grief is now something that is embraced, practiced, discussed, studied, dissected and displayed in ways unimaginable just a few decades ago. Obviously, grief – as a privately felt emotion – can still be a lonely feeling that leaves its hapless victims vulnerable and isolated.

Grief as a social emotion

As mentioned above, grief is an integral part of the human life experience. Everybody eventually dies and hence grief inevitably enters our lives and becomes part of the way we organize our lives and experience the world. This has always been the case and grief is therefore something that we must expect to encounter and experience at some point in life. As indicated above, it seems as if modern society's routine sequestration of death and grief is now being replaced by contemporary society's increasing concern with existential issues and emotionality, as has been suggested by many contemporary social thinkers (e.g., Giddens 1991). Thus, in recent years a rising public and academic interest in the phenomenon of grief has emerged, as shown earlier, resulting in a growing portion of so-called grief research being produced and published. Regarding the former, the public awareness of and interest in grief has been by bolstered by a steadily growing number of articles in national and international newspapers, films and documentaries devoted to the topic of grief and bereavement experiences. The academic interest in grief has been spurred by the coming diagnosis of 'Prolonged Grief Disorder', which will appear in the ICD-11 (published in 2018), new societal and cultural practices of grief, a disciplinary interest in charting and unfolding new research areas, and so on. All of this has attracted the interest of scholars within the social sciences and the humanities. However, quite a lot of the research conducted in the field of grief and bereavement is primarily psychologically oriented or psychiatrically driven.

This book seeks to rectify this by providing a more explicitly sociological perspective on grief in contemporary society. Sociology is concerned with unearthing and understanding exactly the social aspects of life – and not least the relationship between social history, social structure and individual life experiences (at times described as the 'sociological imagination'). In this way, sociology – along with it neighbouring disciplines – is well-suited to shed light on and enhance our understanding of emotions and feelings in general and perhaps grief in particular because sociology does not regard emotions as something solely and exclusively originating in, belonging to, or being experienced or displayed by the individual human being.

Although it has been suggested that grief is *not* an emotion or a feeling (see, e.g., Goldie 2011), we instead propose and emphasize that grief is *indeed* – in all its experiential facets and dimensions – an emotion. Grief is something we *feel*. This does not mean that grief is not *also* something we *do*, something we *think* or something we are capable of *verbalising*, but fundamentally grief is an emotional human experience. Most sociological perspectives and theories dealing with grief have been keen to show how grief is indeed a so-called social emotion. Even though we may in everyday life often associate grief with a very individual, personal and indeed also lonely emotional experience, grief is in fact a social emotion. By this is meant that there are so many social components of the grieving experience and process that it is difficult to individualize the feeling (see, e.g., Jacobsen 2018; Jacobsen and Petersen 2018; Jakoby 2012). Just think of the – at times quite complex and extended – process of preparing for a person's imminent death; it involves so many emotional, practical, financial and ceremonial considerations and the cooperation of so many different people. Or think of the social bond existing between the dying or dead person and the bereaved well beyond the moment of death, or the social nature of the funeral ceremony, the community of grieving family members, friends and colleagues, the involvement of various groups of professionals in the dying and grieving process and so on. Since death tears a hole (some larger than others) in the social fabric, grief becomes a social emotional experience shaped by the fact that a death touches so many different people who each share, organize, negotiate, handle and cope with death and grief in their way.

The social dimension of grief can also be captured by pointing out how grief in a phenomenological sense can be understood as a 'presence in absence' (Fuchs 2018), meaning that the physically absent (and dead) person even after death often remains present – fondly as well as painfully – in our thoughts, memories, feelings, recollections and actions. We might call this the continued presence of the 'living dead' in our lives. So even though the person we grieve in a physical sense is no more, his or her presence is emotionally, psychologically and socially felt – as absence – by the bereaved sometimes even decades after death. Another dualism besides 'presence-absence' that can illustrate the social dimension of grief is 'feeling-display'. It is important to stress that besides its 'feeling side' (grief as an emotion that is felt by the individual or group), grief – like so many other emotions – also contains a 'display side' (Lofland 1985:173) that is perhaps particularly evident in the dramaturgy and manifestation of public grief. Grief is therefore not only an individual emotion experienced by an individual human being. Grief can also be, and most often is, a culturally shared and sanctioned feeling of loss that is somehow performed or put on display for others to witness. To grieve in a good/healthy or bad/unhealthy manner is thus not a question of some naturally given quality inherent in individual human beings – it is a matter of the social and cultural construction of grief. As American sociologist Arlie R. Hochschild once aptly stated: 'The ways in which people think they have grieved poorly suggests what a remarkable achievement it is to grieve well – without violating the astonishingly exact standards we draw from culture to impose on feeling' (Hochschild 1983:68). Moreover, grief is also a target, and increasingly so, of diagnostic endeavours and various treatment regimens that in many ways assist in transforming grief from a normal emotional response to loss into a 'disease' or a 'pathology' requiring some kind of professional intervention (Granek 2010). In such a process (at times called 'medicalization', 'therapeutization' or 'pathologization'), any notion of 'natural grief' is in danger of being substituted, in the name of professional expertise, with a gaze searching incessantly for symptoms, abnormalities, identifiable stages and possibilities for treatment and alleviation. In this way, the disciplines of medicine and psychiatry have become the new vanguards in what has been called the 'policing' of grief (Walter 2000), and this thus inaugurates an overall shift from grief as predominantly a clerical/pastoral concern to grief as a preoccupation of the professions of medicine and psychiatry. Ever since the publication of Sigmund Freud's (1917/1957) groundbreaking essay on mourning and melancholia, grief has been the object of intense psychological and medical scrutiny. However, we want to stress, following the words of British sociologist Tony Walter, that 'grief is a natural human reaction, not a mental illness. Mental health should not be allowed to define good grief, any more than medical expertise should define a good death' (Walter 2017:89). The torrents of literature on managing and coping with grief and the multitude of theories that at times in reductionist fashion provide proverbial one-liners or rigid stage models of the grieving process have not necessarily made it much easier for people to experience loss. As once observed by American psychologist Edgar N. Jackson: 'It may well be easier to confront the dynamics of grief in theory than in the form of the baffling, and often contradictory behavior of a person in the midst of a grief experience' (Jackson 1977:9).

To summarize, even though grieving and mourning our dead is a universal human practice, the way we do it differs considerably based on history, culture and society. Thus, in this edited volume we would like to give voice to various social and cultural perspectives on grief. Our contention is that the relative shortage of social and cultural perspectives on grief is detrimental to a fuller understanding of many important facets and dimensions of grief. Grief is, after all, also a social emotion. Hence, we have invited internationally acclaimed scholars within different social science and humanistic disciplines to contribute by providing perspectives on and engaging in discussions about the social and cultural aspects of grief. This is what this book aspires to do. This collection attempts to point specifically to the sociality of grief – to the many different social factors and cultural facets that surround and shape our individual understanding and experience of grief.

About this book

As should be evident from the above, admittedly rudimentary, analytical framework, this book is about grief as a historical, cultural and social phenomenon or 'construct' as we often say within the social sciences. By this it is meant that grief as an emotion – in many different (some direct, others more subtle) ways – is informed and shaped by the society in which it unfolds and in which it is experienced and displayed. This does not mean, however, that discussions of death as part of the contemporary medical, therapeutic or diagnostical professions – in which grief is often objectified and given a pathological twist – are not of relevance to this book. Quite the contrary, the book will show that all the many different perspectives on grief – including those developed in highly specialized or professionalized contexts – in many ways mirror the social contexts in which they are invoked and employed. The view underpinning this book is that the social world of grief – the way grief is felt, displayed, talked about, sanctioned and treated – consists of very diversified experiences and practices, which goes to show that the way death and dying (and also immortality) is constructed and understood has an impact on the way we grieve and mourn our dead and vice versa.

The book is divided into four thematic sections, each of them dealing with different aspects and dimensions of grief as a historical, cultural and social emotion. The first section contains chapters dealing with general and long-term historical changes in our understanding of grief and relates this to wider social transformations and cross-cultural factors. Chapter 1 is written by *Peter N. Stearns* and deals with the historical changes taking place in our understanding of grief from premodern and traditional societies to contemporary modern society. Drawing on rich historical material, Stearns documents how the evolution of grief has changed quite considerably over the past few centuries. He shows that whereas premodern agricultural societies generated some common beliefs and practices designed to minimize extensive grieving, modern society first relied on a more expressive attitude towards grief, then later had a change of heart and instead began to constrain the emotion in order to allow for individual adjustment and smoother social relationships. In the wake of this, from the 1960s onwards, we have seen an attack on the modernist approach to grief, without, however, dislodging the contemporary cultural framework entirely. The chapter thus illustrates how our understanding and practice of grief does not stand still but is constantly in the process of adjusting to changes and concerns taking place in society at large. In chapter 2 by *Paul C. Rosenblatt*, the author draws on the cross-cultural and historical literature on grieving in order to critique acultural and ahistorical assumptions that underlie some parts of academic and clinical writings that say or imply that everyone grieves in rather the same way. The author also suggests that the pathologising in contemporary academic and clinical writings of grieving may have roots in the demands of the contemporary economy and of powerful societal actors. Instead, it is proposed that we need to appreciate grief in its specific historical and social context, which frames the way grief is experienced and understood. This historical feat continues in chapter 3 by *Patricia Jalland*, who provides important insights into how the two world wars during the 20th century had a profound and cumulative impact on the way society grieves for its dead. By focusing on the changes in practices, attitudes and emotions, Jalland digs into the ruptures brought about by the massive losses and casualties during the two world wars on the way we grieve our war dead. She points out that particularly following World War II there occurred an increasing silencing of grief in England on the individual, family and community levels of society, which was also mirrored in the early contributions to 'grief studies'. The author ends the chapter by showing how we have witnessed a revival of expressive grieving since the 1960s.

The chapters contained in the second section of the book all relate to grief as a literary topic and analyze how grief is described and presented in contemporary popular fiction and professional literature. In chapter 4 by *Kjersti Bale* and *Hilde Bondevik* the analytical point of departure is taken in the study of two American novels, where 'magical thinking' appears to control anxiety and grief associated with the loss of a loved one: Jesmyn Ward's *Sing, Unburied, Sing* (2017) and George Saunders' *Lincoln in the Bardo* (2017). By exploring these two novels, the chapter illustrates how fiction can process collective grief through the examination of individual grief. Bale and Bondevik hence seek to illustrate how literature treats grief and bereavement in ways that complement the medical understanding of them. Thus, they argue that while the diagnostic manuals give medical science's observational view of grief, by linking to ways of thinking and a language that goes beyond a rational approach, fiction can illuminate grief as it is experienced, give it a form, reflect on it and contextualize it. Chapter 5 is written by *Nina R. Jakoby* and *Fiona A. Anderau* and centres on an analysis of the bereavement literature published in the wake of disaster, specifically the tsunami in the Indian Ocean in 2004 that killed hundreds of thousands of people. Jakoby and Anderau draw on the autobiographical account of Sonali Deraniyagala and by way of a qualitative analysis of online literary reviews show how this book and its reception can inform us about the social regulation and public feeling rules pertaining to grief in contemporary society. The authors show how certain themes such as grief work and recovery, deviant feelings and behaviour, social class and the 'luxury of grief', and finally therapeutic narrative and literary genre can be used as a lens in understanding the normative embeddedness of experiences and representations of grief. In chapter 6 by *Christian Riegel*, the author examines – by looking at two key novels, *Obasan* (1981) by Joy Kogawa and *Extremely Loud & Incredibly Close* (2005) by Jonathan Safran Foer – how novelists contend with the turbulent terrain of fraught grief of the late 20th and early 21st centuries. In writing about loss, Riegel states in his chapter, these authors explore mourning as a type of work or labour that unfolds as a process of mourning, and he shows how their resulting novels become products of that mourning, what one can describe as an artefact of their work. Thus, Riegel argues, these novels operate as memorial structures for their readers, enacting an ethical relationship so that readers engage with significant traumatic experiences of loss of the period, and learn about the nature of loss and about how to find in cultural expression useful models of coping.

The third section of the book looks into different, more or less specific forms of the grief experience – for example, relating to parental bereavement, spontaneous memorialization and human-animal bonding. Chapter 7 by *Mary Ellen Macdonald* explores if and how death is taboo and denied in contemporary society, based on reflections from a decade of anthropological research on parental bereavement and child death. The chapter starts out with a delineation of the discursive construction of grief in contemporary society showing how a certain understanding of grief prevails that underpins a neoliberal ideology of productivity, management, coping and so no. Macdonald believes that our lack of a more nuanced language reflects and reproduces stigmatising societal responses to child death and that the many different '-izations' of grief reproduce a certain limited understanding of what grief is and how it feels. In the chapter, the author also invokes the idea of 'ghosts' and 'absent presences' that may help us better understand how parents relate to their deceased children. In chapter 8, *Jack Santino* examines the emergence of a new kind of public ritual expression of grief and grievance. In the chapter, Santino suggests that the public memorialization of death almost always addresses social issues, while utilising familiar funereal symbols and tropes to commemorate deceased individuals. He denotes these commemorative phenomena as 'spontaneous shrines', and in the chapter he examines the implications, and appropriateness, of this term. As he states, spontaneous shrines emerged in the late 20th century to mark a certain type of death – violent, untimely or unnecessary. The causes of such deaths are themselves matters of public concern and range from driving fatalities to terrorism. By conducting extensive research on these phenomena in Northern Ireland, France and the United States, Santino draws on these experiences – as well as including research more broadly – in his analysis. Chapter 9 by *Douglas J. Davies* departs from the other chapters as he deals with grief in relation to the loss of a pet. Douglas begins the chapter by exploring theoretical questions of emotions, grief and life contexts, beginning with a brief description and critical analysis of both the long-established attachment and loss theory, and the more recent continuing bonds theory as applied to human-human grief and, by extension, to their potential application within the context of the death of a pet. Douglas ventures into this endeavour by including his previously developed idea of 'echoing grief', a concept that refers to the experience of some aspects of grief – caused by the loss of a loved human being – that are being retained in a pet that the surviving person has shared with the deceased. The main question raised by Douglas is how the death of the animal brings an echoing emotion of grief originating in the previous death of a partner.

The book's final section contains chapters using grief as a perspective from which to criticize different aspects of contemporary society, particularly looking at the social pathologies of, for example, the suffocation, medicalization and individualization of grief. In this way, grief can be seen as a useful lens through which to analyze and critique different, more or less general, aspects of contemporary society. Chapter 10 by *Allan V. Horwitz* examines the process by which grief has become a medicalized phenomenon. More specifically, Horwitz takes his point of departure in the fact that the 'bereavement exclusion' in previous DSMs explicitly excluded grieving people, who otherwise met the criteria for Major Depressive Disorder, from obtaining a diagnosis. In the latest version of the DSM – DSM-5 – this exclusion has been eliminated. In the chapter, Horwitz traces – by examining some of the major controversies of specific empirical findings that suggest that the bereavement exclusion should stay put – how the elimination of the bereavement exclusion from the DSM-5 was legitimized. In Horwitz's perspective, the end result has greatly increased what he refers to as the inappropriate medicalization of normal distress. In his analysis, the medicalization of bereavement provides a prime example of the continuing inability of the psychiatric profession to develop a coherent definition of what a mental disorder is. In chapter 11, *Tashel C. Bordere* writes about the ways in which grief is disenfranchised and suffocated among bereaved African American populations. Bordere situates African Americans' bereavement within social and cultural contexts examining complications to grief and mourning processes that occur as they navigate various institutions (e.g., educational and health care systems). In the chapter, Bordere addresses and discusses how suffocated grief – what she also refers to as specific types of grief being societally penalized and stigmatized – occurs and how this is balanced with patterns of resilience demonstrated amid historical and present-day death and non-death losses. Further, Bordere outlines opportunities and suggested practices for grief enfranchisement, inclusion and culturally conscientious practice in research, policy and clinical work. The book's final chapter, chapter 12 by *Michael Hviid Jacobsen* and *Anders Petersen*, critically explores and discusses the notion of the individualization of grief in contemporary society. The authors look into the way in which the overall individualization of society has also impacted our understanding of grief. They are critical of the tendency to make grief an individual (and psychiatric or psychological) matter, as if it was something belonging to, being experienced and expressed by and requiring the treatment of an individual person. Such a perspective, they claim, routinely overlooks the many important ways in which grief is a social emotion. Instead, the authors insist that such an individualized colonization of grief needs to be replaced with a perspective acknowledging the many social roots, processes and consequences of grief, and they illustrate this by pointing to three social dimensions of grief: the relational character of identity formation, the social stratification of grief, and finally the stigmatization of grief. In this way, this final chapter returns to some of the aforementioned understandings underpinning the development of this book: that *grief is an emotion that needs to be analyzed and appreciated within its historical, social and cultural context.*

It is our hope that this volume will prove useful for scholars, students and practitioners alike within the fields of grief research and grief therapy, and beyond. We hope it will provide food for thought in the many discussions about what grief is, how we can understand it, how we can deal with it and how we may perhaps learn to live with it that currently seem to preoccupy so many people inside and outside academia. The book does *not* aspire to tell people how to grieve or how to cope with loss. It is rarely a good or advisable idea to dictate to people how to live their lives. Nowhere has this insight perhaps been more pertinent and appropriate than when it comes to defining or deciding how people should mourn the loss of their loved ones. As American psychologist Herman Feifel once so rightly contended:

> We should beware of promulgating a coercive orthodoxy of how to mourn. In the last analysis, an 'appropriate' mourning is one that is acceptable to or tolerated by the mourner, not one so designated by either the helping professions, significant others or the community. Individual differences and respect for personhood must be our principal guides.
>
> (Feifel 1988:3)

Thus, this book does not contain any recommendations, pathways or prophylaxes for how to deal with death and grief. It simply testifies to the fact that death and grief are here to stay and that we need to understand them within their historical, cultural and social context. Just as it is unlikely that death should suddenly disappear (even though José Saramago's novel *Death at Intervals* from 2008 satirically speculates on this possibility), it is also unlikely that the experience of grief should ever stop being an integral part of human life. Perhaps grief is simply something we will have to learn to live with and come to terms with?

References

Aidt, Naja Marie (2017): *Har døden taget noget fra dig så giv det tilbage: Carls bog.* Copenhagen: Gyldendal.

Almeida, Rochelle (2004): *The Politics of Mourning: Grief Management in Cross-Cultural Fiction.* Madison: Farleigh Dickinson University Press.

Ariès, Philippe (1974a): *Western Attitudes Toward Death from the Middle Ages to the Present.* Baltimore: Johns Hopkins University Press.

Ariès, Philippe (1974b): 'The Reversal of Death – Changes in Attitudes Toward Death in Western Societies'. *American Quarterly*, 26 (5):536–560.

Ariès, Philippe (1981): *The Hour of Our Death.* London: Allen Lane.

Ariès, Philippe (1985): *Images of Man and Death.* Boston: Harvard University Press.

Armstrong, Richard (2012): *Mourning Films: A Critical Study of Loss and Grieving in Cinema.* Jefferson, NC: McFarland & Company.

Bauman, Zygmunt (1992): *Mortality, Immortality and other Life Strategies.* Cambridge: Polity Press.

Beck, Ulrich (2002): 'Death of One's Own, Life of One's Own: Hopes from Transience', in Ulrich Beck and Elisabeth Beck-Gernsheim (eds.): *Individualization*. London: Sage Publications, pp. 151–156.

Berridge, Kate (2002): *Vigor Mortis: The End of the Death Taboo*. London: Profile Books.

Butler, Judith (2016): *Frames of War: When Is Life Grievable?* London: Verso.

Cacciatore, Joanne (2017): *Bearing the Unbearable: Love, Loss, and the Heartbreaking Path of Grief*. Somerville, MA: Wisdom Publications.

Cannadine, David (1981): 'War and Death, Grief and Mourning in Modern Britain', in Joachim Whaley (ed.): *Mirrors of Mortality: Studies in the Social History of Death*. London: Europa Publications, pp. 187–242.

Davey, Richard (1890/2013): *A History of Mourning*. London: Jay's.

Devine, Megan (2017): *It's OK That You're Not OK: Meeting Grief and Loss in a Culture That Doesn't Understand*. Louisville, CO: Sounds True.

Doss, Erika (2010): *Memorial Mania: Public Feeling in America*. Chicago: University of Chicago Press.

Feifel, Herman (1988): 'Grief and Bereavement: Overview and Perspective'. *Bereavement Care*, 7 (1):2–4.

Fong, Jack (2017): *The Death Café Movement: Exploring the Horizons of Mortality*. London: Palgrave/Macmillan.

Freud, Sigmund (1917/1957): 'Mourning and Melancholia', in James Strachey (ed.): *The Standard Edition of the Complete Psychological Works of Sigmund Freud* (Volume XIV). London: Hogarth Press, pp. 243–258.

Fuchs, Thomas (2018): 'Presence in Absence: The Ambiguous Phenomenology of Grief'. *Phenomenology and the Cognitive Sciences*, 17 (1):43–63.

Gawande, Atul (2015): *Being Mortal: Illness, Medicine and What Matters in the End*. London: Profile Books.

Giddens, Anthony (1991): *Modernity and Self-Identity – Self and Society in the Late Modern Age*. Cambridge: Polity Press.

Gilbert, Sandra M. (2007): *Death's Door – Modern Dying and the Way We Grieve*. New York: W. W. Norton and Company.

Goldie, Peter (2011): 'Grief: A Narrative Account'. *Ratio (New Series)*, 24:119–137.

Gorer, Geoffrey (1955): 'The Pornography of Death'. *Encounter*, 5 (October issue):49–52.

Gorer, Geoffrey (1965): *Death, Grief and Mourning*. New York: Doubleday.

Granek, Leeat (2010): 'Grief as Pathology: The Evolution of Grief Theory in Psychology from Freud to the Present'. *History of Psychology*, 13 (1):46–73.

Hochschild, Arlie R. (1983): *The Managed Heart: Commercialization of Human Feeling*. Berkeley, CA: University of California Press.

Jackson, Edgar N. (1977): *The Many Faces of Grief*. London: SCM Press.

Jacobsen, Michael Hviid (2016): '"Spectacular Death" – Proposing a New Fifth Phase to Philippe Ariès's Admirable History of Death'. *Humanities*, 5 (19):1–20.

Jacobsen, Michael Hviid (2018): 'Sorgens sociologi – sorgen som et spejlbillede på samfundets syn på døden' ['The Sociology of Grief – Grief as a Mirror Image of Society's Perspective on Death'], in Michael Hviid Jacobsen, Mai-Britt Guldin and Christian Juul Busch (eds.): *Giv sorgen ord – sorgkultur i forandring* [*Give Sorrow Words – Changes in the Culture of Grief*]. Copenhagen: Munksgaard, pp. 41–62.

Jacobsen, Michael Hviid and Anders Petersen (2018): 'Sorgens Socialitet – en sociologisk kommentar til psykologiseringen og medikaliseringen af menneskelige følelser' ['The Sociality of Grief – A Sociological Comment to the Psychologisation and Medicalisation of Human Emotions']. *Psyke & Logos*, 39 (1):55–73.

Jakoby, Nina R. (2012): 'Grief as a Social Emotion: Theoretical Perspectives'. *Death Studies*, 36 (8):679–711.

Jakoby, Nina R. (2015): 'The Self and Significant Others: Toward a Sociology of Loss'. *Illness, Crisis and Loss*, 23 (2):129–174.

Jalland, Patricia (1999): 'Victorian Death and Its Decline: 1850–1918', in Peter C. Jupp and Clare Gittings (eds.): *Death in England: An Illustrated History*. Manchester: Manchester University Press, pp. 230–255.

Kellehear, Allan (1984): 'Are We a 'Death-Denying' Society? A Sociological Review'. *Social Science and Medicine*, 18 (9):713–723.

Kellehear, Allan (2007): *A Social History of Dying*. Cambridge: Cambridge University Press.

Kerrigan, Michael (2007): *The History of Death*. Guilford, CN: The Lyons Press.

Kjær, Esben (2016): *Min usynlige søn: Kunsten at leve med sine døde resten af livet*. Copenhagen: Gyldendal.

Lewis, C. S. (1961/1984): *A Grief Observed*. New York: Walker and Company.

Lifton, Robert J. and Eric Olson (1974): *Living and Dying*. New York: Praeger.

Lofland, Lyn H. (1985): 'The Social Shaping of Emotion: The Case of Grief'. *Symbolic Interaction*, 8 (2):171–190.

McIlwain, Charlton D. (2005): *When Death Goes Pop – Death, Media and the Remaking of Community*. New York: Peter Lang.

Medawar, Peter B. (1961): 'Obituary: Peter Alfred Gorer, 1907–1961'. *The Royal Society* (Biographical Memoirs of Fellow of the Royal Society), 1, November, pp. 94–109.

Mitford, Jessica (1963): *The American Way of Death*. New York: Simon and Schuster.

Morse, Tal (2017): *The Mourning News: Reporting Violent Death in the Global Age*. New York: Peter Lang.

Noys, Benjamin (2005): *The Culture of Death*. Oxford: Berg.

O'Mahony, Seamus (2016): *The Way We Die Now*. London: Head of Zeus.

Petersen, Anders and Michael Hviid Jacobsen (2018): 'Grief – The Painfulness of Permanent Human Absence', in Michael Hviid Jacobsen (ed.): *Emotions, Everyday Life and Sociology*. London: Routledge, pp. 191–208.

Porter, Max (2015): *Grief is the Thing with Feathers*. London: Faber and Faber.

Robert, Martin and Laura Tradii (2017): 'Do We Deny Death? I: Critiques of the Death-Denial Thesis'. *Mortality*, DOI: 10.1080/13576275.2017.1415318.

Samuel, Julia (2017): *Grief Works – Stories of Life, Death and Surviving*. London: Penguin Books.

Saramago, José (2008): *Death at Intervals*. New York: Vintage Books.

Schillace, Brandy (2015): *Death's Summer Coat*. London: Elliott and Thompson Ltd.

Sprang, Ginny and John McNeil (1995): *The Many Faces of Bereavement*. New York: Brunner/Mazel Inc.

Stannard, David (1977): *The Puritan Way of Death*. New York: Oxford University Press.

Stearns, Peter N. (2007): *Revolutions in Sorrow: The American Experience of Death in a Global Perspective*. Boulder, CO: Paradigm Publishers.

Stone, Philip R. (2018): 'Dark Tourism in an Age of 'Spectacular Death'', in Philip R. Stone et al. (eds.): *The Palgrave Handbook of Dark Tourism Studies*. London: Palgrave/Macmillan, pp. 189–210.

Stroebe, Margaret S. (2018): 'The Poetry of Grief: Beyond Scientific Portrayal'. *Omega: Journal of Death and Dying*, 78 (1):67–96.

Tradii, Laura and Martin Robert (2017): 'Do We Deny Death? II: Critiques of the Death-Denial Thesis'. *Mortality*, DOI: 10.1080/13576275.2017.1415319.

Walter, Tony (1991): 'Modern Death: Taboo or Not Taboo?'. *Sociology*, 25 (2):293–310.

Walter, Tony (1994): *The Revival of Death*. London: Routledge.

Walter, Tony (1999): *On Bereavement: The Culture of Grief*. Buckingham: Open University Press.

Walter, Tony (2000): 'Grief Narratives: The Role of Medicine in the Policing of Grief'. *Anthropology & Medicine*, 7:97–114.

Walter, Tony (2007): 'Modern Grief, Postmodern Grief'. *International Review of Sociology*, 17 (1):123–134.

Walter, Tony (2008): 'The New Public Mourning', in Margaret S. Stroebe et al. (eds.): *Handbook of Bereavement Research and Practice*. Washington, DC: American Psychological Association, pp. 241–262.

Walter, Tony (2017): *What Death Means Now*. Bristol: Policy Press.

Whaley, Joachim (1981): 'Introduction', in Joachim Whaley (ed.): *Mirrors of Mortality: Studies in the Social History of Death*. London: Europa Publications, pp. 1–14.

Zimmermann, Camilla and Gary Rodin (2004): 'The Denial of Death Thesis: Sociological Critique and Implications for Palliative Care'. *Palliative Medicine*, 18 (2):121–128.

Part I
Grief and history

1 Grief in modern history

An ongoing evolution

Peter N. Stearns

Introduction

Both the standards applied to grief, and at least some of its most obvious expressions, have changed greatly over the past 250 years. In the Western world a dual transformation occurred. Traditional norms and rituals were first redefined in the 19th century, with a significant facet of Victorian emotional culture devoted to grief and appropriate responses to grief; the shift is quite clear, though its explanation is somewhat more elusive. Then, most obviously in reaction to huge environmental changes associated with the reduction of child mortality and the growing role of professional medicine, grief standards were redefined even more substantially in the early 20th century. While this second adjustment persists in many ways, its contours continue to be modified in societies that seek appropriate ways to combine grief with the latest advances in modern medicine and even psychology.

This chapter, after sketching some characteristic premodern patterns, will deal with the two major stages of modern adjustment in turn: first, the effort to express grief more fully and then the attempt to constrain the emotion in the interests of personal adjustment and smoother social relationships. Sketching this complex evolution also involves considering the causes involved, and the impacts of the recommended emotional styles.

Grief is, of course, a composite emotion, and any history must take into account different combinations of sadness with anger, or fear or (particularly in the past two centuries) guilt. Personality variables complicate the story as well, at any point in time: some individuals find it easier to accommodate the dominant styles of grief than others, and there are also important subcultures to take into account, by social class or ethnicity.

The most important overall challenge, however, in any history of grief, involves the tension between what might be assumed to be a fairly standard human sadness when faced with great loss, regardless of cultural specifics, and the impact of particular value systems and patterns of death that often not only work to channel grief in certain ways but also seek to restrain the emotion. This is a tension that unquestionably continues into the present, as societies seek to smooth some of the rough edges that have resulted from modern attempts to reduce the scope of grief.

The modern history of grief, and the substantial changes involved, have been most extensively studied in Western societies, both in Europe and the United States. But some important literature has emerged for Japan and elsewhere, as many regions, despite divergent traditions, seek to adjust emotional standards to rapid changes in the nature of death and loss, including the growing focus on the later-age segments of the population.

Traditional patterns

When historians first tried to tackle the subject of grief in premodern societies, they tended to seize on, and overemphasize, widespread fatalism. Several pioneering histories of the family, appalled by the high levels of infant and child mortality, assumed that parents must have become inured to the losses involved. One observer even suggested that premodern Western families probably displayed about as much emotion 'as one would expect to find in a bird's nest' (Stone 1979; Shorter 1975). This claim was simply off the mark. Studies of parental diaries or annotations to family Bibles make it clear that the death of a child could be an intensely painful event, carefully noted by fathers and mothers alike at the time and in subsequent, anguished recollections (Vovelle 2000).

Indeed, historians and literary scholars have unearthed some of the most moving expressions of grief available, from written testimonies well before modern times. One study, for example, picks up the vivid commentary by three Japanese men around 1800, as they sought through writing to express a level of pain that simply resisted consolation on the death of a close friend, a wife, or a child (Kim 2015; Bolitho 2003). Similarly a 14th-century English poem, written by an unknown member of the gentry, released the grief felt on the death of a 2-year-old daughter: 'I declare I never knew one so precious. Alas: I lost her in a garden. . . . I mourn, overcome with love, longing for my precious, spotless Pearl' (McNamer 2015). One scholar has argued strongly for the successful expression and management of grief in premodern Europe, which he contrasts with a more troubled approach to death in modern times; and while his evaluation has been disputed, a number of scholars have sought to develop a similar dichotomy (Imhof 1996; Ariès 1981).

Most agricultural societies did generate some common beliefs and practices designed to minimize extensive grief. Many families sought to limit emotional attachments to very young children because of the probability that, on average, up to half of them would die before the age of 2. A Roman author, Epitectus, expressed a common sentiment: 'When you kiss your child, you say to yourself, "Perhaps it will be dead in the morning"'. In some societies (classical Greece and Rome, China) widespread infanticide, as a means of population control, further illustrated and enhanced a degree of callousness (Rawson 2003; Stearns 2006). Many agricultural societies further surrounded themselves with abundant symbols of death – as in locating graveyards and sombre inscriptions in the centre of cities and villages, where they would be encountered as a normal part of daily existence – again promoting a certain level of emotional acceptance of the inevitable.

Agricultural conditions, and high rates of death, almost certainly inhibited any extensive sense of guilt when a family member died, and here too restraint particularly applied to children. Families in early modern Western Europe that sought various remedies for serious illness, including consultations with doctors, almost never bothered with this kind of recourse when a child was suffering – there simply seemed to be no point in challenging the dictates of God and nature. Considerable fatalism, at least on the part of husbands and fathers, may also have accompanied reactions to the frequent deaths of women in childbirth.

Even for adults, males above all, a further characteristic in many agricultural societies may have helped restrain grief upon the imminence of death: a definition of a 'good death' was clearly available, featuring an older adult suffering from a wasting illness. The experience of this kind of good death extended over several weeks, involving progressive wasting but not necessarily intense pain. In the process, both the victim and his family would have the opportunity to resolve any existing grievances and bid farewell, confident that appropriate rituals were being observed (Imhof 1996). Finally, of course, religious solace was a vital element in a family's experience of a 'good death', where the presence of a religious official would help assure all parties that God's will was being observed (Vovelle 2000; Houlbrooke 1981; Cressy 1997). Buddhist rituals, for example, heavily invested in providing comfort and counseling on the occasion of a death (Irish et al. 1993; Desjarlais 2016).

All three Abrahamic religions stipulated burial sites and practices, including the way a dead body should be dressed. Crying and sorrow might be recognized – many Muslim writers discussed grief quite poignantly, even on the occasion of deaths of children – but excessive wailing or rending of garments was discouraged as offensive to God and community (Jones 1997). Most of the major religions, including of course Hinduism with its beliefs in reincarnation, sought to emphasize the possibility that death could be a sweet release, into a better existence after life has passed (Koslofsky 2000).

Fatalism, plus community and religious pressure to keep grief in bounds, plus widely accepted customs and burial practices presumably could combine not to prevent vivid grief, but to offer reassurance and some channels for appropriate expression. It is important to remember that intense emotion might not be satisfied, as vivid written laments attest. Nor of course was traditional practice immune to change – for instance, the transition from Catholic to less elaborate Protestant rituals during the Reformation. Nevertheless, some sense of a combination of intense and certain frequent grief, and approved forms of expression, remains valid. It was this combination that would begin to be challenged by a new set of beliefs and practices in the Western world by the late 18th/early 19th centuries (Badone 1989; McManners 1985).

The Victorian approach

References to grief in written materials in the English language began to increase rapidly in relative frequency from the middle of the 18th century onward (see Figure 1.1). Obviously, changes in relative frequency of reference are at best suggestive; they do not demonstrate that grief itself was on the rise (or later, on the wane). But they do point to possible changes in relevant emotional standards, which other evidence on the whole bears out.

For both discussions and rituals attached to grief did shift in the Western world in the great cultural transitions of the late 18th century. Writers of various sorts began to discuss the emotion with growing fervour, and what data we have suggest that the shift affected private letters (a rising genre in any event) as well as published materials. Images of mourning proliferated, and women, particularly, increasingly became the family agents in dealing appropriately with death and loss. Some girls' schools taught their students to emphasize figures of women draped over the tombstones of husbands or sons as they practiced their needle-work. By the 1870s in the United States, girls could order dolls complete with coffins and mourning clothes, another indication of the new importance attached to preparing appropriate expressions of and responses to grief (Farrell 1980; Rosen-blatt 1983; Stearns 1996).

The emotion was often hauled out for discussion and praise in 19th-century family manuals. Even the temporary absence of a loved one might be compared to death, as in Nathaniel Hawthorne's letter to Sarah Peabody in 1940: 'Where thou are not, there it is a sort of death'. But it was real death that seized emotional centre stage. It was the frequent subject of novels, which, like Louisa Alcott's *Little Women*, focused on the tragedy of family loss through wasting disease (Lystra 1989; Miller 1882). Parlour songs, literally in the hundreds, were filled with the sorrows of losing a loved one. Grief peppered materials prepared for children, who needed to be prepared for the elaborate experience of contemporary grief. Thus, *McGuffey's Reader*, in its 1866 edition, offered lessons on the response to death: 'How still the baby lies/I cannot hear his breath/I cannot see his eyes/ They tell me this is death' (McGuffey 1866). The emotion was clearly painful, but it also seemed essential to reflect the new intensity of family life. As a Protestant manual put it in 1882: 'It may truly be said that no home ever reaches its highest

Figure 1.1 Frequency of the term 'grief' in English, 1700–2008, Google Ngram Viewer, accessed on April 26, 2018.

blessedness and sweetness of love and its richest fulfillment of joy till sorrow enters its life in some way' (Miller 1882; Evans 1888; Finley 1872; Alcott 1868; Stannard 1975; Jackson 1977).

A new wave of etiquette books picked up on the theme, suggesting that the grief emphasis was not merely a conceit of Romantic-age novelists and songwriters. The books and columns offered elaborate instructions on how to visit a bereaved family, to respect their deep grief while also extending support (Kasson 1991).

Finally, insofar as the historian can judge, real people – however guided by the fictional conceits – now needed to express intense grief themselves – more commonly (aided of course by growing literacy) than had been the case in the premodern past. References to 'bitter tears' were standard. An 1897 diary reference captured the common sentiment: 'Jacob is dead. Tears blind my eyes as I write. . . . Now he is at rest, my darling Jacob. Hope to meet you in heaven. God help me to bear my sorrow'. And intense grief was often recalled, by men and women alike, through remembrance even years after the loss, in recollections that could have 'crushing effect'. Recurrent visits to gravesites mixed relief with renewed sorrow (Wells 1994).

Not surprisingly, death rituals themselves became markedly more elaborate, though appropriate emotional interpretation may be challenging. Signs of mourning became more substantial. Gravestones themselves – now for children as well, an innovation – became far more expensive and showy. Some of this, admittedly, represented an intriguing 19th-century expression of rising consumerism, with expenditures designed to express emotion and honour the dead, but also impress the community at large. But the grief component could be very real. In a fascinating new expression of grief – and what would much later be called a search for closure – Americans after the brutal Civil War began to seek out dead sons, brothers and husbands in battlefield graves, and a new industry of modern embalming sprang up to cater to their needs to return the bodies for a proper burial back home. Here – admittedly encouraged by the advent of the railway, which facilitated searches, and also a new interest in embalming – was a first indication of the new grief expressions attached to deaths in combat that would gain further currency – and motivate considerable expenditure – in the 20th century (Faust 2008).

Several factors fed Victorian grief, again beyond the encouragement provided by lachrymose popular songs and novels. Three components can be suggested, operating in combination. First, traditional management of death became more repellent in several ways. New concerns about disease and hygiene prompted a massive relocation of cemeteries from the later 18th century onward, to keep them as a distance from population centres. Death in this sense became less familiar, its reminders less omnipresent. By the later 19th century revulsion at death would be further reflected, and encouraged, by new practices such as embalming, and a rivalry among funeral directors to make bodies as lifelike as possible; and by the emergence of funeral professionals, who took over the arrangements and began to move preparation from the home to new, dedicated centers. Less intimate familiarity with death as a routine (further encouraged, with urbanization, by removal from the experience of frequent animal death), increasing distaste and desire for concealment, certainly had their own emotional contours – including new levels of disgust. But the process might contribute to more vivid grief as well (Corbin 1986).

Second, most obviously, new grief expressions followed directly from the growing emphasis on familial love and affection, which became increasingly common currency particularly in middle-class experiences from the mid-18th century onward (Farrell 1980; Hohenschuh 1900; Burton 1908). Marriages were increasingly organized around romantic courtship, rather than mere parental arrangement. Of course, the shift hardly guaranteed enduring love, but it certainly encouraged an impulse to claim attachment, and corresponding sorrow at loss. One historical assessment thus notes a shift among upper-class men in the American South, from the considerable fatalism that wives' deaths in childbirth seemed to occasion in the 18th century, to more vigorous sympathy and sorrow after 1800 (Dye and Smith 1986; Ulrich 1982; Lewis 1983; Hoffert 1987; Lockridge and Lewis 1988).

The same sentimental attachment certainly applied to the emotional culture surrounding children. As birth rates declined and ideas of childish innocence gained ground, parental, and particularly maternal, love was certainly encouraged by a new style of parental advice, providing the context in which new outpourings of grief, and intensified rituals, could apply to the loss of a child (Mintz 2004). The rise of the novel also encouraged grief in dealing with the death of loved ones (McManners 1985).

Third, grief became more entangled with guilt – that is, with a growing sense that certain kinds of death should be prevented. Enlightenment ideas encouraged a growing belief that traditional death rates should give way to earthly progress. A well-ordered, science-driven society should surely be able to cut into the loss and suffering that had so long burdened humankind. Enlightenment intellectuals themselves were notoriously fascinated by longevity studies, hoping to find clues to the prolongation of life more generally. And while there is no reason to claim widespread conversion to the extremes of progressive expectations, there were signs of change. Thus many people expressed growing discomfort with the customary rates of maternal mortality: a modern society should be able to do better – which could in turn suggest that perhaps a survivor – for example, the husband whose wife died giving birth – should have been able to do more.

This new complexity applied particularly to the deaths of children, through the medium of the proliferation of women's magazines that catered to the middle classes from the 1830s onward, supplemented by a variety of popular health manuals like Dr. Bull's *Hints to Mothers*, which went through 15 editions in Britain between 1833 and 1877. These new outlets were hardly official representatives of Enlightenment ideology, and in the case of the magazines often owed their popularity to recipes and clothing styles rather than emotional advice. But they did begin to introduce a new cautionary note about children, arguing that careful mothers could and should now be responsible for healthy and durable offspring, with explicit statements that current high levels of child mortality were neither 'natural nor inevitable', but the fruit of heedless parenting. Too many mothers, articles commonly warned, did not feed their infants properly, or layered them with too many clothes and blankets – sometimes, tragically and unintentionally, causing their death. Widely publicized cautions also increasingly applied to the care needed in the early months of pregnancy, giving at least some women yet another area of responsibility should anything go wrong (Branca 1975).

A new and arguably disorienting distance from death; a vague belief that some proper modern arrangements should reduce death itself before later age, and an attendant sense of guilt; and most obviously the new emphasis on love and attachment – here were the components for intensified grief, or a need to exhibit appropriate signs of grief, and obviously the source of rising commentary on the emotion as well. While a precise causation formula cannot be ventured, each of the three strands can be explicitly documented and each could contribute to a new and often more intense sense of grief – with claims of love, obviously, most clearly at the forefront.

And all three factors, finally, applied to reactions in a context where actual death rates remained quite high. Modest reductions in mortality rates may have occurred, particularly amid the comfortable middle classes, but there was as yet no revolutionary decline. Few families, unless infertile, would be spared the death of at least one child, and many continued to suffer more frequently. This in turn provided the context in which the new attitudes towards death, a certain sense of guilt, and heightened family affection promoted the novel experience and apparatus of Victorian grief.[1]

Victorianism revisited: the 20th-century redefinitions of grief

During the early 20th century, Victorian grief standards were extensively revisited and indeed directly criticized. At an extreme, 19th-century culture was virtually turned upside down, concerning both grief itself and the rituals surrounding it. Some continuities admittedly modified the transition, but the shift was significant nevertheless – and it established a new emotional framework that in some ways operates in Western culture still:

- Several factors prompted the reconsideration. Western emotional culture more generally was facing significant modifications that had particular bearing on grief. Informality increased, from manners to posture to styles of dress (Wouters 2007). This was a general change, but it obviously had strong implications for the rather formal Victorian routines of mourning and funerals.
- Growing consumerism encouraged an increasingly sharp division between 'positive' and 'negative' emotions, with accompanying preference for identifying and emphasizing emotions which caused good feeling and contentment; more difficult emotions were correspondingly reproved. The concurrent rise of psychological expertise also contributed to reassessments of negative emotions, which a healthy personality should be able to restrain but for which therapeutic assistance might be required where restraint failed (Shields and Koster 1989; Horney 1999).

But the big changes took shape outside the arena of emotional culture directly, as death itself was revolutionized in several respects. Here was the transformation that explains the abruptness and magnitude of the new approaches to grief.

Throughout the Western world the death rate for infants and children plummeted between 1880 and 1920, from about 30% of all children born to 5% and falling. By the 1920s, the average family no longer had to expect at least one child to die; and correspondingly, most children could now grow up without direct experience of death, except perhaps the passing of grandparents who, however, increasingly lived apart from the nuclear unit. Additionally, between the 1920s and 1950s the occurrence of death relocated from home to hospital (Wrigley 1969; Schofield et al. 1991; Gillis et al. 1992; Coale and Watkins 1986; Evans 1987).

These various changes inevitably affected grief standards. There were, quite simply, fewer occasions that demanded grief, in the ordinary lifespan. Tensions between the emphasis on family affection and mortality rates lessened. Serious illness was now increasingly negotiated with doctors and hospital personnel, outside a familial environment and with religious authorities taking a secondary role. The classic definition of a good death itself shifted: with leading killers now shifting towards cancer and heart disease, personal preferences refocused towards hopes for a sudden demise rather than the kind of lingering passing that had previously facilitated emotional adjustments for the family.

New grief issues arose in consequence. How could the now-rare death of a child be managed emotionally? What was the proper emotional response to sudden death? What kinds of emotions would be evoked by hospital settings and medical professionals for whom death was regarded as failure?

Again, some continuities persisted. Particularly in the United States the professional funeral home, complete with fairly expensive coffins and embalmed bodies, still offered rituals for family and friends, usually supplemented by religious services. It was quite possible to regard these procedures as a satisfactory if sad framework for emotional farewells, with a sense that the departed had been treated with appropriate care and dignity (Laderman 2003).

But the emphasis on change and critique was more obvious. A number of observers, at the time and since, proclaimed that contemporary Western societies were making death into a modern taboo, seeking at all costs to avoid the emotions that might accompany contemplation of one's own death or reactions to the loss of friends or family members. And while the taboo idea went too far, it legitimately highlighted a situation in which previous emotional standards were substantially revisited. The *Fortnightly Review* summed up a common early 20th-century sentiment: 'Death is disappearing from our thoughts. . . . Perhaps the most distinctive tone of the modern spirit is the practical disappearance of the thought of death as a significant influence bearing on practical life' (Gorer 1977). A significant amount of literature grew up that argued for the elimination of any significant emotional pain attached to death (Marriott-Watson 1901; Jacobs 1899; 'A New Medical Conception of Death' 1909; Metchnikoff and Smith 1910).

Grief, in this setting, must be reevaluated. 'Probably nothing is sadder in life than the thought of all the hours that are spent in grieving over what is past and irreparable'. A healthy, modern person should be able to handle death without significant emotional baggage, in deliberate contrast to his or her Victorian antecedent. More than passing melancholy, more than a day or two of tears, suggested 'something morbid, either mental or physical' – and this now should be attacked with professional medical or psychological attention. 'When a woman cannot rouse herself . . . from her grief there is need for the care of a physician' (Inge 1911; 'The Great Adventure' 1913; Belfield 1907; 'At the End of the Journey' 1902). By the 1930s and 1940s, a whole category of 'grief work' had developed in the therapeutic community, based on the common assumption that normal people should be able to handle grief quickly and moderately (Fisguill 1914; 'The German Idea of Death' 1915; 'Editor's Diary' 1907; Taylor 1911). A new term, 'Chronic Grief Syndrome', was now applied to any enduring emotional dependency (Wouters 1990). Even etiquette recommendations were transformed. Whereas Victorian manuals had emphasized the careful steps appropriate for consoling a grieving family, good manners now turned on the griever herself, who should know better than to burden others with her emotional baggage (Post 1934; Vanderbilt 1952).

Along with these new attitudes and therapeutic responses, several other changes compounded the effort to moderate grief. Doctors, newly responsible for dealing with death in hospital but not trained in emotion management, often tried to simplify their emotional interactions by concealing terminal illness from the patient and often from the surrounding family as well. Emotion should be focused on fighting death, not preparing for its advent. Here was another complication in actual encounters with death, particularly until some modification after the 1950s (Ariès 1981; Houlbrooke 1989; Kübler-Ross 1975; Illich 1976; Kaufman 2005; Gilbert 2005).

Children – no longer exposed to frequent death in any event – began to be treated differently. Whereas Victorian culture had urged training in grief, particularly for girls, the new advice (somewhat contradictorily) tended to argue that grief and funerals might be too intense for tender youngsters, and that they might best be kept away. This, of course, might complicate grief experiences when they were later seriously encountered in adulthood (Death of family pets, however, might offer some contact with grief, becoming a newly important family focus.) (Fromme 1956; Birney 1905; Metcalf 1947; 'In the Midst of Life' 1945; Chaloner 1932; Fahs 1942; Green 1947).

The most important changes, however, together with the new attitudes to grief itself, involved the progressive truncation of mourning rituals, along with whatever comfort they might previously have provided. The use of special black clothing or armbands to represent grief declined rapidly, from the 1920s onward, as did the reliance on black-edged cards to announce a death. Funerals became more informal, and, beginning in Britain and Western Europe, the increasing popularity of cremation added another challenge to ritual tradition. Employers became increasingly reluctant to allow more than a day or two for mourning – not much beyond the time necessary for the funeral itself. And all of this occurred in a context where, for many families, the last days of a dying relative were spent in the intensive care units of hospitals, surrounding by medical professionals and the intimidating technology of life support (Mitford 1963).

These trends affected death and ritual in societies outside the West as well. The Japanese, for example, continued to rely heavily on Buddhist beliefs and rituals in dealing with death in the family. Buddhist counselling might cushion loss, and rituals such as the careful preservation of the graves of relatives accompanied a continued sense that the spirits of the dead persisted amid the living; Japan did not experience a Victorian-like intensification of grief in the late 19th/early 20th centuries. By the later 20th century, however, the traditional cultural framework was challenged by the increasing occurrence of death in the hospital environment, where medical practices might take precedence over family visits. Traditional consolations were also affected by changes in Japanese family life (along with the highest longevity rates in the world): the rapid decline of the birth rate left many older Japanese living alone, their deaths sometimes unnoticed for days. As in the West, even when mourning rituals were available they were increasingly cut short – one day for a wake, for example, rather than the customary three or four. These developments created a host of new tensions, including a widespread preference, among doctors, for concealing the imminence of death in order to avoid excessive emotionalism. Some studies suggested that Japanese anxiety about death, and uncertainty about appropriate emotional reactions, were greater than in the West. And Japanese culture was much more firmly set against reliance on psychological therapy to ease the emotional pain of death (Becker 2009).

In the West itself, the combination of attacks on excessive grief and the decline of traditional rituals towards the middle of the 20th century began to generate a number of further responses. Many groups, of course, worked hard to retain past practices, usually associated with religion. Jewish Americans, for example, usually continued sittings for several nights after a death, along with performing periodic ceremonies to remember lost relatives; many argued that these continuities eased grief considerably. The African American subculture's encouragement of more open emotion around death, in addition to new rituals, including placement of personal items with the dead body in order to facilitate passage to the next life, might help with the expression of emotion as well (Smith 2005).

Individuals affected with great grief – beyond the norms of the mainstream culture – worked for new solutions of their own, often, of course, including therapy. One striking innovation, from the 1950s onward, involved the creation of grief groups – under headings like 'Thanatos' or 'Compassionate Friends' – in major cities, where strangers whose only link was their shared experience of special grief could come together to provide mutual comfort. Groups of this sort were particularly current for people dealing with the deaths of children or young spouses, where the loss was no longer cushioned by any sense that society at large was sharing the experience or was capable of providing more than routine sympathy. This pattern clearly highlighted the changes in the larger culture, the extent that death before later age had become unusual – reducing the sense of shared pain – and the additional burden of guilt when an individual had to confront a loss. Few parents, for example, could avoid a crushing sense of responsibility when a child died, and many marriages now collapsed under the resultant weight of a grief-guilt combination (Davis 1996; Kübler-Ross 1975; Illich 1976; Sawyer 1982; Dickenson and Johnson 1993; Riley 1983; Stroebe et al. 1992; Wouters 1990).

Explicit attacks on the modernist approach to death and grief emerged amid the cultural ferment of the 1960s, without, however, dislodging the contemporary cultural framework entirely. Both in Europe and in the United States, a number of writers and intellectuals directly challenged what they saw as a shallow medical culture, urging more attention to death and the emotions that accompanied it. Elisabeth Kübler-Ross and others revisited the death-fighting impulses of physicians and hospitals, and indeed medical training did shift a bit to encourage more attention to grief and attendant emotions. Western doctors began to deal more openly and sympathetically with dying patients and their families. Courses on death and dying sprang up in many universities, creating greater awareness of the need for emotional spaces where grief could be expressed and confronted. A new series of books on mourning became available (Ariès 1981; Houlbrooke 1989; Kübler-Ross 1975; Illich 1976).

The result, overall, was a modification more than a reversal of the modernist impulses. Children were less likely to be barred from funerals, but many families continued to prefer euphemisms – such as 'passing' – rather than discussing death directly. Groups like the American Cancer society maintained a clear death fighting stance: 'In no way do we want to be associated with a book on death. We want to emphasize the positive aspects of cancer only'. Many patients complained, as a result, that their sorrows and anxieties could not be adequately expressed, as friends and medical personnel urged an optimistic outlook (Stearns 2007; Homans 2000).

Grief and guilt most clearly complicated approaches to terminal illness in many hospitals, even where elderly patients were involved. Relatives – sometimes amid mutual disagreement – often pressed for heroic measures to maintain life, even in cases where the patient had previously signed DNR, or Do Not Resuscitate, documents. They were sometimes abetted by hospital personnel guided by concerns about lawsuits for negligence as well as a continued commitment to maintaining life. Grief, as a result, was still complicated by a need to be sure that every possible medical measure was being taken (often at great expense) and, as a result, by interactions with a dying relative in the sterile and intimidating atmosphere of a hospital intensive care unit. Contemporary definitions of a good death – unless it was sudden and unexpected – remained elusive.

Some additional efforts reflected the need for further innovation around the grief-death nexus. The most important development, which was launched in Britain in 1967 and quickly spread to the United States and elsewhere, was the hospice movement. Hospice personnel sought to provide an alternative to the death-fighting approach in cases of clearly terminal illness, offering spaces and assistance where a dying patient could be protected from undue pain but without heroic medical measures beyond this. Relatives could visit freely, and indeed where possible the patient spent final days or weeks in his or her own home. The focus was on a dignified death for the individual and maximum possible inter-action with friends and family to express but also to cushion the grief process. The hospice approach gained ground only gradually, however, amid a continued impulse to prefer heroic medicine as a means of prolonging life and reducing the guilt of anxious relatives. Continued ignorance of the hospice alternative – in one poll, 75% of all Americans were unaware that hospices could provide home care – and in many cases uncertainties about insurance coverage, also complicated the picture (Saunders and Kastenbaum 1997).

Two other developments in the late 20th/early 21st centuries reflected impor-tant issues surrounding death and grief. Tolerance for deaths in military combat continued to decrease, particularly after the vivid and disturbing reportage dur-ing the Vietnam War. Particularly in the United States, involved in a number of conflicts over the past quarter century, the military worked hard both to limit casualties and to acknowledge public concern. Efforts to retrieve the bodies of the fallen – an outgrowth of modern grief that had begun with the Civil War – intensi-fied. However, during the wars in Afghanistan and Iraq after 2003, the American military for several years sought to bring most dead personnel back at night, to limit public reaction – a testimony to the potential political impact of collective grief. Public grief and guilt surrounding wartime casualties were also expressed through a growing array of public ceremonies honouring the heroism of the mili-tary (Stearns 2007).

Finally, beginning in the late 20th century, a new movement of public grief began to respond to certain kinds of individual or collective tragedies. The deaths of several public figures – mainly from the domains of politics or entertainment – began to occasion mass outpourings of sorrow. Public gatherings were supple-mented by donations of flowers, teddy bears and other symbolic items around an appropriate site. Widespread mourning around the death of Princess Diana, in 1997, was an early example of the new public grief impulse. Important manifesta-tions also have occurred around some, though not all, of the mass shootings that have and continue to bedevil the United States (for example, the killing of a num-ber of students at Virginia Tech in 2007), and as a reaction to some of the terrorist attacks (both in Europe and the United States).

The new movement of public grief clearly reflected the growing role of media in calling attention to certain tragedies and carefully and vividly reporting grief responses. It surely responded to anger and dismay at failures to prevent mass violence – including the lack of gun control measures in the United States. It reflected deep beliefs that certain kinds of death – of the young, but also of people from the middle and upper classes – were particularly inappropriate, calling for a grief response despite the lack of any real personal connection. Did the new fashion also express frustrations with the continued barriers to grief expression in other settings?

Conclusion

Grief has generated an exceptionally active history over the past 250 years. New cultural currents, as in the West, have prompted reconsideration of traditional rituals and emotional responses – in some cases, alternatively encouraging and constraining grief. In the process, emotional components of grief, and particularly a growing sense of guilt when death could not be prevented, may have shifted as well. Massive changes in the actual facts of death – in child mortality rates, in the rise of hospitals and new life support technology – have challenged grief customs even more widely. There is every reason to encourage more comparative inquiry into the variety of cultural responses. The common theme, obviously, highlights some need to reevaluate grief and its expressions. There is every indication that this reevaluation process continues, as societies experiment with additional emotional responses. The rapid ageing of many populations – from East Asia to the West – may suggest further challenges to grief in the near future.

Overall, people dealing with grief over the past two centuries – both moralists and experts advising about grief standards, and many family members coping with the emotion – have been reacting to several broad changes that to some extent cut across the Victorian and post-Victorian decades. Greater emphasis on affection in the family has joined with hopes that the traditional incidence of death could be reduced. The growing role of doctors has combined with significant changes in the rates and physical experience of death. The history of the complex grief reactions that resulted sheds important light on modern emotional history, but also suggest crucial factors to consider in evaluating grief today.

Note

1 It should also be noted that the Western experience was at this point distinctive in several ways. In the 19th century itself, Enlightenment expectations and the emphasis on family affection had yet to win much attention beyond Western culture. And the Western demographic trajectory was unusual, by global standards, in that falling birth rates preceded major changes in infant death rates. In every other major region, 20th-century shifts altered mortality levels before substantial birth rate adjustments, which could in turn affect some of the emotional reactions attached – though the patterns warrant further inquiry.

References

(1902): 'At the End of the Journey'. *Outlook*, 70, January, p. 216.
(1907): 'Editor's Diary'. *North American Review*, 186, October, pp. 307–308.
(1909): 'A New Medical Conception of Death'. *Current Literature*, 47, October, p. 453.
(1915): 'The German Idea of Death'. *Living Age*, 286, August, pp. 523–529.
(1945): 'In the Midst of Life'. *Parents' Magazine*, 20, September, p. 142.
Alcott, Louisa May (1868). *Little Women*. The Easton Press: New York.
Ariès, Philippe (1981): *The Hour of Our Death*. New York: Vintage Books.
Badone, Ellen (1989): *The Appointed Hour: Death, Worldview and Social Change in Brittany*. Berkeley, CA: University of California Press.
Becker, Carl (2009): 'Aging, Dying and Bereavement in Contemporary Japan', in *Frontiers of Japanese Philosophy 4: Facing the 21st Century*. Nagoya: Nazan Institute for Religion and Culture, pp. 90–118.
Belfield, Jane (1907): 'The Passing: An Emotional Monotone'. *Lippincott's Magazine*, 80, September, p. 374.

Birney, Theodore (1905): *Childhood*. New York: Frederick A. Stokes.

Bolitho, Harold (2003): *Bereavement and Consolation: Testimonies from Tokugawa Japan*. New Haven: Yale University Press.

Branca, Patricia (1975): *Silent Sisterhood: Middle-Class Women in the Victorian Home*. Pittsburgh: Carnegie-Mellon Press.

Burton, A. P. (1908): 'An Experience Hour'. *NFDA*: 100–103.

Chaloner, Lynn (1932): 'When Children Ask about Death'. *Parents' Magazine*, 7, April.

Coale, Ansley and Susan Watkins (eds.) (1986): *The Decline of Fertility in Europe*. Princeton: Princeton University Press.

Corbin, Alain (1986): *The Foul and the Fragrant: Odor and the French Social Imagination*. Cambridge, MA: Harvard University Press.

Cressy, David (1997): *Birth, Marriage and Death: Ritual, Religion and the Life-Cycle in Tudor and Stuart England*. Oxford: Oxford University Press.

Davis, Christie (1996): 'Dirt, Death, Decay and Dissolution: American Denial and British Avoidance', in Glennys Howarth and Peter C. Jupp (eds.): *Contemporary Issues in the Sociology of Death, Dying and Disposal*. New York: Palgrave, pp. 60–71.

Desjarlais, Robert (2016): *Subject to Death: Life and Loss in a Buddhist World*. Chicago: University of Chicago Press.

Dickenson, Donna and Malcolm Johnson (eds.) (1993): *Death, Dying and Bereavement*. London: Singer.

Dye, Nancy Schrom and Daniel Blake Smith (1986): 'Mother Love and Infant Death, 1750–1920'. *Journal of American History*, 73:329–353.

Evans, Richard (1987): *Death in Hamburg: Society and Politics in the Cholera Years, 1830–1910*. New York: Oxford University Press.

Evans, Richard (1888): 'The Golden Stein'. in *From Analytical Fourth Reader*. New York.

Fahs, Sophie (1942): 'When Children Confront Death'. *Parents' Magazine*, 18, April, p. 34.

Farrell, James (1980): *Inventing the American Way of Death, 1830–1920*. Philadelphia: Temple University Press.

Faust, Drew (2008): *This Republic of Suffering: Death and the American Civil War*. New York: Vintage Books.

Finley, Martha (1872): *Elsie's Girlhood*. New York: Dodd, Mead and Company.

Fisguill, Richard (1914): 'Death and La Mort'. *North American Review*, 199, January, pp. 95–107.

Fromme, Allan (1956): *The Parents' Handbook*. New York: Simon & Schuster.

Gilbert, Sandra (2005): *Death's Door: Modern Dying and the Ways We Grieve*. New York: W. W. Norton.

Gillis, John, David Levine and Louise Tilly (eds.) (1992): *The European Experience of Declining Fertility*. Oxford: Blackwell.

Gorer, Geoffrey (1977): *Death, Grief and Mourning*. New York: Arno Press.

Green, Mary M. (1947): 'When Death Came to School'. *Parents' Magazine*, 22, April, p. 20.

Hoffert, Sylvia (1987): '"A Very Peculiar Sorrow": Attitudes Toward Infant Death in the Urban Northeast, 1800–1860'. *American Quarterly*, 39:601–616.

Hohenschuh, W. P. (1900): *The Modern Funeral: Its Management*. New York: Trade Periodical Company.

Homans, Peter (ed.) (2000): *Symbolic Loss: The Ambiguity of Mourning and Memory at Century's End*. Charlottesville: University Press of Virginia.

Horney, Karen (1999): *The Therapeutic Process: Essays and Lectures*. New Haven, CT: Yale University Press.

Houlbrooke, Ralph (1981): *Death, Religion and the Family in England, 1480–1750*. Oxford: Oxford University Press.

Houlbrooke, Ralph (ed.) (1989): *Death, Ritual and Bereavement*. London: Routledge.

Illich, Ivan (1976): *Medical Nemesis: The Expropriation of Health*. London: Marion Boyars.

Imhof, Arthur E. (1996): *Lost Worlds: How Our European Ancestors Coped with Everyday Life and Why Life is So Hard Today*. Charlottesville: University of Virginia.

Inge, W. R. (1911): 'The Vesper Hour'. *Chautauqua*, 62, April, p. 260.

Irish, Donald, F. Kathleen Lundquist and Vivian Jenkins (eds.) (1993): *Ethnic Variations in Dying, Death and Grief: Diversity and Universality*. New York: Routledge.

Jackson, Charles (ed.) (1977): *Passing: The Vision of Death in America*. Greenwood, CT: Greenwood Press.

Jacobs, Joseph (1899): 'The Dying of Death'. *Fortnightly Review*, 72, August, pp. 246–269.

Jones, Constance (1997): *R.I.P.: The Complete Book of Death and Dying*. New York: HarperCollins.

Kasson, John F. (1991): *Rudeness and Civility: Manners in Nineteenth-Century Urban America*. New York: Hill and Wang.

Kaufman, Sharon (2005): *. . . And a Time to Die: How American Hospitals Shape the End of Life*. New York: Scribner.

Kim, Hyunchul (2015): 'Making Relations, Managing Grief: The Expression and Control of Emotions in Japanese Death Rituals'. *The Asia Pacific Journal of Anthropology*, 16 (1):17–35.

Koslofsky, Craig M. (2000): *The Reformation of the Dead: Death and Ritual in Early Modern Germany, 1450–1700*. New York: St. Martin's Press.

Kübler-Ross, Elisabeth (ed.) (1975): *Death: The Final Stage of Growth*. New York: Prentice-Hall.

Laderman, Gary (2003): *Rest in Peace: Cultural History of Death and the Funeral Home in Twentieth-Century America*. New York: Oxford University Press.

Lewis, Jan (1983): *Pursuit of Happiness: Family Values in Jefferson's Virginia*. New York: Cambridge University Press.

Lockridge, Kenneth and Jan Lewis (1988): 'Sally Has Been Sick: Pregnancy and Family Limitations among Virginia Gentry Women, 1780–1830'. *Journal of Social History*, 22:5–19.

Lystra, Karen (1989): *Searching the Heart: Women, Men and Romantic Love in Nineteenth-Century America*. New York: Oxford University Press.

Marriott-Watson, H. B. (1901): 'Some Thoughts on Pain and Death'. *North American Review*, 173, October, pp. 540–553.

McGuffey, W. M. H. (1866): *McGuffey's Fourth Eclectic Reader*. New York: Wilson, Hinkle and Co.

McManners, John (1985): *Death and the Enlightenment: Changing Attitudes to Death among Christians and Unbelievers in Eighteenth-Century France*. New York: Oxford University Press.

McNamer, Sarah (2015): 'The Literariness of Literature and the History of Emotion'. *PMLA*, 130 (5):1433–1422.

Metcalf, Dorry (1947): *Bringing Up Children*. New York: Modern Library.

Metchnikoff, Elie and Henry Smith (1910): 'Why Not Live Forever?'. *Cosmopolitan*, 44, September, pp. 436–446.

Miller, J. R. (1882): *Homemaking*. Philadelphia: Presbyterian Board of Publication.

Mintz, Steven (2004): *Hucks' Raft: A History of American Childhood*. Cambridge: Harvard University Press.

Mitford, Jessica (1963): *The American Way of Death*. New York: Norton.

Post, Emily (1934): *Etiquette: The Blue Book of Social Usage*. New York: Random House.

Rawson, Beryl (2003): *Children and Childhood in Roman Italy*. New York: Oxford University Press.

Riley, John W. (1983): 'Dying and the Meanings of Death'. *Annual Review of Sociology*, 9:191–216.

Rosenblatt, Paul C. (1983): *Bitter, Bitter Tears: Nineteenth-Century Diarists and Twentieth-Century Grief Theories*. Minneapolis: University of Minnesota Press.

Saunders, Cicely M. and Robert Kastenbaum (1997): *Hospice Care on the International Scene*. New York: Springer.

Sawyer, Darwin (1982): 'Public Attitudes Toward Life and Death'. *Public Opinion Quarterly*, 46:521–533.

Schofield, Roger, David Reher and Alain Bideau (eds.) (1991): *The Decline of Mortality in Europe*. New York: Oxford University Press.

Shields, Stephanie A. and Beth A. Koster (1989): 'Emotional Stereotyping of Parents in Child Rearing Manuals, 1915–1980'. *Social Psychology Quarterly*, 52 (1):44–55.

Shorter, Edward (1975): *The Making of the Modern Family*. New York: Basic Books.

Smith, Suzanne (2005): 'Laid Out in Big Mamma's Kitchen: African Americans and the Personalized Theme Funeral', in Peter N. Stearns (eds.): *American Behavioral History: An Introduction*. New York: New York University Press, pp. 159–180.

Stannard, David (1975): *Death in America*. Philadelphia: University of Pennsylvania Press.

Stearns, Peter N. (1996): *American Cool: Constructing a Twentieth-Century Emotional Style*. New York: New York University Press.

Stearns, Peter N. (2006): *Childhood in World History*. New York: Routledge.

Stearns, Peter N. (2007): *Revolutions in Sorrow: The American Experience of Death in Global Perspective*. Boulder, CO: Paradigm Publishers.

Stone, Lawrence (1979): *The Family, Sex and Marriage in England, 1500–1800*. New York: Harper & Row.

Stroebe, Margaret S. et al. (1992): 'Broken Hearts in Broken Bonds'. *American Psychologist*, 47:1205–1212.

Taylor, Arthur (1911): 'Pioneer Inquiries into Burial Lots'. *Survey*, 28, September, pp. 825–824.

Ulrich, Laurel Thatcher (1982): *Good Wives: Images and Reality in the Lives of Women in Northern New England, 1650–1750*. New York: Vintage Books.

Vanderbilt, Amy (1952): *New Complete Book of Etiquette*. New York: Doubleday.

Vovelle, Michel (2000): *La mort et l'Occident*. Paris: Gallimard.

Wells, Robert V. (1994): 'Taming the 'King of Terrors': Rituals and Death in Schenectady, New York, 1844–1890'. *Journal of Social History*, 27:717–734.

Wouters, Cas (1990): 'Changing Regimes of Power and Emotion at the End of Life'. *Netherlands Journal of Sociology*, 26:151–155.

Wouters, Cas (2007): *Informalization: Manners and Emotions Since 1890*. Thousand Oaks, CA: Sage Publications.

Wrigley, E. A. (1969): *Population and History*. New York: McGraw-Hill.

2 Diversity in human grieving

Historical and cross-cultural perspectives

Paul C. Rosenblatt

Introduction

In this chapter, I will argue that it is not valid to set standards for healthy grieving for all people no matter what their cultural background. Establishing standards, as DSM-V does in defining 'complicated grief', makes little sense in the light of evidence, summarized in this chapter, about cultural and historical diversity in grieving. I argue that contemporary standards for 'healthy' grieving are not based on concrete health realities such as those for physical illnesses but are based on metaphors derived from our experience of physical illness. I also argue that historical studies of grief show that the standards for public expressions of grief and possibly for private grieving can change quickly as people with the power to make changes in how people grieve push for changes. That leads to an examination of the forces in modern society that may underlie grief being defined as unhealthy that goes on 'too long' or is 'too intense'. I argue that two dominant aspects of modern society may at least in part underlie the standard for healthy grieving that defines prolonged and intense grief as unhealthy. There are the demands of the modern economy for workers to get back to work after a loss and to do their work well, and the desire of those with great power in society to silence people grieving losses arising from the decisions and actions of those with great power.

Problems with generalizations about grief

It is common in psychology and related fields to write about grief in a generalizing language which implies that there is an essential grief that is universal in humans across cultures and time. For example, the DSM-V (American Psychiatric Association 2013) and many writings about 'complicated grief' set standards for evaluating grief that ignore the very different ways people grieve from culture to culture (Rosenblatt 2013, 2017). The generalizing approach allows grief experts to make strong statements about what is healthy for grieving humans seemingly in any culture and any historical era. For example, standards for post-traumatic growth following a significant loss have generally been written as though experts who are cultural outsiders can and even should be in a position to evaluate what is 'growth' in any culture following trauma (Kashyap and Hussain 2018). The use of generalizing language is rooted in a Western cultural tradition of seeing all humans as sharing a basic psychology and also one of devaluing the knowledge of people in diverse cultures and from diverse geographic and historical locations who lack credentials as academic or clinical experts. The generalizing approach employs a language and an epistemology that delegitimizes, obscures, and ignores information that does not fit the universalizing language. But there are many cross-cultural and historical studies showing that human grieving has been and is quite diverse. People universally experience loss, but they are quite variable in emotional and cognitive response to loss and how that response affects their everyday lives.

This chapter argues for dealing with bereaved people in their own cultural terms. They have their own culture-based understandings of what a loss means to them. They have their own understandings of what their problems are as a result of a death, and those problems may not be so much emotional as relational (with the living or with the dead), spiritual, or practical. We do not do people a service by defining their loss for them. We do not do them a service by imposing our terms and meanings on them for what has occurred and what is going on with them. Indeed, we may do great harm by ignoring or dismissing their terms and meanings. From this perspective, our knowledge of the clinical and academic grief literature can make trouble for us, making us poor listeners and poor at relating to many people who are hurting.

Cultural diversity in grief challenges generalizations about 'healthy' grief

When we write about reactions to loss and define what healthy grieving is, it is difficult to escape our own language and cultural standards for grieving. But establishing for people from diverse cultures what healthy grieving is and labelling certain kinds of grieving as unhealthy and even signs of mental illness based on our own language and culture smacks of cultural insensitivity and even cultural policing. It is arguably unkind and harmful to impose the standards of one culture on people from other cultures.

Imposing the standards of one culture on diverse others is a serious problem in a diverse country like the United States. The large public hospital in my own community has a website in 36 different languages and there are translators in the hospital or who can quickly be reached for more than 200 languages. With such cultural diversity it is risky and insensitive to claim that we know what proper grieving should be for people from all cultures. Even treating someone with a physical injury like a torn knee ligament may set up many cultural issues, for example, about the gender of medical staff touching the patient or what to do if the patient believes the injury was caused by witchcraft. But for someone whose grief seems too intense, too long term, or too muted by the standards of mental health professionals who advocate culturally oblivious standards for evaluating grief, there is great risk of imposing cultural standards on a person whose upbringing and family and community standards call for, demand, expect, or even reward the way they are grieving.

Labelling grieving that according to some academic psychology views is deviant and unhealthy as an illness does not make it an illness like one due to injury, bacterial or viral infection, blockage of blood vessels, and the like that have a demonstrable physical basis. Arguably when a particular expression of grief is considered symptomatic of illness concepts drawn from physical illness are being applied metaphorically (Rosenblatt and Bowman 2013). There is not a physical reality to be assessed, like a torn ligament.

Considering grief as a thing, as though it were a concrete, knowable object like a pencil, obscures the extent to which it is not a knowable thing. That is, making grief a thing makes 'grief' an ontological metaphor (Rosenblatt and Bowman 2013); this makes it easy to use concepts and language normally applied to concrete things. But the great risk in treating grief as though it were concrete is that we lose track of its mutability, its lack of boundedness, and its unknowability. And if we are drawn into thinking of grief as though it were as concrete and real as, say, a fractured toe, we also can be drawn into writing and talking as though all humans grieve in the same way. But people in many cultures have common ways of grieving that differ greatly from grieving in Western cultures. Given that, it seems ethnocentric, insensitive, and rude to say the standards of one culture are the proper ones for other cultures.

Culturally normal grief that is pathological in common mental health views

Descriptions of normal grieving from many cultures challenge DSM-V standards of what healthy grieving is and what cultural categories make sense in understanding grief. The following examples, drawn from the ethnographic literature, illustrate the risks in cross-cultural application of DSM-V standards for complicated grief (Rosenblatt 2013, 2017). In DSM-V people are said to have complicated grief if they grieve too long (longer, say, than six months), grieve too intensely, or seem not to be grieving enough. These DSM-V standards are widely endorsed in the academic and clinical literature, and are used as guides to referral and treatment, though they certainly have their critics (e.g., Boener et al. 2013; Horwitz 2015; Horwitz and Wakefield 2007; Schurman 2017; Wakefield 2013).

Sesile Smørholm (2016) wrote about mothers in an economically marginal part of Lusaka, Zambia, who had experienced the death of a young child. In certain contexts the bereaved mothers were encouraged to grieve in silence, not to talk about the child, not to cry, and not to think much about the child. Smørholm saw those standards for mother's grieving as reflecting ideas in their culture of health, well-being, and what is proper for the spirit of the deceased child. The mothers may seem to an outsider to have no feeling for their child's death, but the mothers were doing what is proper, and there were times when they cried and talked about how much they missed the child and how much they hurt. The periods of maternal silence are encouraged by people around the mothers, and the silence has cultural meanings. Treating it as though it were an individual pathology would be inappropriate, given that the pattern of behaviour is widely shared in the society and embedded in the social and cultural milieu that pervades the life of the mothers.

Similar examples of grief that seem pathologically attenuated or muted but that are normal and make sense in cultural context come from several Indonesian cultures. Among the Toraja (Hollan 1992; Wellenkamp 1988) it is usual not to express much grief after the first few days of grieving a death. In the Toraja assumptive system, grieving that way makes a person safer from harm caused by the ancestors or spirits. Similarly, Hindu Balinese (Wikan 1990) do not express grief in public and quite possibly in private. Expressing sadness and other feelings of loss is seen in that culture as cutting one off from the gods (so they will not attend to one's prayers) and as making one vulnerable to sorcery by malicious humans.

There are also cultures in which normal grieving may carry on far longer and with more intensity than is considered proper by DSM-V standards. For example, mothers in the slums of Cairo, Egypt, who have experienced the death of a child may grieve in mute numbness for years after the child's death, and the Cairenes around such mothers understand and accept that grieving as proper (Wikan 1980).

Central aspects of the death-related realities in some cultures are so outside the realities of many clinical writings in the mental health and bereavement field that they are not even mentioned in many clinical writings. For me, that is a sign that those who rely on the mental health bereavement literature need to tread carefully in working with culturally diverse clients. How much help can one provide if the person one is trying to help is working with an assumptive system that is outside one's own experience and clinical knowledge base? Consider, for example, that when a death is believed to be caused by sorcery or witchcraft, as are some deaths among the Lihir or Papua New Guinea (Hemer 2010) and the Waorani of Ecuador (Robarchek and Robarchek 2005), bereavement can involve great anger, an intense search for who might have caused the sorcery, and possibly revenge killing of the apparent sorcerer.

There are cultures where the standards people hold for the bereaved are like those that are common in the Western mental health literature, but the underlying assumptions make the similarity in standards only superficial. For example, Catherine Lutz (1985) wrote that the Ifaluk, in the Caroline Islands of Micronesia, see a person whose grieving goes on too long as not suffering from an intrapsychic problem but having not replaced the lost person with another person who is adequate. Thus, the underlying expectation is not of emotionally coming to terms with the loss but of finding a replacement relationship.

I might be wrong, but it seems to me that the mainstream bereavement literature generally assumes that a person grieving the death of an important person in her or his life, the death of a spouse, for example, is primarily grieving that person's death. But what if one is instead primarily grieving the consequences of the death? Are we not on shaky ground in trying to help someone whose grieving realities do not fit our assumptive system? Consider, for example, that grieving in some cultural settings may be as much or more about economic losses resulting from a death than about the end of a person's life. For example, some widows in Zulu culture in South Africa may not so much grieve a husband's death as grieve the loss of economic support (Rosenblatt and Nkosi 2007). Moreover, some widows in some sub-Saharan African cultures may not only lose the economic support provided by their husband but lose the land they farm, the house they live in, and their material goods because at their husband's death all that may revert to ownership by his patrilineal kin (Cattell 1997).

It seems to me that often it is assumed in the mainstream grief literature that grieving people express their feelings through words and culturally common emotional signs such as crying and depression. But what if the standard language of grieving in a culture involves physical symptoms, for example, a headache (e.g., a community in Nicaragua, Yarris 2011)? Working within the framework of the clinical literature on grieving it might be easy to ignore or misunderstand a language (such as headaches) that is not legitimated in that literature as a language of grief.

As these examples indicate, there is not cross-cultural uniformity in how people grieve and what is proper and normal grieving. I know of no aspect of grief that is invariant across cultures. And from a perspective on culture, one could argue that it is an expression of culture when professionals and scholars cloak a culturally based view of grief with claims of panhuman applicability. Understanding the cultural foundations of culturally oblivious diagnostic categorizing with regard to grief might help us to be more open to the diversity of grieving.

Historical studies challenge generalizations about healthy grief

Not only do cross-cultural studies of grief challenge common standards for healthy grieving, so do a number of historical studies of grief. According to Johann Louw and Willem van Hoorn (2014), many scholars write as though grief has been the same throughout history, but that presumption is questionable. In fact, grief has many different histories, included histories providing views of grief (in some historical contexts) that would be considered quite odd and perhaps not healthy by the standards of contemporary Western psychology. Thus, one can see the same thing historically as cross-culturally, grief phenomena that challenge the narrowness of common mental health standards in the contemporary literature, seeing those standards as located in a particular historical and cultural era (Barclay and Reynolds 2016; McNamara and McIlvenna 2014; Rosenwein 2016; Strange 2005; Stroebe et al.1992).

What do scholars who assume that grief has been rather the same over the years (e.g., Houlbrooke 1998) make of the diversity of expressions of grief historically? The answer is in part that some scholars seem to draw a distinction between grief (feelings of sadness and the like following a death) and mourning (external, often ritualized and culturally shaped if not prescribed ways of showing to others that one has experienced a loss). That means that in some eras and places the demands of mourning may suppress expressions of grief in public and greatly limit the duration of public grieving, while in other eras and places the expectations of mourning may demand strong expressions of grief in public and a quite long period of public grieving. Then the implication is that what is underneath the limits or demands of mourning in any era is more or less the same as in any other era and place. That gets to a fundamental problem with data on what seems to be grief, particularly with historical data which ordinarily do not allow us to know how much of what we are given as historical evidence (for example, written documents or art) reflects inner feelings. But I think even if a body of historical materials, and the analysis of those materials, is entirely or substantially about mourning, the materials can still give us perspectives on grief. That is so because even when it is impossible or difficult to distinguish between grief and mourning in historical material, historical material is helpful in giving a sense of the power of cultural standards to regulate what is considered normal grieving. For example, my research with 19th century diaries from the United States and Canada (Rosenblatt 1983) indicated that for many diarists grieving too much or too long was seen as inappropriate because it seemed to question God's decisions about who should die when and to deny that the deceased had gone to heaven, which was considered a much better place than earth. I could also tell from some diary material that grieving too much was not simply an issue of public display of mourning but a matter of personal conflict between the pain of loss and deeply felt religious belief.

In examining historical studies of grief it is obvious that the context of grief could be quite different in other eras and places from what is common in the modern world, so then what grief was about in some times and places might be partly or even completely outside the assumptive framework of contemporary mental health writings. For example, the grief of a widow in the 19th-century United States (Rosenblatt 1983; Steele 1998) and in 17th-and 18th-century Britain (Houlbrooke 1998:190–191) could be, like that of some grieving sub-Saharan widows cited above (Cattell 1997), tangled in cultural rules that defined men as the owners of farmland, houses, and other assets. That could make grief over the death of a husband very much about the loss of the material basis of a woman's life. Also, in the United States in the 19th century, women were tasked with carrying much more of the burden of mourning than were men, formally expressing and symbolizing loss over a substantial period of time (Steele 1998). That put women in a place of expressing relatively strong and prolonged feelings of grief and men in a place of possibly having to suppress grieving. And either pattern might seem pathological by the standards of some mental health writings from our own era.

Grief in ancient times and modern mental health standards

Not so different from contemporary mental health standards, mourning practices which included time limits on the public expression of loss were well known and well-regulated in ancient Greece and Rome (Konstan 2006:252–253). There was also an expectation that people would get over their grief after a reasonable amount of time (Konstan 2006:250). But the mourning practices that were culturally appropriate and that gave people ways to express and communicate their feelings, if they had them, could get into zones that would seem strange by common mental health standards. For example, some ancient Greeks lamented, ululated, tore out their hair, and beat their breasts (Konstan 2006:244). Further challenging the common contemporary mental health definition of what is healthy grieving, to the extent that ancient Athenians thought of a death as not an evil it was not something to be grieved (Konstan 2006:253–254). Death was to be expected, and if a dying person seemed not unhappy, the death would bring but little sadness to the survivors, and that minimal level of sadness might enter into the problematic range by modern mental health standards. There would be sadness if the dying person had been unhappy about dying, but then the sadness might, for the ancient Athenians, be more of a pitying than a matter of grieving.

Historical mourning expectations that coerced or blunted grieving

Congruent with what was said earlier in this chapter about mourning versus grieving, there is evidence from some eras and cultures of mourning expectations that coerced or blunted expressions of grief so that people acted in public and perhaps in private in ways that might not fit their inner feelings. Mourning practices could coerce expressions of sentiments a person did not have (Lerner 1975). For example, Thomas Dixon (2015) asserted that in 18th-century Britain there were constraints on weeping such that men were limited quite a bit and both genders were limited as to where it was proper to weep. Dixon further argued that men's weeping has been seen as effeminate, weak, and manipulative throughout Western history, and that has been a constraint on male weeping. There also is reason to think that in some situations, for example, in Victorian and Edwardian Britain, anger was very rare in grieving widows in part because anger was socially disapproved of and to some extent blocked by religious ideology (Jalland 1996:238–239).

With mourning expectations being coercive, people who have experienced a loss may be required to say they loved someone who died whom they did not love and to act sad about a death about which they were relieved or even elated. They may have had to observe restraints on their activities, wear mourning clothing, and look serious in public when they were experiencing no grief feelings that fit those constraints. Jeffrey C. Lerner (1975) argued that in the United States and Britain of 100-plus years ago the more or less required wearing of mourning clothing especially for people of higher social classes, coupled with the inconvenience and expense of wearing mourning, pushed many people to stop wearing mourning. He also argued that in Britain during World War I another force for ending the wearing of mourning was the common feeling, fostered by the mass media and the government, that soldiers who died in the war were heroes, and that their deaths should be celebrated rather than mourned. Public grieving for their deaths was even seen as an unpatriotic discounting of their heroism. However, David Cannadine (1981:218) and Patricia Jalland (2010) argued that Britons pulled away from wearing mourning at that time (and during World War II) in part because there were so many war dead. Wearing mourning did not distinguish one from people around one; it could be assumed that everyone was mourning. Grieving openly could be seen as selfish when so many others grieved silently (Jalland 2010:157). Thus, a case can be made that there were social forces in England during and after the wars that led to suppressed public expressions of mourning becoming the norm (Jalland 2010, 2013). Furthermore, Jalland (2006) observed rather the same phenomena for Australians during and after the war years. Although there is now decreased emphasis on suppressed public expressions of grieving in Australia and England and greater valuing of people speaking about their losses and express-ing feelings (Jalland 2006, 2013), the past rooted in part in what happened as the result of two world wars may still be reflected in mental health standards in Aus-tralia and Britain concerning what is healthy grieving. In fact, I would argue that even if there is objective research and judicious interpretation of the research driv-ing mental health standards for grieving, the standards are at least partly driven by historical forces in the culture.

Recent historical changes affecting grief and standards for healthy grief

Writings like those of Jalland, Lerner, and Cannadine make clear that we do not have to compare contemporary grief with grief in the ancient past to see historical change in grief. In fact, grief has changed considerably in relatively recent times in Britain, the United States, and Australia. Jalland (2010) not only saw the two world wars as driving that change but also such other driving forces as marked changes in religion and health care. Related to that, Peter N. Stearns (1994:148–164) and scholars he cited wrote about how Victorians in Britain embraced grief and gave it room to be consuming in a person's life. But by the 1890s there was a growing sense in Victorian Britain of grief as unpleasant, with a menacing poten-tial to pull a person out of normal realities. Among factors that Stearns said under-lay the change, four that stand out are a dramatic decline in child death rates, the confrontation of Victorian religious beliefs by scientific ways of looking at things in which ideas about evolution had a powerful impact, the religious idea that since reunion in heaven with deceased loved ones will occur there is no need to grieve their death intensely, and for those who die in old age death is a welcome release from decrepitude. Still another thread of argument against grieving intensely and long was the idea that it was time-wasting, that instead of dwelling on the past one would do well to get on with life. Along with that was the sense that something was wrong if one grieved strongly for very long, and it might take medications or psychotherapy to repair what was amiss that led to such grieving. That idea from more than 100 years ago, a cultural idea that closely resembles DSM-V implica-tions about grief and mental health, puts medicine and psychology in support of a cultural ideology about properly limited grieving. And, of course, that echoes lines of thought nowadays, including the idea of complicated grief, grieving too long or too intensely, being a sign of need for mental health intervention. In fact, as of his 1994 book, Stearns was still seeing the dominant cultural standard for grief in the United States being one of a stiff upper lip, limited grief, and grief well-controlled. And he was seeing the major line of thought about therapy with the bereaved as a matter of helping grieving people to cut ties with the deceased and get into an active work life, social life, and general life without being held back or limited by grieving. No wonder we are still arguing in the grief field about whether grieving relatively long or relatively intensely is a bad thing. We are being pushed by the larger culture to take a stance against longer term and/ or more intense grieving. On the other hand, if the social pressures worked on everyone, there would not be so much concern about 'healing' people with 'complicated grief' because there would not be people to heal. And we would not have a burgeoning of support groups for people with long-term grieving issues over the death of a child or spouse (Stearns 1994:247).

What drives contemporary ideas about grieving?

The discussion so far in this chapter makes clear that contemporary grieving in Western society and contemporary mental health standards about grief reflect a particular culture in a moment of time. The theories and realities offered in psychology and related fields no doubt lead to some people receiving much needed help, but those theories and realities are embedded in a particular culture and history in ways that should make us cautious about using them (Gone 2011). We need to be alert to aspects of contemporary life that drive and limit ideas about grieving. What are those aspects? Two seem to me to be crucial.

The demands of the modern economy: From a critical theory perspective, setting standards of healthy grieving that greatly limit both the duration and the strong expression of grief can be seen as in service to employers in the modern economy who need workers to get back to work (Granek 2014). From that perspective, it is not at all surprising that the DSM-V and the literature on complicated grief raise strong concerns about people who grieve too long or too much. The work of those people is needed. My interviews of 29 bereaved parent couples made clear to me how powerfully money-earning work shapes and limits how and when people grieve. As I wrote in a report of that research:

> Parent narratives make crystal clear the primacy of money-earning work in U.S. society. Money-earning work limits, controls, organizes, suppresses, and shapes the grief process. Grieving parents who have money-earning jobs seem almost always to have to return soon to work, almost always in a week or less. They seem not to have other possibilities offered to them and, in many cases, do not include in their narratives an account of serious thoughts, immediately following the child death, about quitting the job or demanding long term leave in which to grieve. The U.S. seems to be a society where workers must work and in which employers, the community, the government, the church community, health insurers, and other institutions and collectivities express not the least interest in excusing a person who is deeply bereaved from work or in providing a time for the strong feelings, confusion, and so

on of early bereavement to be carried out without the requirement of wage-earning work. These constraints and forces in bereavement are underlined by the occasional parent who is grateful for the few extra days of sick leave or family leave that are granted after the child's death.

(Rosenblatt 2000:225–226)

Two grieving fathers who could not get back to doing the job well almost immediately were fired or came close to being fired. One lost his job because in his grief he could not meet the sales quota set by his employer and another would have lost his job if he had not complied with his boss's insistence that he see a grief therapist.

The demands of the modern economy also have the effect of segregating where one grieves. One is expected not to grieve at work. In fact, people who drive to work may grieve while they drive (Rosenblatt 2004), keep their grief under wraps at work, and release it again when they drive home from work. Arguably, modern capitalism requires workers to be emotionally controlled, and perhaps it should be no surprise that modern psychology has set standards for healthy grieving, through DSM-V, that support what capitalism requires of workers.

Sheltering the harm-doers of the larger system: The larger political and economic system, with its injustices, racism, wars, indifference to climate change, colonialism, neocolonialism, and lack of regulation or faulty regulation of great harm-doing, causes many deaths (Granek 2014). From this perspective, the regulation of grief in ways that mute and punish strong expressions of grief and prolonged grieving can be understood as protecting those who benefit economically from the larger system (Granek 2014). That is, standards of grieving that call for therapy and medication for those who intensely grieve deaths caused by the system or grieve those losses for a long time can be understood as defending the system and in service to it. And to the extent that the standard-setting sources on grief pathology and grief therapy are mute about these issues, they can be understood to say that systemic injustice, negligence, and the like do not matter or that anyone who grieves intensely or for a rather long time about losses linked to injustices, negligence, and the like needs counselling, medication, or other treatments. That can be taken as saying that the problem is in grieving persons and not in the system with its injustice, negligence and so on – a system that itself has caused great and widespread loss. So, for example, we know that African American grief can be entangled in past and current social justice issues connected to racism as a cause of death and racism that limited the life of a deceased loved one (Rosenblatt and Wallace 2005a, 2005b). And we know that Native Americans have hundreds of years of historical trauma and recent and current sources of injustice entangled in high rates of deaths and other losses (Ball and O'Nell 2016; Brave Heart and Debruyn 1998; Tafoya and DelVecchio 2005). Framing African American or Native American grief intensity or grief for an extended period of time as complicated grief misses the magnitude and the ongoing nature of their losses and all that these losses are entangled in, and can add to the loss and trauma they experience. And such losses are not unique to African Americans and Native Americans.

There have been and are ongoing so many different wars, genocides, destructions of ways of life, forced removals of populations, deaths caused by corporate and government negligence, and the like causing grief to many people.

Culture, grief, and writing about grief

Whatever people do or do not do in grieving is inextricably entangled in culture. People are regulated by culture, do what they do or do not because of culture, and give meanings to what they do or do not based on culture. All writings about grief, including this chapter, are saturated with cultural shoulds and cultural meanings. The fact that there are writings like this chapter and also writings that argue that grief is the same everywhere and that the DSM-V view of grief is universally valid reflects contradictions in Western culture. The culture includes forces that push for the respect of diversity and for caution in deciding what is pathological and forces that push for simple generalizations and strict, universal standards for labelling some behaviours or feelings as pathological. One can resolve the contradiction personally, but that does not mean that contradictions in the culture have gone away or can go away.

The contradictions push into a wider range of areas that touch on grief than have been addressed so far in this chapter. For example, there is cross-cultural and historical evidence that for those living in poverty the impact of a death could be economically devastating in ways that might differentiate their grieving from those not in poverty (e.g., Rosenblatt and Nkosi 2007; Strange 2005:194–208). And to the extent that contemporary mental health standards for what is healthy grieving have nothing to say about the grief of those in poverty, they may in a sense stigmatize those who are very poor and whose grief is strongly affected by economic loss that impacts whether they have a place to live, enough food, or adequate support in old age.

The mourning versus grief distinction drawn earlier in this chapter highlights the problems we all have in understanding what is going on with someone who has experienced a loss. But perhaps the distinction is not so significant in dealing with the aftermaths of a death for people in some times and places. Johann Louw and Willem van Hoorn (2014) argued that the emotionally rich, self-aware response to loss arose in historically recent times (the second half of the 19th century in Western Europe), and it is only after that way of being was common that psychological analysis of emotions, including grief, could come into existence. This does not mean that the ancients experienced nothing like grief, but it implies that grief was not their focus or what they would converse about, consider important, have the language to talk about, or value knowing about. And so the distinction between grief and mourning might not be very useful in dealing with at least some ancients.

This chapter implies that we lack the footing to understand or confidently label in our own language what is going on with people from cultures other than our own or with people from other eras. And yet I would not dismiss the usefulness of various approaches to helping people who are grieving. Grieving people may hurt with great intensity, and sometimes people want or need help or understanding. It is arguably a good thing for people to receive help if they need and want it. And if mental health professionals can help some grieving people, that is very good. Still, this chapter makes a strong case for people being understood in their culture-saturated terms and being helped and understood in ways that make sense to them and fit the culture(s) in which they are rooted.

Conclusion

I have argued in this chapter that it is a mistake to define 'healthy grief' as though culture and historical era did not matter. There is considerable variability across cultures and eras in what is normal and healthy grieving. Blanket assertions about what is healthy grief, for example the DSM-V standards defining complicated grief, are inconsistent with cross-cultural and historical evidence and perhaps are maintained only because counterfactual research reports are ignored or dismissed. Perhaps that is accomplished in part by defining very narrowly what counts as evidence and who has the credentials to have their words taken seriously. But in reality it would benefit vast numbers of bereaved people if their helpers were well-attuned to their own limitations, biases, and areas of obliviousness and were knowledgeable about cultural diversity and about the force in Western society that pushes for defining grieving too long or too intensely as illness.

References

American Psychiatric Association (2013): *Diagnostic and Statistical Manual of Mental Disorders* (5th Edition). Washington, DC: American Psychiatric Publications.
Ball, Tom and Theresa D. O'Nell (2016): 'Square Pegs and Round Holes: Understanding Historical Trauma in Two Native American Communities', in Devon E. Hinton and Byron J. Good (eds.): *Culture and PTSD: Trauma in Global and Historical Perspective*. Philadelphia: University of Pennsylvania Press, pp. 334–358.
Barclay, Katie and Kimberly Reynolds (2016): 'Introduction: Small Graves: Histories of Childhood, Death, and Emotion', in Katie Barclay, Kimberly Reynolds and Ciara Rawnsley (eds.): *Death, Emotion and Childhood in Premodern Europe: Palgrave Studies in the History of Childhood*. London: Palgrave Macmillan, pp. 1–24.
Boener, Kathrin, Anthony D. Mancini and George Bonanno (2013): 'On the Nature and Prevalence of Uncomplicated and Complicated Patterns of Grief', in Margaret S. Stroebe, Henk Schut, and Jan van den Bout (eds.): *Complicated Grief: Scientific Foundations for Health Professionals*. New York: Routledge, pp. 55–67.
Brave Heart, Maria Yellow Horse and Lemyra DeBruyn (1998): 'The American Indian Holocaust: Healing Historical Unresolved Grief'. *American Indian and Alaska Native Mental Health Research*, 8 (2):60–82.
Cannadine, David (1981): 'War and Death, Grief and Mourning in Modern Britain', in Joachim Whaley (ed.): *Mirrors of Mortality: Studies in the Social History of Death*. New York: St. Martin's Press, pp. 187–242.

Cattell, Maria G. (1997): 'African Widows, Culture, and Social Change: Case Studies from Kenya', in Jay Sokolovsky (ed.): *The Cultural Context of Aging: Worldwide Perspectives* (2nd Edition). Westport, CT: Bergin and Garvey, pp. 71–98.

Dixon, Thomas (2015): 'Weeping in Space: Tears, Feelings, and Enthusiasm in Eighteenth-Century Britain', in Susan Broomhall (ed.): *Spaces for Feelings: Emotions and Sociabilities in Britain, 1650–1850*. New York: Routledge, pp. 137–158.

Gone, Joseph P. (2011): 'Is Psychological Science A-Cultural?'. *Cultural Diversity and Ethnic Minority Psychology*, 17 (3):234–242.

Granek, Leeat (2014): 'Mourning Sickness: The Politicizations of Grief'. *Review of General Psychology*, 18 (2):61–68.

Hemer, Susan R. (2010): 'Grief as Social Experience: Death and Bereavement in Lihir, Papua New Guinea'. *Australian Journal of Anthropology*, 21 (3):281–297.

Hollan, Douglas (1992): 'Emotion Work and Value of Emotional Equanimity among the Toraja'. *Ethnology*, 31 (1):45–56.

Horwitz, Allan V. (2015): 'The DSM-5 and the Continuing Transformation of Normal Sadness into Depressive Disorder'. *Emotion Review*, 7 (3):209–215.

Horwitz, Allan V. and Wakefield, Jerome C. (2007): *The Loss of Sadness: How Psychiatry Transformed Normal Sorrow into Depressive Disorder*. New York: Oxford University Press.

Houlbrooke, Ralph A. (1998): *Death, Religion and the Family in England, 1480–1750*. Oxford: Clarendon Press.

Jalland, Patricia (1996): *Death in the Victorian Family*. New York: Oxford University Press.

Jalland, Patricia (2006): *Changing Ways of Death in Twentieth-Century Australia: War, Medicine and the Funeral Business*. Sydney: University of New South Wales Press.

Jalland, Patricia (2010): *Death in War and Peace*. New York: Oxford University Press.

Jalland, Patricia (2013): 'A Culture of Silent Grief? The Transformation of Bereavement Care in 20th Century England'. *Bereavement Care*, 32 (1):16–22.

Kashyap, Shivali and Dilwar Hussain (2018): 'Cross-Cultural Challenges to the Construct 'Posttraumatic Growth''. *Journal of Loss and Trauma*, 23 (1):51–69.

Konstan, David (2006): *The Emotions of the Ancient Greeks: Studies in Aristotle and Classical Literature*. Toronto: University of Toronto Press.

Lerner, Jeffrey C. (1975): 'Changes in Attitudes toward Death: The Widow in Great Britain in the Early Twentieth Century', in Bernard Schoenberg et al. (eds.): *Bereavement: Its Psychosocial Aspects*. New York: Columbia University Press, pp. 91–118.

Louw, Johann and Willem van Hoorn (2014): 'Historical – Psychological Reflections on Emotion and Human Subjectivity'. *South African Journal of Psychology*, 44 (2):205–215.

Lutz, Catherine (1985): 'Depression and the Translation of Emotional Worlds', in Arthur Kleinman and Byron Good (eds.): *Culture and Depression: Studies in the Anthropology and Cross-Cultural Psychiatry of Affect and Disorder*. Berkeley, CA: University of California Press, pp. 63–100.

McNamara, Rebecca F. and Una McIlvenna (2014): 'Medieval and Early Modern Emotional Responses to Death and Dying'. *Parergon*, 31 (2):1–10.

Robarchek, Clayton and Carole Robarchek (2005): 'Waorani Grief and the Witch-Killer's Rage: Worldview, Emotion, and Anthropological Explanation'. *Ethos*, 33 (2):205–230.

Rosenblatt, Paul C. (1983): *Bitter, Bitter Tears: Nineteenth Century Diarists and Twentieth Century Grief Theories*. Minneapolis: University of Minnesota Press.

Rosenblatt, Paul C. (2000): *Parent Grief: Narratives of Loss and Relationship*. Philadelphia: Brunner/Mazel.

Rosenblatt, Paul C. (2004): 'Grieving while Driving'. *Death Studies*, 28 (7):679–686.

Rosenblatt, Paul C. (2013): 'The Concept of Complicated Grief: Lessons from other Cultures', in Margaret S. Stroebe, Henk Schut and Jan van den Bout (eds.): *Complicated Grief: Scientific Foundations for Health Professionals*. New York: Routledge, pp. 27–39.

Rosenblatt, Paul C. (2017): 'Complicated Grief: A Cross-Cultural Perspective', in Kenneth J. Doka and Amy S. Tucci (eds.): *When Grief Is Complicated*. Washington, DC: Hospice Foundation of America, pp. 43–54.

Rosenblatt, Paul C. and Beverly R. Wallace (2005a): *African American Grief*. New York: Routledge.

Rosenblatt, Paul C. and Beverly R. Wallace (2005b): 'Narratives of Grieving African-Americans about Racism in the Lives of Deceased Family Members'. *Death Studies*, 29 (3):217–235.

Rosenblatt, Paul C. and Busisiwe Catherine Nkosi (2007): 'South African Zulu Widows in a Time of Poverty and Social Change'. *Death Studies*, 31 (1):67–85.

Rosenblatt, Paul C. and Ted Bowman (2013): 'Alternative Approaches to Conceptualizing Grief: A Conversation'. *Bereavement Care*, 32 (2):82–85.

Rosenwein, Barbara H. (2016): *Generations of Feeling: A History of Emotions, 600–1700*. Cambridge: Cambridge University Press.

Schurman, Donna L. (2017): 'Is Grief Complicated? The Dangers of a Label', in Kenneth J. Doka and Amy S. Tucci (eds.): *When Grief is Complicated*. Washington, DC: Hospice Foundation of America, pp. 55–69.

Smørholm, Sesile (2016): 'Suffering Peacefully: Experiences of Infancy Death in Contemporary Zambia'. *Ethos*, 44 (3):333–351.

Stearns, Peter N. (1994): *American Cool: Constructing a Twentieth Century Emotional Style*. New York: New York University Press.

Steele, Jeffrey (1998): 'The Gender and Racial Politics of Mourning in Antebellum America', in Peter N. Stearns and Jan Lewis (eds.): *An Emotional History of the United States*. New York: New York University Press, pp. 91–106.

Strange, Julie-Marie (2005): *Death, Grief and Poverty in Britain, 1870–1914*. New York: Cambridge University Press.

Stroebe, Margaret S., Mary M. Gergen, Kenneth J. Gergen and Wolfgang Stroebe (1992): 'Broken Hearts or Broken Bonds: Love and Death in Historical Perspective'. *American Psychologist*, 47 (10):1205–1212.

Tafoya, Nadine and Ann DelVecchio (2005): 'Back to the Future: An Examination of the Native American Holocaust Experience', in Monica McGoldrick, Joe Giordano, and Nydia Garcia-Preto (eds.): *Ethnicity and Family Therapy* (3rd Edition). New York: Guilford. pp. 55–63.

Wakefield, Jerome (2013): 'Is Complicated/Prolonged Grief a Disorder? Why the Proposal to Add a Category of Complicated Grief Disorder to the DSM-5 Is Conceptually and Empirically Unsound', in Margaret S. Stroebe, Henk Schut, and Jan van den Bout (eds.): *Complicated Grief: Scientific Foundations for Health Professionals*. New York: Routledge, pp. 99–114.

Wellenkamp, Jane C. (1988): 'Notions of Grief and Catharsis among the Toraja'. *American Ethnologist*, 15 (3):486–500.

Wikan, Unni (1980): *Life among the Poor in Cairo*. London: Tavistock.

Wikan, Unni (1990): *Managing Turbulent Hearts: A Balinese Formula for Living*. Chicago, IL: University of Chicago Press.

Yarris, Kristin Elizabeth (2011): 'The Pain of 'Thinking Too Much': Dolor de Cerebro and the Embodiment of Social Hardship among Nicaraguan Women'. *Ethos*, 39 (2):226–248.

3   The impact of the two world wars on cultures of grieving

Grief in England, 1914–1980

Patricia Jalland

Introduction

Cultural norms relating to grief and bereavement have been transformed over the last hundred years, by demographic and medical change, the decline of religion and by the two world wars. In this chapter, I will analyze the slow and complex shift in the cultures of grieving in England in the fifty years after the Great War as a consequence of the two world wars – from a Victorian culture, where death was often accepted and emotions openly expressed, to an officially required culture of emotional avoidance, minimal ritual and private sorrow. The revival of expressive grieving from the 1960s, predominantly among the middle class, was a slow and sustained recovery from the extreme cultural impacts of the two world wars.

In the 19th century, mourning rituals had made the grieving experience more meaningful for many and helped to meet the emotional needs of the bereaved. Christianity still played a powerful part in the lives and deaths of many Victorians, offering hope of immortality and encouraging expression of sorrow in overtly emotional terms. After 1914, religious faith became one of several important variables and gradually played a less influential role. A fall in mortality from infectious diseases and a significant rise in life expectancy marked a sharp divide between the 19th and 20th centuries. People expected to live longer and their babies to survive. Moreover, the advance of secularization altered the meanings, the emotions and the significance ascribed to mortality, as the belief in divine judgement and an afterlife declined (Jalland 2010:15–34, 1996).

The mass slaughter of the First World War brought intense and prolonged communal grief and a powerful reaction against Victorian ways of death. Victorian family rituals seemed inadequate and inappropriate during and after World War I, particularly in the absence of the bodies, which were buried and lost on the battlefields (Cannadine 1981). Soldiers' burial in England had been prohibited from 1915, so grieving families had no funerals or graves at home as a focus for sorrow. Traditional mourning rituals were unable to cope and declined dramatically during the war and afterwards, as did Victorian-style deathbeds.

In the following I will demonstrate how the two world wars had a profound and cumulative impact, with overwhelming communal grief for the war dead. Emotions were already blunted by the mass war deaths, while soldiers had repeatedly asked families not to grieve for them if they died. In the interwar years and beyond, there were no more prolonged deathbed scenes as death gradually moved from home to hospital and bereavement rituals declined. The Second World War marked a far deeper break with the past than the Great War; it represented a watershed in the emotional and ritualized culture of grieving in England. The change in cultural norms affecting family bereavement was more intense, widespread and long-lasting from the 1940s. Open and expressive sorrow was strongly discouraged in favour of a pervasive model of suppressed privatized grieving, which became entrenched in the nation's psyche for the next thirty years or so. The cultural prescription which privileged stoicism in the face of loss had long affected upper-middle-class men, soldiers in wartime, the unskilled working classes and the poor. But in the next thirty years it became even more influential and was internalized by many more bereaved women as well as men in the English community (Jalland 2010).

The revival of expressive grieving from the 1960s was primarily among the educated middle class, particularly among women in the cities, the large towns and the south. The creation of grief studies in the 1960s and 1970s helped to reframe the possibilities of different cultures of grieving – beyond silence and denial. Social scientists emphasized and normalized the complexity of cultures of grieving, and the cultural value of personal as well as social mourning rituals.

The impact of World War I and the influenza pandemic

World War I had a profound impact on changing attitudes, emotions and practices relating to grief and bereavement. The massive mortality of British servicemen in World War I has been estimated by Jay Winter at close to three-quarters of a million (Winter 1986:70–97). One in eight was killed. Almost three-quarters of war wounds were caused by artillery shells, which often turned septic (Jalland 2010:17). The sheer number and nature of war deaths were appalling, and communal grief at the front and at home was overwhelming. Yet soldiers and bereaved families largely repressed their grief and coped in silence (Raphael 1986). Soldiers had to minimize their grief at the death of comrades, and encourage their families to do the same. Despite the massacre at the Battle of the Somme in July 1916, the *Barnsley Chronicle* (15 July 1916) remained confident such huge losses would be borne 'with Spartan courage'. Personal grief was sacrificed in the midst of so much death and with such minimal ritual.

While conventional practices for dealing with death and loss were patently inadequate under the immediate impact of World War I, new and innovative communal ways were devised to commemorate the dead soldiers. These included the remarkable public rituals at the Cenotaph, popular visits to the Tomb of the Unknown Warrior in Westminster Abbey and Armistice Day Commemorations. Local civic war memorials, erected across the country, brought comfort to many bereaved families who lived far from London (Cannadine 1981; Gregory 1994, chapter 1).

The global death toll from the influenza pandemic in 1918–1919 was at least twice that of the war, yet 'the flu was rapidly relegated to obscurity' (Reid 2005). The Great War overshadowed the worldwide epidemic, even though there were about thirty million influenza deaths globally, perhaps even fifty million. The impact of the war explained the virulence of the epidemic and England's weak response (Patterson and Pyle 1991). The measures required to fight a lethal military war were inappropriate to counter disease, and medicine had no cure and no really effective treatment. The over two hundred thousand British people killed by the pandemic tended to be seen as war victims, but they were not commemorated in the interwar years as were the 560,00–577,000 dead soldiers (Jalland 2010:32). The memory of the killer epidemic was subsumed in that of the war. People wished to celebrate victory in November 1918, not dwell on the horrors of the pandemic. The vast numbers of war deaths had already blunted the emotions of survivors, A terrible war subdued the normal community responses to an enormous loss of life at home.

The need to seek personal consolation and to come to terms with the intense emotions of grief and despair still remained for individuals and families, even though new communal forms of grieving had been created. The public commemoration of dead soldiers in England often had little appeal for the families of missing soldiers, with no known graves. These families needed solace most of all. Pilgrimages to the former battlefields could help to satisfy some of these personal needs for grieving. The Bickersteth family was one of many to make repeated ritualized pilgrimages to the newly created war cemeteries. They visited the presumed grave of Lieutenant Morris Bickersteth, killed on the first day of the battle of the Somme, on 1 July 1916. Morris's body was probably blown to bits and he was posted missing for months, until the family learned his presumed remains had been moved to a cemetery near the battlefield where he died. The devout Anglican Bickersteth family described their many visits in the interwar years as 'sacred pilgrimages' to a 'holy place' where they felt close to Morris's spirit. These visits evoked intense emotions, as revealed in the family's poignant and lengthy accounts of their four pilgrimages in the 1920s and 1930s. Religion, spirituality and memory as well as intense grief, played vital roles in such pilgrimages. Most pilgrims believed they were closest to the spirits of their dead on the battlefields where they lay, perceived as sacred places where heroic soldiers sacrificed their lives for their country (Bickersteth 1919).

The role of memory was almost as vital in the process of mourning as that of religion. The heart of the Bickersteths's pilgrimages was Morris's grave, with his name inscribed on the headstone. Morris's brothers were war veterans who were also still grieving intensely for fallen comrades, who had shared their war trauma. They were haunted by survival guilt and horrific memories. The Bickersteth family saw their visits as 'sacred pilgrimages' fought for 'the ideals of liberty and freedom'. For the Bickersteth brothers, remembering the war and its dead was a vital part of grieving which helped them come to terms with their own painful and complex wartime past (Bickersteth 1919; Jalland 2010:60–82).

The continuing power of spiritualism was another source of comfort to many bereaved families during and after the war. Spiritualism became a popular source of consolation in wartime both for soldiers at the front and bereaved families at home. It encouraged belief in communication with the spirits of the dead through mediums. Spiritualism offered an outlet for intense sorrow during the war and in the two decades of intense mourning which followed. Spiritualism held special meaning for families mourning the vast army of soldiers whose bodies were never found. The movement gained mass appeal during the war and its numbers reached a peak in the 1930s with about a quarter of a million members (Nelson 1969:155–165). While its power lasted it carried comfort to bereaved parents; these included Rudyard Kipling, and Mary Countess of Wemyss, who visited a spiritualist to contact the two sons she lost in the war (Jalland 2010:51). As Jay Winter notes, the power of spiritualism declined in the later 1930s when many mourners at last came to terms with their grief (Winter 1995:58–63).

The interwar years: continuity, disasters and change

In the interwar years, responses to death and bereavement varied widely, by class, region and religion, and in a complex manner. Older traditions were more resilient among the lower working classes, older people and women. In the North of England, the Midlands and the Celtic fringe, there were powerful continuities with the stoical working-class culture of death and loss before 1914 (Strange 2005:195, 252–255). Older traditions were often surprisingly resilient in these areas.

Ritualized and emotional grieving remained an important aspect of family bereavement in working-class Lancashire between the wars, retaining a vitality often missing in middle- and upper-class families. Elizabeth Roberts's interviews with 160 older women in Preston, Barrow and Lancaster reveal that spiritual beliefs and folk religion were still influential, while families accepted the loss of babies and children stoically but with no lack of feeling. The performance of long-established rituals was seen as vitally important in providing comfort. From 1800 to 1940 death, like birth, remained in the experienced care of female family members and neighbours. Continuity with the past was still powerful and emotional responses strong. A respected neighbourhood layer-out washed the body, dressed it in a clean nightgown and placed pennies on the eyes, a loving procedure offering sympathy and respect. The body in the open coffin was kept at home in the front parlour, surrounded by flowers, with curtains drawn, as family and neighbours paid their last respects (Roberts 1989). These working-class rituals retained the emotional depth of the late 19th century.

A 'good send-off' at a crowded, respectable funeral was considered especially important in Lancashire between the wars. Funerals were acknowledged to serve the needs of the living, allowing the family to confront the reality of the death and commence the grieving process. There was no lack of emotion but an expectation that it would be constrained, out of respect. The funeral tea with ham sandwiches was prepared for mourners after the funeral by the neighbours, providing a time for family solidarity and emotional reminiscences about the dead person. The family then went into mourning for many months, wearing black clothes and reducing their social activity. As Roberts notes:

> People were given time to grieve, indeed they were expected to grieve. There appears to have been little expectation that they should smile brightly and pretend nothing happened. The dead were constantly remembered, they were talked about, their photographs were displayed and their graves visited.
>
> (Roberts 1989)

Family members went to the cemetery most Sunday afternoons to tend the graves: 'And [the dead] went on living, so to speak, in conversation and memory for some considerable time' (Roberts 1989:188–207).

The coalminers in the north of England and Wales experienced more deaths in peacetime than the rest of the working classes and responded in ways that were deeply rooted in the past. Their ways of grieving were very different from those described by Roberts in other parts of the North. They were also powerfully affected by their dreadful war experiences. They had faced appalling pit disasters frequently, losing about a thousand men annually in the five years up to 1931. Miners were often compared to soldiers in the trenches in the Great War, in which a quarter of miners enlisted. In the interwar mining catastrophes, as in the Great War, suppression of emotion was common and necessary to help men survive the ordeal (Jalland 2010:84–86).

Strict cultural conventions governed the behaviour of the mining communities and the press in dealing with bereavement. The role models for the bereaved families were the miners and the soldiers of the Great War – an entirely masculine model. The long 'watch of agony' at the pithead was maintained by stoical families seeking to suppress their distress. Crowds of thousands would wait in silence for news, day and night. As bodies were recovered, the colliery yards were 'crowded with dry-eyed but woebegone women'. Even at the dreaded public ritual of identifying the bodies there were usually 'no emotional scenes' and widows maintained a 'dignified calm'. The newspapers respected the privacy of the bereaved to a degree inconceivable today (Jalland 2010:86–92).

The emotional needs of so many bereaved mining families were not recognized as they were elsewhere in the north or as they would be today. Support mechanisms such as bereavement counselling and mutual help groups were phenomena of the future. Family sorrow was intense, but it took place behind the drawn blinds and closed doors of little cottages: families dealt with their loss privately as best they could, with limited neighbourly support. We can only speculate on the negative effect of so many violent pit deaths on the consoling family rituals practised elsewhere in the north, such as the laying-out of the corpse and the wake held around it. The circumstances of pit deaths often made such social rituals impossible, especially as many victims' remains were buried in the pit. Widows were likely to be pauperized by the loss of breadwinners and bereaved families were often obliged by poverty to move away (Jalland 2010:86–92).

However, from the 1940s the important roles of layer-out, family and community were increasingly replaced by the formal professional care of doctors, nurses and funeral directors. With the introduction of the National Health Service in 1948, health care became more a matter for the hospital, and home nursing was supervised by the district nurse (Roberts 1984, 1989:205–206; Adams 1993). Although working-class attitudes to death changed very slowly over decades, many old customs were gradually abandoned or attenuated. But the rate of change varied greatly by region and class. A surprising number of rituals described by Roberts survived among the northern working classes into the 1960s, albeit often in a reduced form.

The Second World War, the atomic bombs and silent grief in England

In World War II, Winston Churchill appealed for national courage and stoicism during the German air blitz on British cities. The dark side of the blitz story, with its high mortality and mass graves, was sanitized to sustain morale in the interests of survival. The British defence forces again provided the stoical model for the country to follow, with the celebrated stiff upper lip and determination to conceal emotion. The government encouraged civilians not to dwell on the intense distress of individual bereaved people. British propaganda and press censorship strove to maintain good humour, courage and positive morale in the community in the face of the blitz and flying bombs. Emotional 'breakdown' amounted to cowardice in this stereotypical model, and victims of air raids were given no encouragement to express or report psychological trauma (Calder 1991:121–122).

Until early 1945, the human cost of the war in Britain fell heavily on the civilian population. Numerous families were wounded by intense sorrow that they felt required to repress in the interests of morale, sometimes for years. Families in target areas in East London were expected to 'take it' in silence, and display outward stoicism and courage. On 7 September 1940, German bombs killed 430 people, followed by 770 during the next two nights, leaving the London docks blazing. A family account in the Imperial War Museum in London reveals the broader impact of these first air raids. The Furniaux family took refuge in a public air raid shelter in poverty-stricken Shoreditch in the East End, the chief target. About forty people were killed and many more wounded when a bomb exploded, causing utter chaos. Flo Furniaux and her two children were among the many dead, and were buried in a mass common grave with other victims, all of whom were denied the dignity of individual graves and memorials. Flo's sister, Rosie, was badly wounded and received a hospital bill, like most other victims, which she refused to pay. In later years, Rosie was still angry that her family had received no counselling or compensation, while there was no plaque in London to commemorate the sacrifice of victims of the blitz in so many families (Furniaux 1940).

The families of young men in RAF Bomber Command were also required to be courageous and stoical. Revd. G. H. Martin was an Anglican chaplain with RAF Bomber Command in 1944, based in Cambridgeshire. His numerous files in the Imperial War Museum on 'Missing Personnel' make depressing reading, containing a wealth of correspondence from the relatives of hundreds of airmen categorized as missing or believed dead. The responses of these families still make a powerful impact on the reader by their courage, anguish and stoicism, which vastly understates their own grief and suffering. The families insisted their beloved sons or husbands would have wished them to be strong and stoical, implying that expressive and emotional grief was self-indulgent and unhelpful to the war effort. In many cases, lost airmen had asked their wives to keep a 'stiff upper lip' if they were killed. Most wives made heroic efforts to emulate the masculine code of meeting death with stoicism and fortitude, bringing their female patterns of grieving into line with those of men (Martin 1944). Many of the missing men remained so forever, and families suffered in silence for years, hiding their sorrow, with no certainty of their men's deaths and continuing mental images of their likely fate in burning planes.

The events of World War II led to increasing silences in response to loss among bereaved families of Blitz victims, RAF Bomber Command crews and other casualties of war. The community coped with the huge losses of both wars by a complex mixture of remembering and forgetting, which are also contradictory aspects of the grief process. But the emphasis was more on remembering after the Great War and forgetting after the Second World War. The English already had a traditional reserve about expression of emotions, more marked among men and particular groups such as the upper class and the lower levels of the working class. This emotional constraint was enhanced by the impact of both world wars, but more so by the Second World War.

During the interwar years the Armistice Day ritual had tried to make sense of the suffering of the Great War in terms of the traditional elevated ideals of patriotism and sacrifice, often expressed in emotional Christian language. But that ended in bitter disillusionment once it was clear that the Great War had failed to prevent another war. It was far more difficult in 1945 to find symbolic meaning for the slaughter after the mass deaths of civilians, the Holocaust and the dropping of the atomic bombs. As Jay Winter observed: 'After Hiroshima and Auschwitz, the earlier commemorative effort simply could not be duplicated. . . . After 1945, older forms of the language of the sacred faded, and so had the optimism, the faith in human nature on which it rested' (Winter 1995:8–9, 203, 228). Moreover, the mood in England in 1945 was to support the Labour Party's positive agenda in building a new welfare state, rather than dwelling on the catastrophe of war with its mass casualties. And so, instead of erecting new monuments in 1945, names of the Second World War dead were generally added to those of 1918.

The American decision to use atomic bombs on the two Japanese cities of Hiroshima and Nagasaki in August 1945 ended the war quickly, as intended. It also immediately raised the awful spectre of 'the total extinction of human civilization', as the Emperor of Japan warned. The prospect of nuclear warfare from August 1945 adds a quite awesome dimension to the story of death and grief in war and peace. On 6 August 1945 the American bomber *Enola Gay* dropped an atomic bomb on Hiroshima. The English philosopher Bertrand Russell wrote:

'The prospect for the human race is sombre beyond all precedent. . . . In the next war, if atomic bombs are used on both sides, it is to be expected that all large cities will be wiped out' (Russell 1945).

There was widespread fear of potential global destruction from 1945 to the early 1960s. As Samuel Brittan recalled in the *Spectator* in 2001 (14 April): 'The fear of mutual annihilation in horrifying circumstances was a dominating concern between the Hiroshima bomb in 1945 and the detonation of the first H-bomb in 1954'. The 'Russell-Einstein Manifesto' warned in July 1955 that one H-bomb could obliterate vast cities like London and New York, while many H-bombs could bring global death, sudden for the minority and 'a slow torture of disease and disintegration for the majority' (Russell 1945). Bertrand Russell became a leading figure in the Campaign for Nuclear Disarmament, which started in Britain in 1958 as a powerful protest movement. It subsequently declined because most people preferred not to dwell on the prospect of nuclear annihilation. Increasingly the costs of war appeared to exceed the rewards.

Those two decades of existential fear of universal nuclear death coincided with a period of profound silence about death and grief at an individual, family and community level in England. As Adrian Gregory observed: 'There was a new silence in 1945, the silence after Auschwitz and the silence after Hiroshima. The silence in which nothing meaningful could be said' (Gregory 1994:222). Writing in *New Society* in 1965 (29 April) Richard Hoggart had a similar view of the impact of the war and of the atomic bombs:

> Perhaps we talk less about death *not* because we are running away from it but because in the light of recent experience, we have all too fully accepted it – as massively impersonal, imminent and immanent, and perhaps as meaningless.
> (Hoggart 1965)

In 1971, A. Alvarez noted: 'Death is everywhere and on such a vast scale that it becomes indifferent, impersonal, inevitable and finally, without any meaning' (Alvarez 1971:199–203). The sense of helplessness and existential dread may have haunted many. The threat of mass extinction had the capacity to make individual domesticated deaths seem even more insignificant. In the broader context of potential nuclear annihilation, personal sorrow for a loved one might seem an indulgence, to be borne quietly alone, powerfully reinforcing those earlier silences in response to wartime deaths.

The Second World War made emotional restraint the customary code for all, regardless of gender, and affected the culture of grieving by women more deeply than men. The gender gap was reduced as women increasingly internalized their sorrow and moved closer to the socially conditioned male patterns of grieving. Women understood during the war that it seemed self-indulgent 'to spread one's own sorrows' when thousands of others were suffering in silence. Many women had taken to heart the wartime prescriptions about the appropriate way to deal with grief: 'You must hide your feelings: you do your mourning quietly, alone. The same as you might do praying'. This shift in female patterns of grieving made a major contribution to the culture of silence about death and loss that was so pervasive after 1945 (Jalland 2010, chapters 7–8; Walter 1999, chapter 10).

It is a special challenge for a historian to explore the nature of a culture of grief characterized by silence, as in the two decades after 1945. The wealth of unpublished family evidence in archives is reduced by 1960 and almost nonexistent beyond 1980. Bereaved people lacked guidelines to help them understand and cope with their grief, except wartime conventions, which dealt with public morale not personal sorrow. They faced their loss before psychiatrists had constructed theories of grief relating to the broader culture. There were no mutual support groups, bereavement counsellors or advice books. Bereaved people were advised to keep busy, and move on, even if their hearts were breaking. They must behave normally and pretend to be cheerful – and grieve privately in silence.

War widows received little attention or community support in the 1940s and 1950s. Many sought refuge from sorrow in apathy and avoidance, while the community looked away. One war widow spoke to sociologist Peter Marris on the 1960 BBC radio program *The World of the Widow*. She was deeply shocked by her widowhood at age 27: 'I felt completely at sea and it took me a long time to recover my feeling for life at all'. Emotional problems crowded in on her. She had felt obliged 'to put on a good show' because she had no choice and the community did not want to hear about her grief. She noted that most people had no idea what sort of effort it cost widows to 'appear normal on the surface' (BBC 1960).

Audrey Deacon was one of many war widows whose grief lasted for years because she tried to suppress it, while those around her colluded in the silence. When her husband, Terry Deacon, an army officer, was killed in 1943, she threw herself into frenetic war work in the Women's Royal Naval Service. As Audrey noted in her diary, the Normandy landings allowed her to block her grief through hard work and exhaustion. In September 1945, fifteen months after Terry's death, she noted: 'I'm not facing life', though 'I don't actively want to die now'. Audrey acknowledged that she had lived without purpose, 'in a blind unthinking state of numbness mentally'. Years later, in 1948, Audrey admitted that she had failed to 'assimilate the catastrophe' into her life and give it some meaning, relapsing instead into a prolonged state of apathy. After several years of depression she slowly recovered with the help of religious consolation and a successful career in social welfare (Deacon 1940–1945).

Audrey Deacon's story was common among war widows who found refuge from grief in apathy and avoidance while the community looked away. Margaret Torrie, a Quaker and pacifist, became aware of the suffering of such widows during the 1950s in the course of her work at the Citizens Advice Bureau. Consequently, in 1959 she established the Cruse Bereavement Care organization for widows, initially to provide practical services and meeting places, with associated doctors and social workers. Margaret was supported in this endeavour by her husband, Dr Torrie, a psychiatrist, whose own therapeutic work had made him aware of the need. In 1960 the Torries were interviewed for the BBC programme *The World of the Widow*, which explained the results of Peter Marris's sociological research into the nature of grief (see Marris 1958). The Torries emphasized the little-known fact that the painful symptoms of grief were widely experienced and usually normal. They explained that the Cruse organization was urgently needed because so many widows felt completely isolated, as most people avoided the emotive subjects of death and bereavement, which were so little understood (BBC 1960).

Several widows who had joined Cruse were interviewed for Peter Marris's BBC programme. One said she had come to Cruse a month after her husband died: 'It's done me wonders – I don't know what I would have done without it', since it allowed her to share similar troubles with other widows, who offered sympathy and advice (BBC 1960). Dr and Mrs Torrie were delighted with Cruse's early achievements, but they emphasized that Cruse had to be professional: 'We want a serious counselling service', and not 'a party of wailing women'. The Torries succeeded in gaining the confidence of the medical profession, statutory groups, and voluntary societies (BBC 1960).

As the eminent psychiatrist, Dr Colin Murray Parkes noted, Cruse 'provided the opportunity to develop a network of bereavement care across the whole of the United Kingdom', training members of the caring professions and volunteer counsellors in the required skills (Parkes 1972/1986:17, 186–187). Cruse ultimately achieved remarkable success, becoming Britain's leading bereavement agency, placing increasing focus on psychological and emotional counselling. The service was extended to widowers in 1980 and to all bereaved people in 1987 (Richards 2009). By the 1990s Cruse had become a largely secular organization in which sympathetic understanding, psychological counselling and well-tested grief theories largely replaced religious faith (Parkes 1972/1986; Walter 1999:196–198).

The creation of grief studies: Geoffrey Gorer, C. S. Lewis and Colin Murray Parkes

As late as 1963, the social anthropologist Geoffrey Gorer was so concerned about the community's wish to avoid the subjects of death and bereavement that he undertook an extensive social investigation. This was published two years later as *Death, Grief and Mourning in Contemporary Britain*. Gorer was partly motivated to write his book by the harrowing experience of his brother's death from cancer in 1961, leaving a distressed young widow and two children. His widowed sister-in-law dealt with her bereavement by trying to behave as if nothing had happened, taking her children for a picnic instead of attending the cremation ceremony. Elizabeth could not bear the prospect of losing emotional control and allowing others to observe her grief. There were no rituals and she was unable to mention her husband for months, even to her own children. Elizabeth believed her friends avoided her as if she was a leper. She was only socially acceptable if she pretended nothing had happened: 'She did not wear black clothes, nor ritualize her grief; she let herself be almost literally eaten up with grief, when she most needed help and comfort she was left alone'. Elizabeth eventually required longer-term psychiatric help to deal with unresolved grief (Gorer 1965:216–218).

Gorer argued in his book that societies without mourning rituals and rules of behaviour in bereavement were dysfunctional. He deplored their loss in England after 1914, since they had once provided vital support for the bereaved: without them many widows, like Elizabeth, would hide their grief. Gorer found that rituals were preserved more tenaciously among the working classes, having been largely abandoned by the middle and upper classes since 1914, especially in the southeast of England. His results suggested that the vast majority of middle- and upper-class people in 1963 acted in public as if nothing had happened after a death. Giving way to grief was stigmatized as morbid and unhealthy (Gorer 1965:218–225).

Gorer concluded that many women in particular would deny their feelings to themselves as well as in public, and fight against giving them expression. This could lead to prolonged or chronic grief, identified by Colin Murray Parkes as intense and lasting many years. Parkes thought chronic grief had become a more common problem in the 1950s and 1960s among people who kept 'a stiff upper lip' in grief. It could involve years of continued pining for the lost loved one, severe distress and social isolation (Gorer 1965:224–228; Parkes 1972/1986). Gorer identified 15% of his eighty interviewees as 'in despair', convinced they would never recover. Many readers wrote to Gorer in the 1960s, endorsing his picture of widows in despair among the middle classes in the south of England. Gorer's contribution to the history of grief was substantial, but ironically his book was largely ignored in the 1960s because of the continuing silences about which he protested (Gorer 1965:224–232).

Even Christianity and the churches offered little leadership for the bereaved until the publication of C.S. Lewis's book *A Grief Observed*, in 1961. This was written after his wife, Joy, died, and later popularized by Richard Attenborough's film *Shadowlands* (1993). Lewis's book offered an elegant and harrowing analysis of his own personal experience of bereavement. It became an instant best seller, telling readers what grief was actually like for Lewis. It has sold well ever since, helping many thousands. Lewis's book demonstrated the complexities that profound religious faith could add to the grieving experience, and also suggested the longer-term consolations of faith for believers. It had much more influence as a popular guide to grief in the 1960s and 1970s than the works of the early social science experts. It is a reflection on the profound silence surrounding the culture of death and grief up to the 1960s that even Lewis, a celebrated Christian writer on the problem of pain, had earlier completely avoided the issue of grief. It is also significant that Lewis began his book because his personal need was desperate, and little emotional support was available from his family or friends (Lewis 1961).

There is some justification for the argument that the cultural leadership relating to death and grief slowly shifted from the churches to medicine, psychology and sociology. Yet the churches have survived in England and continue to offer comfort to the bereaved, which is reinforced more recently by new immigrants' ways of dealing with grief in a multicultural society since the 1970s. We also need to take into account the survival of folk religion in rural and more isolated areas, such as Staithes in Yorkshire, where they perpetuate a popular belief in a God and an ill-defined afterlife not drawn directly from the bible. Its features included reunion with dead loved ones and belief in ghosts and spirits of the dead (see Clark 1982).

The first British psychiatrist to introduce the lay person to grief was Colin Murray Parkes in his classic 1972 book, *Bereavement: Studies of Grief in Adult Life*. This offered an invaluable analytical framework for the symptoms of grief, drawn from his own extensive empirical research and clinical experience. Parkes's book was a unique and pioneering account and subsequent editions have stood the test of time. He emphasized that the phases of grieving were not a neat progression of fixed stages, but varied significantly between individuals: 'Grief is a painful process of change, by which someone gradually gives up one world and enters another' (Parkes 1972/1986:18, 223–225).

The revival of expressive grieving since the 1960s

The revival of expressive grieving has been a significant change since the 1960s, led principally by middle-class women. This is a striking reversal of the process over the previous fifty years, whereby women tended to follow men's more restrained pattern of grieving. This change in English cultural norms began in the 1960s, as one facet of a so-called counterculture or 'expressive revolution'. Significant changes in the cultural, intellectual and social climate encouraged more liberal attitudes and greater freedom of emotional expression, the latter affecting women more than men. A shift in ideas, attitudes and modes of behaviour included a new receptiveness to more permissive ideas from the United States, with middle-class women and the caring professions most strongly affected (Walter 1999:168–184; Jalland 2010:252–254; Martin 1981, chapters1, 9–10).

Expressive grieving became more common from the 1960s, encouraged by the growth of the popular bereavement counselling movement. Cruse counsellors for widows focused on the individual, working through the phases of grief in one-to-one sessions or in groups. Many bereavement counsellors and their clients were women, and the care they offered encouraged the expression of emotions.

By contrast, mutual help groups such as Compassionate Friends for bereaved parents saw themselves as communities in which common experiences of loss could best be shared with others suffering in the same way. The oral testimony of Val Hazel describes the support she found in a mutual help group after her 9-year-old son, Jeff, died from a rare brain tumour in 1976. After the funeral Val found that people outside the family tried to avoid her because they didn't know what to say and thought that she should grieve quietly at home. But Val needed to talk about Jeff, and she found the ideal outlet for her feelings in sharing her emotions with other bereaved parents she had met at St Bartholomew's Hospital. She was in touch with many such parents 'all in the same boat. . . . And we just rang each other and we were talking about the children endlessly. And it wasn't all doom and gloom'. This informal mutual help group was invaluable because other bereaved people could sometimes help more than family or friends. Her husband, John, found bereavement particularly challenging because he internalized his emotions: 'He's a very quiet person anyway, who does hide feelings. And I think he found it extremely difficult, not being able to let go of his feelings' (Hazel 1991). This reflects many British men's social conditioning to contain their feelings in bereavement and to focus more on solving practical problems.

Many more people have expressed their emotions openly in England since the 1960s, but the influence of expressive grieving should not be overstated. Those affected were more likely to be educated middle-class people, particularly women, from the cities, large towns and the south. Meanwhile, white working-class families in the north, the Celtic fringe and rural areas were more likely to retain vestiges of their traditional ways of mourning. Their ritualized grieving continued to provide solace through funerals, even as medical care was professionalized and funeral directors increasingly managed the funeral process. Cultures of grief continued to be shaped by cultures of class in England, as part of the profound historical legacies of class and region in modern British life.

Conclusion

In this chapter, I have explored the impact of the two world wars on cultures of grieving in England. While the mass deaths of World War I brought intense and prolonged communal grief, the Second World War intensified the dominant social paradigm of suppressed and privatized grieving. This culture of private grief was only challenged from the 1960s with the revival of expressive grieving, primarily among the middle class.

In the last twenty years important new research areas have been developed, notably a substantial theoretical literature on grief and bereavement which has been published by social scientists. More emphasis has been placed on diversity in grieving and less on prescriptive stages and time limits. In 1993, the psychiatrist Paul C. Rosenblatt observed that grief is shaped by its social context: 'Cultures differ widely in defining death and in defining what is an appropriate expression of grief' (Rosenblatt 1993:102–111). This observation is exemplified in my study of the specific cultures of grieving in modern England. Further, different national cultures create different cultures of grieving. Experiences of death and grief in England cannot be simply applied to other Western countries, which have their own specific historical cultures which shape their own cultures of grieving (e.g., the impact of Catholicism and immigrant cultures in France).

Thus, a number of experts over the last two decades have suggested that people may show their emotions in a variety of ways; patterns of behaviour may change over time and across gender and different cultures. Margaret S. Stroebe and Henk Schut proposed that grief is not a simple universal process with a succession of fixed stages. Instead, healthy oscillation is needed, between dwelling on the death, the grief and the emotions on the one hand, and dealing with the practical consequences on the other (Stroebe and Schut 1999). Such theories are now passed on to bereaved people by helpful counsellors and practical advice manuals. Fewer people today should suffer as Audrey Deacon and many others did up to the 1940s and 1950s.

Geoffrey Gorer proposed in 1965 that new and inspiring secular mourning rituals were needed to help the bereaved (Gorer 1965:76–77, 110–116). He would no doubt have approved of the revival of expressive grieving from the late 1960s and the new enthusiasm for celebrating the life of the deceased at remembrance ceremonies. He might also have welcomed the later green burial movement, though perhaps not the ubiquitous roadside memorials. Gorer's own failure to propose appropriate new rituals underscored the challenges involved in a more secular and individualized society. Different views about socially acceptable behaviour expressing the emotion of grief reflect our changing cultural boundaries. The public expression of private grief and the nature of the most appropriate bereavement care remain contested, deeply influenced by our social and cultural history.

References

Adams, Sheila (1993): 'A Gendered History of the Social Management of Death in Foleshill, Coventry, during the Inter-War Years', in David Clark (ed.): *The Sociology of Death*. Oxford: Blackwell, pp. 149–168.

Alvarez, A. (1971): *The Savage God. A Study in Suicide*. London: Weidenfeld and Nicolson.

BBC (1960): 'The World of the Widow': Interviews with Dr and Mrs Torrie at Cruse Club, Bowlby Papers, PP/BOW/F5/1/box 41. London: Wellcome Institute.

Bickersteth, E. (1919): 'Tour of the Battlefields, 28 June to 3 July', in *Bickersteth Diaries, BIC 1/10, CCC*. Cambridge: Churchill College.

Brittan, Samuel (2001): 'In Defence of the Late Bertrand Russell'. *The Spectator*, April 14.

Calder, Angus (1991): *The Myth of the Blitz*. London: Pimlico.

Cannadine, David (1981): 'War and Death, Grief and Mourning in Modern Britain', in Joachim Whaley (ed.): *Mirrors of Mortality*. London: Europa, pp. 187–242.

Clark, David (1982): *Between Pulpit and Pew: Folk Religion in a North Yorkshire Fishing Village*. Cambridge: Cambridge University Press.

Deacon, A. D. (nee Hawkins) (1940–1945): '*Diary of a WREN, 1940–45: The Second World War Diaries of Mrs A. D. Deacon*', 89/17/1. London: Imperial War Museum.

Furniaux, R. (1940): *Miscellaneous, 180 [27087]*. London: Imperial War Museum.

Gorer, Geoffrey (1965): *Death, Grief and Mourning in Contemporary Britain*. London: Cresset Press.

Gregory, Adrian (1994): *The Silence of Memory: Armistice Day 1919–1946*. Oxford: Berg.

Hazel, V. (1991): *Interview, in 'Perspective for Living', H913/04 2:32'12*. London: British Library.

Jalland, Patricia (1996): *Death in the Victorian Family*. Oxford: Oxford University Press.

Jalland, Patricia (2010): *Death in War and Peace. A History of Loss and Grief in England, 1914–1970*. Oxford: Oxford University Press.

Lewis, C. S. (1961): *A Grief Observed*. London: Faber and Faber.

Marris, Peter (1958): *Widows and Their Families*. London: Routledge and Kegan Paul.

Martin, Bernice (1981): *The Sociology of Contemporary Cultural Change*. Oxford: Blackwell.

Martin, G. H. (1944): '*Missing Personnel*', 93/48/1–2. London: Imperial War Museum.

Nelson, Geoffrey K. (1969): *Spiritualism and Society*. London: Routledge and Kegan Paul.

Parkes, Colin Murray (1972/1986): *Bereavement. Studies of Grief in Adult Life*. London: Tavistock/Penguin Books.

Patterson, K. David and Gerald F. Pyle (1991): 'The Geography and Mortality of the 1918 Influenza Pandemic'. *Bulletin of the History of Medicine*, 65 (1):4–21.

Raphael, Beverley (1986): *When Disaster Strikes: How Individuals and Communities Cope with Catastrophe*. New York: Basic Books.

Reid, Alice (2005): 'The Effects of the 1918–1919 Influenza Pandemic on Infant and Child Health in Derbyshire'. *Medical History*, 49 (1):29–54.

Richards, Sarah (ed.) (2009): *Voices of Cruse 1959–2009*. London: Cruse Bereavement Care.

Roberts, Elizabeth (1984): *A Woman's Place: An Oral History of Working Class Women, 1890–1940*. Oxford: Blackwell.

Roberts, Elizabeth (1989): 'The Lancashire Way of Death', in Ralph Houlbrooke (ed.): *Death, Ritual and Bereavement*. London: Routledge, pp. 188–207.

Rosenblatt, Paul C. (1993): 'Grief: The Social Context of Private Feelings', in Margaret S. Stroebe, Wolfgang Stroebe, and Robert O. Hansson (eds.): *Handbook of Bereavement: Theory, Research and Intervention*. Cambridge: Cambridge University Press, pp. 102–111.

Russell, Bertrand (1945): 'The Bomb and Civilisation', in *The Russell Editorial Project* (Volume 22). Canada: McMaster University.

Strange, Julie Marie (2005): *Death, Grief and Poverty in Britain, 1870–1914*. Cambridge: Cambridge University Press.

Stroebe, Margaret S. and Henk Schut (1999): 'The Dual Process Model of Coping with Bereavement'. *Death Studies*, 23:197–224.

Walter, Tony (1999): *On Bereavement: The Culture of Grief*. Buckingham: Open University Press.

Winter, J. M. (1986): *The Great War and the British People*. Basingstoke: Macmillan.

Winter, J. M. (1995): *Sites of Memory, Sites of Mourning. The Great War in European Cultural History*. Cambridge: Cambridge University Press.

Part II
Grief and literature

4 Magical thinking

Experiences of grief and
mourning in George Saunders'
Lincoln in the Bardo and Jesmyn
Ward's *Sing, Unburied, Sing*

Kjersti Bale and Hilde Bondevik

Introduction

Sitting down to have dinner on a late winter evening, the American writer Joan Didion witnesses her husband having a massive stroke that causes his death. Even though the incident comes as a shock, Didion is what the hospital personnel refer to as 'a pretty cool customer'. She is calm, rational, does not scream or break down. Nevertheless, she behaves in ways we normally regard as irrational. When she authorizes an autopsy it is because she thinks that if the cause turns out to be something simple, it might be fixed. Similarly, when she clears the shelves and closets where her husband stacked his clothes and shoes she suddenly becomes aware:

> I could not give away the rest of his shoes.
> I stood there for a moment, then realized why: he would need shoes if he was to return.
> The recognition of this thought by no means eradicated the thought.
> I have still not tried to determine (say, by giving away the shoes) if the thought has lost its power.
>
> (Didion 2012:37)

Didion seems to believe that she has the power to influence future events merely through her thoughts.

Nine months after her husband's death, Didion starts writing the book that has since become an international bestseller, and entitles it *The Year of Magical Thinking* (2005). The term 'magical thinking' indicates the belief that an event is the result of another, without any plausible causality being demonstrated. More-over, magical thinking or 'odd beliefs' have for years been included as a symptom or criterion in diagnostic descriptions of psychosis, especially in schizophrenia (see ICD-10 code F.21 and DSM IV code 301.22).[1] The paperback edition of Didion's book has an endorsement quote from the *Daily Mail*, which says that the book 'will speak to and maybe comfort anyone who has lost forever the one they loved'. The point of departure of this chapter is the assumption that magical thinking is common among people who experience severe grief and even that it might create new and valuable connections of relations and contexts of meaning.

According to medical science, grief is both a symptom of depression and a diagnostic category (in ICD-11, 'Prolonged Grief Disorder'). As such it can be described in scientific, objectifying and generalizing terms. Autobiography, memoir and fiction on the other hand can portray grief as it is experienced, as a subjective feeling and as an integral part of the human condition. In what follows we will examine two American novels in which magical thinking appears in tandem with loss, anxiety, grief and bereavement: George Saunders' *Lincoln in the Bardo* and Jesmyn Ward's *Sing, Unburied, Sing*. Both novels are much praised. *Lincoln in the Bardo* was awarded the 2017 Man Booker Prize, and *Sing, Unburied, Sing* the National Book Award for fiction the same year. In this chapter we want to show how fiction can explore individual as well as collective grief through ways of embodying magical thinking, and thus how fiction can supplement other understandings of grief and bereavement. We claim that fantastic literary devices like the spirits in Saunders' novel and the ghosts in Ward's are summoned to embody a web of connections between the living and the dead, and that grief is the impetus to those connections.

Our reading is led by a special attention to some of the distinct details and topics related to the sociality of grief in our chosen texts. Thus, the readings might be said to have a thematic orientation, of which 'magical thinking' and 'grief' as emotional and relational reactions to loss and absence are of main concern to us. Such a thematic reading also takes into account the social cogito of the literary text – that is, the historical and ideological or political horizon it was part of and further points to. Accordingly, the contextual frameworks in which the texts are written will also be present more implicitly in our interpretations of the novels. In addition, as we emphasize the metonymical aspects of the spirits and the ghosts in the two novels, the reading might also be called rhetorical.

As Didion mentions Sigmund Freud, before we turn to the two novels, we will take a closer look at his description of magical thinking in his essay 'Totem and Taboo' (1913). The essay was written four years earlier than 'Mourning and Melancholia' (Freud 1917/1957). Freud uses the very same model when he explains magical thinking and grief. Both phenomena are regarded as instances of narcissism. Hence a bridge between grief (*trauer*) and magical thinking is indicated, but Freud does not explore the connection. We argue, however, that magical thinking and grief are connected, regardless of narcissism.

Freud on animism and magic

In 'Totem and Taboo', Sigmund Freud approaches the phenomenon of animism. Drawing on works by Herbert Spencer, J. G. Frazer, Andrew Lang, E. B. Taylor and Wilhelm Wundt, he defines animism as a certain 'view of nature and the universe adopted by the primitive races' (Freud 1990:32). According to Freud, animism is the oldest and most primitive explanation of the nature of the universe. He speculates that the chief basis for the animistic *weltanschauung* or worldview must have been the problem of death, and that to primitive man, immortality, the indefinite prolongation of life, must have been the natural way to approach the problem. The belief in souls and demons, which is the essence of animism, hence must come from the impression death makes upon people. Because of this sup-posed connection between animism and death, certain procedures or techniques are used in dealing with spirits. Freud labels them as magic and defines it as a method of subjecting natural phenomena to the will of man, thereby mistaking an ideal connection for a real one.

Freud highlights two different operative factors that underpin his examples: similarity and contiguity. The principle of similarity is operative in rituals like rain dances, in which the action imitates the hoped for result, whereas the principle of contiguity is operative, for example, in the belief that if you have wounded a man you have only to spit on the hand that inflicted the wound, and the pain of the sufferer will be alleviated. In Freud's view, the true essence of magic is 'the misunderstanding which leads it to replace the laws of nature by psychological ones' (Freud 1990:141), which is the principle of the 'omnipotence of thoughts' (Freud 1990:143).

In addition to the animistic *weltanschauung* there are the religious and the scientific *weltanschauungs*. According to Freud, these three pictures of the uni-verse form a chronological and progressive development towards modernity. In this era, projective mechanisms implying that ideal connections are mistaken for real ones are replaced by scientific laws: 'The scientific view of the universe no longer affords any room for human omnipotence; men have acknowledged their smallness and submitted resignedly to death and to the other necessities of nature' (Freud 1990:146). Yet even though animism is a primitive mode of thinking, it persists in modern life: 'Only in art does it still happen that a man who is con-sumed by desires performs something resembling the accomplishment of those desires and that what he does in play produces emotional effects – thanks to artis-tic illusion – just as though it were something real' (Freud 1990:148). Magical thinking by ways of art production is thus regarded as wish fulfilment by proxy.

Freud's conception of how the human mind has developed is normative. He makes a clear distinction between animism on the one hand and rationality and science on the other, in favour of the latter. Yet, during the first half of the 19th century the ambivalence between modernity and magic was under scrutiny among German thinkers. Max Weber pointed out the dangers of meaninglessness in a disenchanted world, and Max Horkheimer and Theodor W. Adorno developed their thoughts on how instrumental reason becomes irrational. Especially after World War II a progress optimism such as Freud's has been heavily criticized (see Adorno in his *Minima Moralia*). Moreover, Zygmunt Bauman has argued that modernity's quest for order and assumed superiority of rationality over irrational action have unforeseen dehumanizing consequences (Bauman 1989). Therefore, we would like to challenge Freud's interpretation of magical thinking. We suggest that instead of a hierarchy of principles at work in how people experience reality, there is a repertoire of principles that are all available to the experiencing human being. Which principles are put to work and which ones dominate depend on the circumstances. Certain contexts can trigger certain principles. Hence similarity and contiguity can be regarded as universal principles of experience. Roman Jakobson has suggested that these very principles correspond to metaphor and metonymy as principles of discourse (Jakobson 1971). There are reasons to be sceptical about reducing the repertoire of principles governing human experience to such a degree (Bredin 1984). Nevertheless, we find it productive to regard magical thinking as a realization of the contiguity principle and as such a recurrent feature in expressions of grief. Instead of regarding the principle of contiguity in art as a primitive mode of thought, we regard art and literature as a field where such principles can be embodied and examined. Such a view can be underpinned by reference to anthropologists such as Stanley J. Tambiah, who has argued that in ritual operations the analogical action (in which he includes both metaphorical and metonymical action) conforms to the 'persuasive' rather than the 'scientific' model (Tambiah 1973/2017:461).

In the following, we maintain that the contiguity principle at work in magical thinking and animism, as described by Joan Didion in *The Year of Magical Thinking* and Freud in 'Totem and Taboo', is coupled with an experience of connectedness and a way of making a certain aspect of reality – namely, the loss of a loved one – accessible to experience. But whereas Didion focuses on individual grief exclusively, we will throw light on grief also as a social phenomenon (see Petersen and Jacobsen 2018:202), on collective grief. Magical thinking will thus be regarded as relational, as a social mode of association.

Lincoln in the Bardo

George Saunders' *Lincoln in the Bardo* represents the relationship between William Lincoln, who died of typhoid fever at the age of only eleven in 1862, and his inconsolably grieving father, Abraham Lincoln. Despite its biographical underpinning, the novel can be described as speculative or fantastic fiction. As indicated in the book's title, the 'bardo' is where we meet Willie. The notion refers to the *Bardo Todrol*, known as the *Tibetan Book of the Dead*, from the 8th century. The 'bardo' is an intermediary state between death and rebirth. The dead person's consciousness remains near the body and seeks release into a form of enlightenment. If the consciousness fails to be released it remains in the physical world as a ghost until the Lord of the Otherworld reviews the demons and desires of the person's former life (Leeming 2001). Although the novel takes inspiration from the *Tibetan Book of the Dead*, the realm where most of the novel takes place is an imaginary construct. Still, the idea that there is an intermediary state between life and death is crucial to the narrative because it is this intermediary spiritual realm that accounts for the magic – that is, for the influence that the dead can have on the living and vice versa, by way of contiguity.

There are a huge number of narrative voices in the novel, which is constructed like a richly populated drama. Hans Vollmann and Roger Bevins III are the first to appear on the scene. Both have suffered brutal and sudden deaths at a moment when life was at its most intense. Vollmann is 46 years old and has recently married a girl of 18. Their marriage is not consummated because Vollmann has not wanted to force himself on her. After a while her distaste abates, but on the very day when their marriage is to be consummated a beam falls from the ceiling, hits him 'just *here*' and kills Hans Vollmann, who is sitting at his desk. Lending a comic aspect to the incident is the fact that in the bardo his spirit assumes the shape of him as naked with an enormous erection.

Richard Bevins III is a young man who slits his wrists when his clandestine lover dumps him for another man. As he lies dying he realizes how beautiful the world is and changes his mind, unfortunately too late. He has several sets of eyes, several noses and multiple sets of hands, which indicate the sensual approach to the world he assumes at his moment of death. 'I am freed now of all fear, hesitation, and timidity, and, once revived, intend to devoutly wander the earth, imbibing, smelling, sampling, loving whomever I please; touching, tasting, standing very still among the beautiful things of this world' (Saunders 2017:27).

Both Hans Vollmann and Richard Bevins III have strong ties to the world of the living. They refuse to accept that they are dead and consistently refer to the coffins in which they are buried with the euphemism 'sick-box'. At nighttime, they can leave their sick-boxes and pass through living people, animals or things. Doing so has effects, such as when Vollmann makes the dogs bark by inducing them to dream of a bear. Thus contiguity is established already at the novel's opening.

The third among the most salient voices in the bardo is Reverend Everly Thomas. Whereas Hans Vollmann is a comic figure and Richard Bevins III a sensual one, Everly Thomas elicits fright, anxiety and terror, even though he always speaks with great calmness and good sense. That is because Thomas keeps a terrible secret; he knows that he is dead. Thomas has seen how Christ's emissary and his angels have weighed two men's hearts and condemned the one to be led into Christ's hall of happiness, the other into a terrible beast's hall of horror. When it is his turn to have his heart weighed and he surmises that he will be condemned to the hall of horror, he runs away. Thomas is not pursued but is warned to tell no one about what he has seen, or else it will be worse on his return. Thus he knows that the place where he, Vollmann and Bevins abide is only intermediary, but he has no idea whatsoever why he has been allotted such a terrible destiny.

When Willie Lincoln arrives at the bardo, the spirits stand in line to speak with him. He brings hope and meaning to their intermediary existence owing to the extraordinary grief his father displays when he returns to the coffin in the crypt to hold his son and speak tenderly to him.

> The holding, the lingering, the kind words whispered directly into the ear?
> My God! My God!
> > the reverend everly thomas
> To be touched so lovingly, so fondly, as if one were still –
> > roger bevins iii
> Healthy.
> > hans vollman
> As if one were still worthy of affection and respect?

It was cheering. It gave us hope.
                    the reverend everly thomas
We were perhaps not so unlovable as we had come to believe.
                    roger bevins iii.
                                        (Saunders 2017:69–70)

Reverend Thomas, Roger Bevins III and Hans Vollman are all grieving for their life on earth and it is the physical nearness, the holding and the touch they lament. Hence they do not want to leave the bardo.

All the spirits in the bardo have deliberately chosen to stay and none of them wants to leave. Therefore a procession of angels who take on different guises depending on the tastes of those they are trying to tempt, mercilessly assault the spirits with the intention of making them leave the bardo. To linger in the bardo is a rebellion against the will of God. Thus the angels behave 'like hunters, seeking for any sign of weakness' (Saunders 2017:93); they are demons who assume familiar forms to lure the spirits over to the other side of the iron fence that demarcates the borders of the bardo. The reverend sees through their illusion:

> At one moment, the angels stepping *en masse* back into a ray of moonlight to impress me with their collective radiance, I glanced up and saw, spread out around the white stone home, a remarkable tableau of suffering: dozens of us, frozen in misery: cowed, prone, crawling, wincing before the travails of the particularized onslaught each was undergoing.
>
>   (Saunders 2017:95)

What seems like a procession that exhibits glory is a trap.

Willie Lincoln is just a child and therefore cannot be expected to resist the onslaught of the angel-demons. The efforts cost him dearly. He loses his breath, his hands are shaking and he loses bodyweight so his cheekbones protrude, his neck becomes like a stick and he has charcoal-dark rings under his eyes. A vine-like plant similar to a cobra but more stone than snake twines around him. Nevertheless he persists and even accuses his three guides of having lied to him to make him leave. Willie wants to stay because of his strong ties to his father. 'Father promised, the boy said. How would that be, if he came back and found me gone?' (Saunders 2017:106).

Because of the contiguity between the living and the dead, Hans Vollmann, Richard Bevins III and Reverend Everly Thomas undertake the task to make Abraham Lincoln go to the mausoleum – 'the white stone home' – a second time, to encourage Willie into his father so he can hear that his father wishes him to be in a bright place, free of suffering. That is why they appear as guides for Willie Lincoln, presumably as a comic parody on Virgil, Beatrice and Bernard de Clair-vaux in Dante's *Divine Comedy*, who conduct Dante through Hell and Purgatory to Paradise. Vollmann and Bevins just want to end Willie's suffering; Thomas probably surmises that the lovable and good-natured child will be let into the 'hall of happiness'. They succeed – that is, when the boy's spirit unites with his father, he realizes that he is dead, and the magical thinking thus makes Willie leave the bardo. That is also the last time Abraham Lincoln visits Willie's coffin, realizing that when he needs to look upon his son, he can do so in his heart. But why does not the novel end there?

The first part of the novel concerns the time from Willie's illness and death until the burial and all ceremonial activities associated with it are over. In the second part, which starts the night after Willie is interred, the scope of the novel is expanded. In addition to the voices of the spirits in the bardo, there is a range of quotes from contemporary sources – some actual, some fictional – such as letters, speeches and memoirs that represent experiences from the Civil War. This displacement from individual grief to the grief of a nation is prepared for earlier in the novel.

When Lincoln comes to the crypt for the first time after the funeral, Willie rushes towards his father.

> Bursting out of the doorway, the lad took off running toward the man, look of joy on his face.
>> roger bevins iii
> Which turned to consternation when the man failed to sweep him up in his arms as, one gathered, must have been their custom.
>> the reverend everly thomas
> The boy instead passing through the man, as the man continued to walk toward the white stone home, sobbing.
>> roger bevins iii.
>
> (Saunders 2017:44)

The scene resonates with the episode in Virgil's *Aeneid* where Aeneas meets his father, Anchises, in the Underworld. When Aeneas tries to embrace his father, the spirit melts from his hands 'like the wind's breath' (Virgil, *Aeneid*, VI, 1935:702). As it is the son who is dead in *Lincoln in the Bardo*, not the father, the situation is reversed. Yet the implicit comparison universalizes the longing for deceased loved ones across cultures and centuries. Virgil and Saunders use similar metaphors – of wind, of passing through.

Regardless of this insubstantiality, the nearness between the dead and the living brings about certain effects. When Willie goes into his father, they can both feel the other:

> Could feel the way his long legs lay How it is to have a beard Taste coffee in the mouth and, though not thinking in words exactly, knew that *the feel of him in my arms had done me good. It has. . . . I had forgotten somewhat already. But here: his exact proportions, his suit smelling of him still, his forelock between my fingers, the heft of him familiar from when he would fall asleep in the parlor and I would carry him up to.*
>
> (Saunders 2017:61, italics in original)

Here the image of the son who tries to embrace his father across the divide between life and death is reversed and turned into the image of the father who embraces the corpse of his son. Yet the hint towards the incident where Aeneas and Anchises meet in the Underworld points to the future of the nation. Abraham Lincoln and Aeneas are both leaders who must lead their people through war to secure the future of their respective (in Aeneas' case future) nations: Aeneas has to conquer the Rutuli to found Lavinium, which in due course is to become part of Rome; Lincoln has to conquer the Confederates to reconstruct the United States.

Saunders quotes from Larry Tagg's *The Unpopular Mr. Lincoln* to highlight the connection between Lincoln's private grief and the grief of the nation: 'As the dead piled up in unimaginable numbers and sorrow was added to sorrow, a nation that had known little of sacrifice blamed Lincoln for a dithering mismanagement of the war effort' (Saunders 2017:232). Furthermore, the war connects the suffering caused by the war with the suffering caused by slavery. Among the spirits in the bardo several have been slaves, such as Elson Farwell, an obedient 'best boy' obsessed with revenge after having fallen ill on an outing and experiencing that the family he serves just leaves him in great pain; and Litzie Wright, so traumatised after having been raped over and over again that she has lost her ability to speak. The hierarchy among the residents is equivalent to the social stratification in real life. Thus suffering is what binds the universe together:

> His [Lincoln's] mind was freshly inclined toward *sorrow*; toward the fact that the world was full of sorrow; that everyone labored under some burden of sorrow; that all were suffering; that whatever way one took in this world, one must try to remember that all were suffering (none content; all wronged, neglected, overlooked, misunderstood), and therefore one must do what one could to lighten the load of those with whom one came into contact; that his current state of sorrow was not uniquely his, not at all, but, rather, its like had been felt, would yet be felt, by scores of others, in all times, in every time, and must not be prolonged or exaggerated, because, in this state, he could be of no help to anyone and, given that his position in the world situated him to be either of great help or great harm, it would not do to stay low, if he could help it.
>
> (Saunders 2017:303–304)

Hans Vollmann is here narrating Lincoln's thoughts by using the very same words that Willie has used earlier, thereby stressing the connectedness: 'All had been wronged Neglected Overlooked Misunderstood' (Saunders 2017:82). The magical thinking thus works both ways; in the bardo as well as in the world of the living, suffering is pervasive and sorrow is what binds people together. In spite of this, Black people in the bardo do not even have sick-boxes, probably a critical comment on the political situation in the contemporary United States since the African American community is both disproportionately at risk for homicide and for experiencing 'disenfranchised grief' – that is socially invalidated, unacknowledged or discouraged grief (see Piazza-Bonin et al. 2015).

The best we can do, then, is to try and lighten the others' burden. This insight seems to be induced into Abraham Lincoln by his son. On the other hand, it is the father's thoughts that make the son realize that he is dead and has to let go. The insight is mirrored in Vollman's and Bevins' intuition that 'Our first huge failing', 'Our initial abandonment of the better nature we had brought with us from that previous place' (Saunders 2017:331), is evident in the cowardice they have shown by not encouraging a suffering 14-year-old girl to leave the bardo. The last thing they do before leaving the bardo themselves is consequently to apologize and help her leave, at last.

The novel ends with Abraham Lincoln riding out into the night with the spirit of Thomas Havens, a former slave, within him, with his mind directed towards the future. Lincoln is such a pivotal figure in the novel because he is like a bridge between particular and collective sorrow: his grief about his son as well as about the Civil War and the slavery in the United States. By alluding to the *Divine Comedy* and the *Aeneid*, Saunders associates his novel with a tradition of literary representations of the Underworld and of contact between the living and the dead. He highlights that sorrow is not individual; it is shared by thousands. What really matters therefore is what we do to lighten the load of those with whom we come into contact. Magical thinking is the poetic device that enables him to examine this connectedness.

Against this backdrop, magical thinking is not so much a primitive way of thinking as a metaphorical construct that points to the bonds and connections there are between people, living and dead, across time and place. Magical thinking is therefore not something to be overcome but rather a device that makes the grieving person able to approach reality, to articulate his or her lived experience of it – that is, of unbroken ties with the deceased. Whereas science relies on principles such as causality and aims at explaining phenomena, magical thinking relies on contiguity and aims at giving meaning to experience. The experience under scrutiny in *Lincoln in the Bardo* is the experience of connection, of bonds between people. The poetic device of magical thinking is what gives reality form and thus transforms it into lived experience.

Sing, Unburied, Sing

Like *Lincoln in the Bardo*, Jesmyn Ward's *Sing, Unburied, Sing* provides a concrete representation of the connections and contiguity between the living and the dead. Dead spirits beseech the living. Yet there is a significant difference between the two novels. In Saunders' novel the spirits of the dead pursue the living because of the bond of love between them, whereas the spirits in Ward's novel haunt the living because they cannot have peace until they are remembered. They have all suffered violent and dreadful deaths. Magic is introduced early in the novel when the protagonist, Jojo, receives a small pouch of items including a feather, an animal's tooth, a rock and a piece of paper saying 'Keep this close' (Ward 2017:71) from his grandfather. It is a gris-gris bag, a talisman, meant to protect Jojo from evil and to bring luck. 'Everything got power' his grandfather explains to him.

'There's a spirit in everything. In the trees, in the moon, in the sun, in the animals. . . . You need all of them, all of that spirit in everything, to have balance' (Ward 2017:73). The small sack is full of things to balance.

Balance also relates to the contiguity between the living and the dead. Jojo as well as his mother and grandmother have the gift of second sight and can in due course see dead spirits and understand what animals express. That network of relationships is connected to two central symbols: water and birds. In what follows we will lay out how this structure of associations and symbols are connected with remembrance in *Sing, Unburied, Sing*. The animism that manifests itself via contiguity between the living and the dead seeks balance, and to obtain balance the living must remember the dead. That memory work is collective.

Whereas Saunders' novel takes place during the first half of the 1860s and is at least partially an historical novel, the setting of *Sing, Unburied, Sing* is contemporary. The fictional events take place sometime after 2010, partly in the fictional town of Bois, near the Mississippi Gulf Coast, and partly on a trip from there to Parchman, the Mississippi State Penitentiary, in the Yazoo Delta. The area is fertile but the people we meet are poor.

Sing, Unburied, Sing is narrated in the present tense with flashbacks, which gives a strong impression of the past living on in the present. There are several narrators and the chapters alternate between them. Seven of the fifteen chapters are narrated by Jojo, a 13-year-old boy who lives with his mother, Leonie, and his 3-year-old sister, Kayla, at the home of his grandparents, whom he calls Mam and Pop. Leonie is Black, and Jojo's father, Michael, is white. There is a road novel in miniature embedded in the novel: we follow Leonie, her children and her friend Misty on their trip to Parchman to bring home Michael, who is being released after three years of imprisonment for cooking methamphetamine. The aforementioned talisman is given to Jojo when he leaves for Parchman. Leonie, a drug addict, is the narrator of five chapters. A focal point of her narrative is how her dead brother, Given, haunts her whenever she is high. Moreover, Leonie's father and Jojo's grandfather River (Pop) are narrators of a story discontinuously told and inserted into Jojo's narrative about River's stay at Parchman between six and seven decades earlier. Finally, the ghost of a 12-year-old boy, Richie, who was killed at Parchman when Pop was confined there, is the narrator of three chapters. Parchman is thus the narrative hub of the novel and the site that links the novel's characters together.

Jojo's family has suffered a terrible loss. Given was shot while only in his senior year. He was an athlete and a football player. Given went hunting with his white teammates and made a bet with Michael's cousin that he could kill a buck with a bow before Michael's cousin could take one down with a rifle. He won, and Michael's cousin, who was drunk, shot him for beating him. The boy's father, Michael's uncle, called on Big Joseph, Michael's father and the town's sheriff. They agreed to call it a hunting accident. The District Attorney agreed to a plea deal that sentenced the cousin to three years in Parchman and two years' probation.

The first time Leonie sees Given's ghost, which she calls Given–not Given, is when Michael has just gone to jail and she is at a party where she takes cocaine: 'I couldn't help wanting to feel the coke go up my nose, shoot straight to my brain, and burn up all the sorrow and despair I felt at Michael being gone' (Ward 2017:51). The appearance of Given's ghost thus entwines several threads – Leonie's attempt at forgetting, her sorrow and despair and the killing of Given; as additionally, the place where Given was shot, eponymously named the Kill, is also where the party takes place. Given–not Given represents this entanglement. Probably because Leonie's drug abuse is an attempt at forgetting, she cannot hear what Given–not Given wants to say to her. 'He tried to talk to me but I couldn't hear him, and he just got more and more frustrated' (Ward 2017:51). It is obvious that he disapproves of her drug abuse.

Several times Pop tells Jojo the story of his imprisonment at Parchman when only 15 years old, just because he happened to be at home alone when a group of white men who had been fighting with his brother, Stag, came to fetch Stag, and took both brothers. Parchman is divided into fifteen camps, or 'work farms', each surrounded by a barbed-wire fence. At the core of Pop's story is an even younger boy, Richie, aged only 12 and the youngest boy in Parchman, imprisoned simply because he stole food to feed his siblings. Richie is skinny and weak-muscled, which makes him unfit to work in the fields at Parchman. River protects Richie as well as he can, but when Richie is beaten almost to death he decides to escape. '*I'm going home*,' River says (Ward 2017:126). What is meant by home is not explained until the end of the novel.

Richie's ghost is introduced into the narrative when Leonie, her family and her friend are on their way home from Parchman. Jojo sees 'a dark skinny boy with a patchy afro and a long neck [who] is standing on my side of the car, looking at Kayla and then looking at me. Kayla cries and whines. "The bird, the bird", she says' (Ward 2017:130–131). The ensuing chapter is the first chapter told by Richie. It is narrated from beyond death. Richie sees a white snake transform into a black scaly bird. When he picks up a scale and keeps it in his hand he can fly like a bird.

Richie wants to go home, and to do so he needs to hear how his own story ends. No one but River can tell him what happened. Jojo and Kayla can both see him, but since Kayla is too young he urges Jojo to make his grandfather finish his story. Finally, Pop tells how Richie died. At the same time as Richie was escaping Parchman, an inmate called Blue raped and abused a woman inmate. Richie discovered him in flagrante, and Blue forced him to run with him. River followed them. When Blue set about assaulting a young white girl, Richie stopped him by hitting him with a tree limb. White men gathered to lynch Blue, who was cut to pieces before he was skinned. River found Richie by following the dogs. He knew the mob would do the same to him, so River killed Richie while telling him he would take him home, and then let the dogs tear into him.

However, learning what happened to him and how his story ended does not satisfy Richie. He is hungry for the love that life has denied him. There is a battle between him and Given over Mam, who is dying of cancer, and whom Richie has come for, 'vengeful as a beat dog', 'pulling all the weight of history behind him' (Ward 2017:264–265). When Leonie, encouraged by her mother, recites a litany to Maman Brigitte, a death god and the only white Voodoo god, symbolized by a black rooster, her mother dies and she and Given leave for good. But not Richie, who still has not come home. 'I can't. Come inside. I tried. Yesterday. There has to be some need, some lack. Like a keyhole' (Ward 2017:281). The key is still the scale that can make him fly; he is told this by a black-feathered bird. And he is not the only one. Jojo sees that the trees' branches are filled with ghosts, perched like birds. They have all suffered terrible deaths. It is Kayla who finally makes them go home. In her very person she represents balance, like the talisman Pop gave to Jojo. 'Her eyes Michael's, her nose Leonie's, the set of her shoulders Pop's, and the way she looks upward, like she is measuring the tree, all Mam. But something about the way she stands, the way she takes all the pieces of everybody and holds them together, is all her. Kayla. '"Go home", she says. . . . Kayla begins to sing' (Ward 2017:284). She gathers all the threads that connect the living and the dead and makes the ghosts 'smile with something like relief, something like remembrance, something like ease' (Ward 2017:284). It is as if Kayla remembers the sound of all water and sings it.

In *Sing, Unburied, Sing* Ward portrays how grief about a loved one, like Given or Mam, is not just an individual feeling. She uses Jojo to show how grief can make us observant, able to see things that bind the living and the dead together. The ghosts in the novel are immaterial relationships made concrete. They are reminders of the collective grief and memory work necessary to balance the nation, to protect it, in contrast to the strategy of forgetting that Leonie and Michael represent. Remembrance is hard work, however, highlighted by how painful it is for Pop to complete the story about Richie. Mam describes his way of telling stories to Jojo:

> 'Your pop don't know how to tell a story straight. You know that? He tell the beginning but don't tell the end. Or he leave out something important in the middle. Or he tell you the beginning without setting up how everything got there. He always been like that'.
>
> I nod.
>
> 'I used to have to piece the things he told me together to get the whole picture'.
>
> (Ward 2017:67)

Jojo experiences the same himself. Twice he tells us, 'Pop's told me some parts of Richie's story over and over again. I've heard the beginning at least too many times to count. There are parts in the middle . . . that I've only heard twice. I ain't never heard the end' (Ward 2017:72). 'Whenever Pop done told me his and Richie's story, he talked in circles' (Ward 2017:248). Piecing the story together to obtain the whole picture is also a task for the reader. Doing so demands alertness to metaphors. We will highlight two: water and birds.

When Pop wants to explain to Mam about his brother, Stag, he uses water as metaphor: 'There's things that move a man. Like currents of water inside. . . . What's in Stag is like water so black and deep you can't see the bottom. . . .

Parchman taught me the same in me' (Ward 2017:68). Moreover, his name is River. Later, water, and especially saltwater, is connected to the goddess Mam is calling on: Our lady of Regla, the Star of the Sea, Yemayá, the goddess of the ocean and saltwater. Those are life-giving waters. Hence for the dead to have peace is to be taken 'across the waters of this world' (Ward 2017:191).

Birds are a recurrent element in the novel. There is a black vulture that circles over Richie in the last chapter; there is the black rooster that symbolizes Maman Brigitte, and Richie as well as the ghosts in the tree look like birds. But most importantly there is the bird from which Richie gets the scale that makes him fly like a bird – that is, 'a bird, but not a bird. No feathers. All black scales' (Ward 2017:135). The scales associate this bird with fish and thus with water. Significantly, the scaly bird is consistently associated with Richie's wish for remembrance and hence with the main theme of the novel. The bird's association with scales and remembrance may hint at the Sankofa bird. Like Pop's gris-gris bag, the Sankofa is a West African symbol, widely used in contemporary American Black culture. 'San' means return, 'ko' means go and 'fa' means look, seek and take; that is, learning from the past while moving forward, which is, so to speak, the key to the novel.

The novel's main motif, which symbolizes the bond between the living and the dead, is tragically the state prison. Leonie's father and uncle, Michael's cousin and Michael himself, all are jailed there for years. An important cause is racial antagonisms: Michael's cousin shoots Given because 'he was supposed to lose' (Ward 2017:50); white guys fight with Stag and have both Stag and River imprisoned; Richie, who is just a child, is sent to jail for having stolen food. On the other hand, there is also Michael, who feels guilty because of his cousin's deed. He himself has to serve time in Parchman because he has been cooking meth to forget an atrocious experience and support his family. Michael worked as a rig welder on the Deepwater Horizon, which blew up in 2010. Since returning home he has suffered from nightmares. He grieves his dead fellow crewmen: 'I knew those men – all eleven of them. Lived with them' (Ward 2017:92). Michael probably suffers from post-traumatic stress disorder (PTSD). At Parchman he experiences violence, stabbings, hangings, overdoses and beatings. 'This ain't no place for no man. Black or White. Don't make no difference. This a place for the dead' (Ward 2017:96).

Our focus has been on how sorrow and grief are countered by a perspective on life and death we have called magical thinking and animism, as well as contiguity between the living and the dead. Key to this network of connections is remembrance. If the United States in general and Mississippi in particular are unable to remember the gruesome deaths that American culture has inflicted on people like Given and Richie, the wound will not heal.

Discussion and conclusion

From 2018 forward, 'Prolonged Grief Disorder' has been its own distinct diagnostic category in ICD-11. This medicalization of grief brings with it the risk of individualization of the emotion and consequently the tendency to ignore the social dimensions and expressions of grief. The fact that grief originates in the loss of a significant other becomes underemphasized (Petersen and Jacobsen 2018:202–203). The kind of sorrow and despair we have been discussing in this chapter are emotions caused by the irretrievable loss of someone dear – Abraham Lincoln's loss of his son, Willie; Leonie's loss of her brother, Given; and River's loss of Richie, who has become like a little brother to him. Such emotions have been labelled 'large griefs' because they 'call the world into question and challenge the very meaning of life' among those who suffer from them (Petersen and Jacobsen 2018:192). Fiction can articulate large griefs as well as represent potentialities for overcoming them and moving forward. In *Lincoln in the Bardo* and *Sing, Unburied, Sing* the bereavements are not individually experienced only, but linked to the mass deaths of several hundreds of men killed in action during the American Civil War and the lynching of thousands of African Americans from the late 19th century on, respectively. In this way, bereavement and reactions to it are also represented as collective phenomena. In *Lincoln in the Bardo*, the great loss of young soldiers gives rise to a collective grief displayed to the readers by way of excerpts from memoirs and letters that express the collective rage, grief and mourning among relatives – in contrast to the lack of equivalent material representing the mourning for dead slaves. In *Sing, Unburied, Sing*, however, the emotive responses to the deaths of the two young boys are concealed, subdued and marked by shame. The memory work necessary to elicit Richie's story especially, but also other stories connected to Parchman, is therefore transferred to a third generation, to River's grandchildren, Jojo and Kayla. Kayla in particular embodies a hope of reconciliation. Both Saunders and Ward use supernatural figures such as spirits and ghosts to express the relationship and thus the contiguity between the living and the dead. They show that what Freud, at least outside of the realm of art, would have dismissed as a primitive way of coping with reality, as a misunderstanding, has to do with meaning rather than with causes. Magical thinking is not false causal action but expressive action, where the expression itself is the fulfilment. As Stanley J. Tambiah has pointed out, metaphorical and metonymical action within the framework of magical rites has to do with persuasion and expansion of meaning and should therefore not be judged in terms of true/false criteria (Tambiah 1973/2017:465) or placed in dualistic categories such as pathological/healthy. Hence, magical thinking is a performative act that offers solutions to existential problems.

The inclusion of 'Prolonged Grief Disorder' in the ICD-11 manual highlights how medicalization of grief entails drawing a line between acknowledged and unacknowledged grief. Magical thinking is not mentioned in the entry and seems to be commonly, if not exclusively, linked to what we have called 'disenfranchised grief'. In this chapter, we have attempted to go beyond the medical understanding of grief and its diagnostic categories based on symptoms to demonstrate how fiction can challenge such an acknowledged understanding of the emotion. By addressing magical thinking as a literary device, we hope to encourage further research on topics such as disenfranchised grief among varying societal groups, and grief and mourning as responses to collective trauma, within the framework of comparative analysis of different types of discourses.

Note

1 In the recently revised versions of the ICD-11 and DSM 5 manuals, the term 'magical thinking' has been deleted.

References

Bauman, Zygmunt (1989): *Modernity and the Holocaust*. New York: Cornell University Press.

Bredin, Hugh (1984): 'Roman Jakobson on Metaphor and Metonymy'. *Philosophy and Literature*, 8 (1):89–103.

Didion, Joan (2005/2012): *The Year of Magical Thinking*. London: Fourth Estate.

Freud, Sigmund (1913/1990): 'Totem and Taboo', in *The Origins of Religion: The Penguin Freud Library* (Volume 13). London: Penguin Books, pp. 43–224.

Freud, Sigmund (1917/1957): 'Mourning and Melancholia', in James Strachey (ed.): *The Standard Edition of the Complete Psychological Works of Sigmund Freud* (Volume XIV). London: Hogarth Press, pp. 237–258.

Jakobson, Roman (1971): 'Two Aspects of Language and Two Types of Aphasic Disturbances', in *Selected Writings* (Volume II). The Hague: Mouton, pp. 239–259.

Leeming, David (2001): *A Dictionary of Asian Mythology*. Oxford: Oxford University Press.

Petersen, Anders and Michael Hviid Jacobsen (2018): 'Grief. The Painfulness of Permanent Human Absence', in Michael Hviid Jacobsen (ed.): *Emotions, Everyday Life and Sociology*. London: Routledge, pp. 191–208.

Piazza-Bonin, Elizabeth, Robert A. Neimeyer, Laurie A. Burke, Meghan E. McDevitt-Murphy and Amanda Young (2015): 'Disenfranchised Grief Following African American Homicide Loss: An Inductive Case Study'. *Omega: Journal of Death and Dying*, 70 (4):404–427.

Saunders, George (2017): *Lincoln in the Bardo*. London: Bloomsbury.

Tambiah, Stanley J. (1973/2017): 'Form and Meaning of Magical Acts: A Point of View'. *HAU: Journal of Ethnographic Theory*, 7 (3):451–473.

Virgil (Publius Vergilius Maro) (1935): *Virgil in Two Volumes* (Volume 1: *Eclogues, Georgics, Aeneid* I – VII) (The Loeb Classical Library). London: Heinemann.

Ward, Jesmyn (2017): *Sing, Unburied, Sing*. London: Bloomsbury Circus.

5 A story of loss

Self-narration of grief and public feeling rules

Nina R. Jakoby and Fiona A. Anderau

Introduction

The Indian Ocean earthquake and tsunami in 2004 killed approximately 230,000 people in fourteen different countries. The link between two separate literatures – bereavement and disaster – has been recently identified as a research deficit (McManus et al. 2017). Taking a closer look at the Indian Ocean tsunami in Sri Lanka, we will concentrate on one particular story of sudden, profound and traumatic loss, which is followed by the deep and desperate grief reaction of one individual. This story of multiple loss, near to unimaginable in its extent, is captured in the autobiography *Wave: A Memoir of Life after the Tsunami* by Sonali Deraniyagala. The 2004 tsunami, striking the southeastern coast of Yala (Sri Lanka) where Deraniyagla was residing, cost her the lives of multiple family members and subsequently also her reference points in helping her navigate the world. On the subject of her autobiography Deraniyagala states: 'This book was my survival; it was my way of reaching into my memory and recovering details of my family and of keeping them with me'.[1] The memoir in its unique accounting of multiple losses conveys valuable insights on the emotion of grief. These insights cannot – and will not – be captured by sociological analysis alone but are also viewed here through the lens of literary theory as the singular individual case cannot be fully accounted for through sociological interpretation. The radicalness of death and the deep and desperate mourning of the survivor disclose core dimensions of grief and highlight the social nature of relationship loss.

Through Deraniyagala's publication of *Wave*, her self-narrated grief is made public to the criticism and judgement of a wider audience. Literary reviews give insight into the social regulation of grief and public feeling rules. They show that although mourning has become highly individualized in modern society, feeling rules still permeate the expression of grief. Based on qualitative content analyzes of reviews on Goodreads, we analyze the social evaluations and the public responses to Deraniyagala's story of loss. We identify four general themes cantered on the existence of feeling rules: (1) grief work and recovery, (2) deviant feelings and behaviour, (3) social class and the 'luxury of grief' as well as (4) the therapeutic narrative and literary genre.

In the following chapter, we will first clarify the link between identity, autobiography and loss as well as provide an overview of the normative discourse regarding the emotion of grief. In a next step, we will elaborate on our methodology for the aforementioned qualitative content analysis. We will then proceed to present our results: first the literary analysis of Deraniyagala's memoir itself followed by the analysis of the online literary reviews found on the social cataloguing site Goodreads. We will end by drawing a conclusion of our findings.

Identity, autobiography and loss

As Kathy Charmaz (1980:282) argues, 'The experience of loss is related to personal identity'. Any significant loss causes a 'crisis of the self' (Charmaz 1997:232). How can we capture the link between identity, autobiography and loss? Death, according to the sociologist Anthony Giddens (1991:203), constitutes a point of no return in which the rational-technical values of modernity are fundamentally rejected and control is revealed to be nothing more than an illusion. Similarly, Zygmunt Bauman (1994:8) equates death to an 'unimaginable other', to the opposite of self, which withdraws itself from any form of communication. Mortality and the ongoing construction of self-identity are seen by Giddens (1991:47) as one of the most central and existential themes of life. Discontinuity in a person's life span, arising through loss and the breaking of social ties, can be explained through his concept of ontological security. Ontological security may be seen as the emotional dimension of identity, characterized through basic emotions such as trust, hope and commitment (Giddens 1991:38). Enforcing this sense of security are the reliability of people and objects as well as routines and habits. Continuity over space and time (i.e., the past, present, future) constitute key characteristics of a reflexive identity and are subsequently also key features in constructing one's biography (Giddens 1991:52–53). The reflexive character of identity may be deemed 'self-referentiality' as it is characterized by a permanent observation of the 'I' in continuous adjustment to the outside (Abels 2010:431):

> The reflexive construction of self-identity depends as much on preparing for the future as on interpreting the past, although the 'reworking' of past events is certainly always important in this process.
>
> (Giddens 1991:85)

Personal continuity, as already stated by Anselm L. Strauss (1959:145), is defined by a 'symbolic order of events', which is structured along a past-present-future timeline and is distinguished through its coherence and unity. The experience of change and loss have to be integrated into this biographical order on which feelings of continuity and discontinuity are hinged (Strauss 1959:146). Losses destroy the subjective meaning of daily life and the underlying 'routine reality' (Berger and Luckmann 2004:27). Crisis situations like deaths erase the self-evident nature of the environment (Schütz and Luckmann 1979). Following Giddens, it can be said that a significant loss destroys the 'protective cocoon' – held erect by daily life routines – and subsequently creates 'existential identity crisis' (Giddens 1991:129).

When the 'other' dies, the social nature of the self becomes painfully obvious. It is not only the loss of a loved human but also a loss of the self, which was constructed through its relationship with the other (Bradbury 1999). A loss generally destroys significant dimensions of the self of the survivor. Thus, Marris states that 'the fundamental crisis of bereavement arises, not from the loss of others, but the loss of self' (Marris 1986:32–33). The loss of a group member has fundamental consequences for the survivor's mental representation of the world – that is, losses cause a 'disintegration of identity' (Marris 1986:38). The concept of loss is supported by counselors who describe grieving as 'falling apart' or 'falling to pieces' during bereavement (Àrnason 2007). The sociological concept of *threads of connectedness* (Lofland 1982, 1985) best describes the multidimensional connections that are disrupted by relationship loss. Lyn H. Lofland highlights the following links between the self and others: role partner, mundane assistance, linkages to others, the creation and maintenance of self, receiving support for comforting myths, reality maintenance as well as the maintenance of possible futures (Lofland 1982:222–231). Thus, the death of a child may be associated with the 'loss of possibility' (Frost et al. 2007) and 'loss of promise' (Ironside 1996). It further refers to the perceived identity as a mother which is disrupted and a loss of dreams or expectations (Frost et al. 2007).

The model of *continuing bonds* (Klass et al. 1996; Walter 1996, 1999) challenges the medical view by highlighting further social dimensions of grief. There are four manifestations of continuing bonds with the deceased that provide continuity with the past: sensing the presence of the dead, talking with the dead, conceiving of the dead as moral guides and talking about the dead (Klass and Walter 2007; see also Unruh 1983). Bereavement is seen as a part of the process of (auto)biography whereas grief is defined as a symbolic code that allows communication of a loss and a narrative reconstruction of biography and self-identity (Walter 1996).

Peter L. Callero (2003:124) highlights the general role of narratives in the process of self-construction commenting that 'when disruption is perceived it must be explained, and narratives provide a framework' and reassert order. As a literary genre, autobiographies have emerged as a nonfictional and yet inevitably constructed auto-diegetic narration in which a self-reflexive subject seeks to understand his/her own life trajectory (Schwalm 2014). Marked by its retrospective telling, past memories are evaluated and selected through the lens of the present and are turned into meaningful plots (Bamberg 2011:7). By ascribing interconnections and causality into one's past and ordering characters along a space and time continuum, the narration constructs the autobiographer's life into a coherent whole and makes sense of contingency (McCarthy 2007). Furthermore, the narration serves as a vital means in the process of identity-formation, as it continuously 'makes claims vis-à-vis the who-am-I question' (Bamberg 2011:7). The autobiography *Wave*, written by Sonali Deraniyagala, reveals the emotional life of the protagonist in terms of a self-narration of loss and grief.

Normative discourse

Psychological models such as stage or phase models of grief (e.g., the 'Kübler-Ross model') understand grief as an individual experience open to pathology (Bradbury 1999). At its core, we find the binary conception of healthy grieving and pathological grief, which includes all deviations from what is considered to be the proper way to grieve. The individualistic conception of grief as a disease can be exemplified by the following definition:

> On the whole, grief resembles a physical injury more closely than any other type of illness. . . . As in the case of a physical injury, the 'wound' gradually heals, at least it usually does. But occasionally complications set in, healing is delayed. . . . In such cases abnormal forms arise.
>
> (Parkes and Prigerson 2011:5)

The perception of grief resembling an illness includes the expectation of intense distress, the importance of 'working through' the loss (in line with grief work and stage models of grief), the necessity of breaking down attachments and the expectation of recovery (see Wortman and Silver 2007). Recovery is seen as the normative aim of grieving (Kauffman 2008).

Societal and cultural norms regarding the inner and outer expression of grief are embedded in what Leeat Granek (2010) and Darcy Harris (2009/2010) see as the 'modern paradigm' and the capitalist economic structure, which promotes values like productivity, competition, consumption, functionality, efficiency and rationality. Mourning, sadness or fear – symbols for vulnerability, weakness and intense emotionality – contradict the aforementioned values of modernity. The aim is the restoration of functionality and the healing or full recovery of intense emotionality.[2] The social and cultural feeling rules of a given society are classified by the term 'emotionology' by Peter N. Stearns and Carol Z. Stearns:

> Emotionology: the attitudes or standards that a society, or a definable group within a society, maintains toward basic emotions and their appropriate expression; ways that institutions reflect and encourage these attitudes in human conduct.
>
> (Stearns and Stearns 1985:813)

These normative feeling expectations are also recognized by Arlie R. Hochschild (1979, 1983). According to Hochschild emotions are guided by feeling rules – that is, socially shared norms – which specify the emotions that individuals should feel or express in a given situation. Feeling rules govern the intensity and duration of emotions, whereas display rules refer to the public expression of emotions. Regarding the emotion of grief, Hochschild argues that 'the ways in which people think they have grieved poorly suggest what a remarkable achievement it is to grieve well' (Hochschild 1983:68). Forms of 'complicated grief' such as chronic, delayed or excessive grief reactions contain implicit feeling rules regarding the intensity and length of grief (Charmaz and Milligan 2006). Even absent grief can be wrong grief and deviate from existing grieving norms (Hochschild 1983). For the English-speaking sphere, Nancy Berns (2011) defines closure as a specific feeling rule in dealing with loss and grief, which at its core implies termination and can adopt multiple meanings such as 'closing a chapter', 'forgetting' or 'forgiving' (Berns 2011:23). With regard to Erving Goffman (1977), closure can also be seen as 'a frame used to explain how we should respond to loss' (Berns 2011:4), which is interwoven in market mechanisms and societal spheres of politics and mass media. Closure is a cultural construct, which offers a new language for feelings associated with mourning and loss.

In her qualitative study of grief management, Sarah Goodrum (2008) refers to the complexity of techniques available to control one's grief. The most common strategies of grief management aimed at bringing emotions into line with normative expectations are restraining grief and pretending to feel good. This may be the management of one's own emotions in terms of deep acting or playing down grief as a display act to reduce others' discomfort (e.g., suffering relatives) and to prevent them from being sad as well (Goodrum 2008:435). Most frequently, the bereaved are advised to distract themselves from grief in order to regain control of their vulnerability and emotions and be able to function again in everyday life (Harris 2009). Expressing grief is often stigmatized as weak or pessimistic. The bereaved are encouraged to return back to life, to function again and face the future (Ironside 1996). Other social responses seem to suggest there is both an expectation that one should grieve a little and a concurrent desire that the mourner not grieve too much (Granek and O'Rourke 2012).

Method

Published literary autobiographies contain firsthand accounts of loss narratives and can generate general knowledge about death and grief by providing accounts of lived experiences. Viewed through the eyes of the researcher, autobiographies can generate new understandings about the grief experience beyond the dominant medical frame of grief (Bandini 2015). By blurring research genres and using autobiographies as qualitative data within a sociology of emotions framework, we are able to uncover new knowledge (Power et al. 2012:39–40). In Deraniyagala's autobiography the depth of human loss is expressed through written means, and it thus provides a rich source of qualitative data to analyze the narrative of loss and grief by identifying plots and general themes.

Memoirs, such as Deraniyagala's *Wave*, foreground a self-narration of loss and grief. Consequently, they also foreground the reconstruction of lost social bonds as the bereaved construct plots to establish the character of the deceased and their own grief. Robert A. Neimeyer and colleagues (2014:489) differentiate between the 'event story' of the loss itself and the importance for the life of the survivor. The 'backstory' represents the relationship with the deceased and the attempt to restore some sense of attachment and continuing bonds. *Wave* represents a 'thanatological resource' (Sofka 1997) in two ways. First, grief narratives emphasize the role of the narrator, 'on how the stories of the bereaved are about themselves as well as about the deceased'. Second, 'narratives make us mindful of plots: of how the bereaved construct plots to establish the character of the deceased; of how plots reflect and shape the relationship between the bereaved and the deceased and the color of the grief of the former' (Àrnason 2000:195–196). Therefore, the autobiography offers a rich and valuable resource of narrative, used as qualitative data, with which the experience of grief and severe loss can be explicated. Deraniyagala's narration of loss in *Wave* will be taken as the subject of our analysis.

Furthermore, autobiographies are intended for public consumption and Deraniyagala's story of loss is subject to public criticism and opinion. Her words are judged by readers (Power et al. 2012:41). In addition to the analysis of Deraniyagala's self-reflection of loss, online literary reviews of her memoir, found on the social cataloguing site Goodreads, further provide us with insight into the social regulation of grief. Therefore, the autobiography offers a fruitful research tool in the field of bereavement research. Opting for two time periods, the analysis focuses on 65 gathered reviews from July 2012 to March 2013 and on 25 reviews gathered from April to July 2018. Our analysis is based on qualitative content analysis (Mayring 1997) using inductive and deductive categories to identify key dimensions of loss and grief as well as sifting out prevalent feeling rules.

Analysing the narrative as well as reviews and critiques of *Wave* provides a 'window into the intimate' *and* a 'window into society' at the same time (Power et al. 2012:42). The questions this chapter asks are therefore twofold: (1) How does the author reflect on the experience of loss and grief? What general insights about human loss can we gain from this unique story of grief? and (2) What do the online reviews reveal about the social feeling rules that permeate the experience of grief in contemporary society?

Results

The loss narrative

Sonali Deraniyagala's 2013 autobiography, *Wave: A Memoir of Life after the Tsunami*, chronicles her enormous loss after losing her entire family in the 2004 Indian Ocean tsunami. The author was born and raised in Sri Lanka before moving to London for her studies and finally settling there with her husband and two children. On one of their annual family trips to her childhood home, the tsunami struck the southeastern coast of Sri Lanka, where Deraniyagala was staying in a national park in Yala with her husband (Steve), her two sons (Vik, Mali) and her parents. With no forewarning of the wave, her family was taken by surprise, and Deraniyagala ended up being the sole survivor. In her memoir, Deraniyagala recounts the aftermath the tsunami had on her life and her experience with grief over a span of seven years. Typical of the literary genre of autobiographies, the narration is a retrospective one, with her as a first-person narrator focalizing her past/younger self. Through this dual structural narration, in which the autobiographical subject is divided into a narrating I and the narrated – that is, experiencing subject – the generic narrative logic of autobiographies is upheld, allowing for the author to recall and reconstruct her memories from a (pseudo-static) present. Thus, the novel is characterized by its high degree of self-reflexivity and psychological introspection, reconstructing and reassessing her past memories retrospectively in what Helga Schwalm (2014) has deemed a 'textual self-fashioning' of one's life. The autobiography can be divided into three plots and thematic structures anchoring the narrative:

1 Beginning: trauma and agony

Deraniyagala's autobiography, *Wave*, opens with a narration of her traumatic survival of the Sri Lankan tsunami and her last brief moments with her family. The story marks it as the central event dividing the author's life into a 'before' and 'after' and the narrative shifts between selected memories of Deraniyagala's family before the wave and memories of her painful realization of loss after. Following the immediate aftermath of the wave, Deraniyagala describes herself as overwhelmed by a feeling of shock, incomprehension and confusion: 'Couldn't I somehow stay suspended in my confusion? . . . I was terrified that tomorrow the truth would start' (Deraniyagala 2013:29). She is flooded by a sense of unreality, her mind unable to properly process the recent happenings. In her stupor, she stays silent, refusing to talk except once inquiring the time from Mette, their former jeep driver. However, instances of anger, bitterness and a sense of unfairness at the fact that other people have survived with seemingly no scratch seep through her dreamlike trance and manifest themselves time and again in her self-posed question: 'Why aren't *they* dead?' (Deraniyagala 2013:21); it's a question she ponders whenever she sees someone from the hotel her family stayed in. She is torn between an ambivalent state of hoping her family has survived, latching on to the sense of unreality of her momentary situation, and stifling her hope and preparing for the worst-case scenario. By crushing her hopes and thus protecting herself from hurt and disappointment, she is effectively managing her emotions. Deraniyagala's narrated feelings and reactions remain ambivalent, even after news arrives confirming the death of her parents, husband and two children. She continues to shift between (almost desperately) clinging to her harsh new reality and seeking comfort and relief in a blurred, distorted truth in which she distances herself from her past. The idea, that the unblurred and harsh truth must be faced and an attitude of cautiousness and vigilance must be adopted in order to avoid 'slipping up' and relearning the painful truth all over again manifests itself throughout various points in the narration.

However, after the early section of her memoir, her need to forget and escape her past dominates. 'Let them, let our life, become as unreal as that wave' (Deraniyagala 2013:44). The narration equates the loss of her family with the loss of her whole world – that is, her points of orientation in the world. After the traumatic loss of her family she has thus to readjust and reposition herself in the world, being confronted with a multitude of 'first times without's', which painfully remind her of the before, of 'that life' (Deraniyagala 2013:35). Unable to separate the ones she has lost from the world she continues to move in, everything constitutes a reminder of her loved ones and as a consequence, she is determined to remove herself from everything. For example, the display of bats and crows is too painful for her and she wishes them extinct, belonging to her old life but not her new one. She also develops a fear of time itself, refusing to look at a clock on Sundays as she does not want to be reminded of the time when her life came to an abrupt halt. Instead, she immerses herself in darkness: 'All that they were missing, I desperately shut out. I was terrified of everything because everything was from that life. . . . Now I had to make myself safe. I had to shrink my sight. I disappeared into darkness. I shut myself in the room. Even with the curtains closed, I pulled the covers over my head' (Deraniyagala 2013:35). By actively trying to stop herself from remembering anything from her past life and thus enhancing her sense of unreality of the past (i.e., doubting that it really happened), she tries to restrict her grief. She distances herself from her memories and subsequently also from her past self and the roles she inhabited. For, with only hazy memories, there is nothing to grieve *for*.

2 Middle: uproar and daze

In the second plot, the narrative continues to pick up on the ambivalence between clinging to the objective truth of her loved ones' deaths and desperately trying to avoid any reminders of her former life. The difference, however, lies in Deraniyagala being portrayed as taking a much more active role in trying to distance herself from her loss and avoiding reminders which might trigger a cascade of memories. She starts excessively drinking, in part to escape her dreams featuring her family, and thus she shifts between momentarily forgetting and relearning the truth all over again when she is sober. She starts mixing alcohol with pills and loses herself in her hallucinations. By looking at images of the wave, images of destruction, dead bodies, mortuaries and mass graves and Googling ways to kill herself she attempts to make herself insane. Further, she seeks escapism by directing all her energy towards a specific goal. For example, on her first time going back to the Yala Safari Beach Hotel, she, at first terrified of finding anything belonging to her loved ones as she is still unable to comprehend their death, starts obsessively searching for any traces she might find of her family. She stops only after effectively achieving her goal and finding Vik's lime-green cotton shirt. After that she finds a new fixation – namely, to harass the Dutch family that moved into her parents' house and are 'infecting' it. She describes how her mostly nightly outings tip the power imbalance in her favour, and she feels more in control again and not helplessly powerless to circumstances. She rationalizes her behaviour by thinking that 'Vik and Mali will be so impressed by her ghostliness' (Deraniyagala 2013:72), with emphasis on the use of *will*, implying their future pleased reaction despite this imagined future being unreachable. The narration remarks that she has been too compliant and numb since the wave, her behaviour at odds with the deranged way one 'should' behave after suffering major losses as she did. Her energy spurt is temporary, however, and she starts spending her days in bed again 'in a daze of Vodka and Ambien', angry at her husband, Steve, for leaving her in this (ghostly) position alone: 'In order to survive this bizarre and brutal truth, do I have to make murky the life I had with them?' (Deraniyagala 2013:114).

Throughout the narrated time, spanning a range of four years, Deraniyagala continues to grapple with the sense of disbelief over what happened. She moves between London, New York and Colombo, reaching out for her family when she is able to and pushing them away when she is overcome by pain and a deep and desperate longing for what she has lost. She adopts a wary and careful attitude in remembering, taking care to not lose herself in her memories. However, this becomes a problem when she is emerged into too familiar surroundings such as her family home in London. Her former life is pressed upon her and she is left feeling helpless, her grasp on reality loosening and her memories coming into sharper focus. Left feeling as if in a daze, Deraniyagala is almost able to delude herself that nothing has changed. As a consequence of this, her trips to London remain brief, her terror of being too close to the life she has lost becoming unbearable, and she wills herself into remembering the fact of her family's demise. The moment the truth escapes her and she moves away. Her apartment in New York serves as a place in which she can reach for her family in a 'safe' way. By removing herself physically, she finds it easier to emotionally distance herself as well. The truth acts as a barrier between her present and past self. By distancing herself from her memories and rejecting her former self, she enhances the feeling of the truth being ungraspable – for how can she grieve her role as a mother when she is unable to imagine she ever occupied that role? So, even though she does remember, it is a misty, hazy remembering to protect herself from the pain of her loss.

3 End: 'There is a difference now'

The final thematic structure is marked by the repeated statement, 'There is a difference now' (e.g., Deraniyagala 2013:132). The difference lies in her attitude towards remembering. Recalling memories of the past does not leave her feeling as fractured as before, and rather than trying to avoid details of her family, she starts to actively long for them. She is able to recall her children's vulnerable sides, whereas before she had ignored this in favour of the humorous and cheeky parts of their personality. By recalling all she has lost, she also feels the distance between her past and present identity diminishing, being able to recognize and acknowledge her past as a part of herself. There is still a discrepancy between the past and present as well as a clear-cut distinction between 'this life' (after the wave) and 'that' (before the wave). However, for the most part she is able to balance her past and present, even finding strength in remembering. Only by keeping her memories of her family alive can she continue to sustain her own sense of self:

> But I have learned that I can only recover myself when I keep them near. If I distance myself from them; and their absence, I am fractured. I am left feeling I've blundered into a stranger's life.

> (Deraniyagala 2013:208)

Although the narrative evokes or draws on the notion of recovery as the normative aim of grieving, recovery is understood in a different sense. More accurately what is meant by the word is actually a 'rediscovery' of her family and reconstructing a connection with them. The key to finding comfort in her memories is to acquire 'balance' – that is, to not completely lose sight of the present but also to not completely distance herself from the past. Grief, sadness or fear have not disappeared or faded away; these emotions, the yearning for her family and the loss of self remain. However, the shock and disbelief have gone and during the course of writing the memoir she has 'rediscovered' her family and experiences an openness for memories and places associated with her family. Nevertheless, she describes it as a 'new sadness' and uses the metaphor of 'distilled loss' to illuminate the new shades of grief:

> Seven years on, and their absence has expanded. Just as our life would have in this time, it has swelled. So this is a new sadness, I think. For I want them as they would be now. I want to be in our life. Seven years on, it is distilled, my loss. For am I not whirling anymore, I am no longer cradled by shock.
> (Deraniyagala 2013:207)

The first and the final paragraphs of the book represent meaningful sections underlying a core theme of the narrative: *identity and loss*, as pointed out in the second chapter. As Charmaz (1980:282) argues, 'The extent of loss depends upon how immersed the identity of the bereaved is in the circumstances within which the loss is felt'. In the beginning Deraniyagala mentions the statement of her friend who stayed in the same hotel in Sri Lanka: 'What you guys have, is a dream' (Deraniyagala 2013:4). And then almost immediately after these words are spoken, they are reversed – the wave comes and destroys this dream. The tsunami ended the life the narrator had known up to that time. At the end, she remembers how her son described and defined her by using the family name of her husband and her social role as mother: '"Mummy Lissenburgh" – me having no identity without these three boys' (Deraniyagala 2013:208). And she recalls her response and protest: '*That's* not me'. At the same time when she allows herself to remember her family and admits the reality of loss, she reflects on her 'post-loss self' (Jakoby 2016). In that sense the memoir ends with a self-narrative – that is, an awareness and reflection on her identity, which is completely marked by her social roles as mother and wife.

Finally, evidence in the text suggests that bereaved individuals are confronted with a variety of grieving norms, which are partly connected to the social role(s) one inhabits or has inhabited. The narrator expresses concern that the narrated grief reactions do not conform to the way a mother is expected to mourn. Deraniyagala's reactions are deemed unnatural, feeble and abhorrent. It is remarked that she would be less bewildered about having been a mother to two children if she had also grieved the way a mother should: 'I might feel more like their mother if I was constantly weeping and screaming and tearing my hair out and clawing the earth, I think sometimes' (Deraniyagala 2013:115). This would thus suggest that her distance from her pre-loss self's social role as a mother is affected (or even partly induced) by her deviance from the 'proper' way a grieving person occupying that role is expected to behave. Feeling rules also become apparent in Deraniyagala's narrated hesitance in telling her story and voicing her grief. In interactions with others she is prone to omit the 'outlandish truth of me' (Deraniyagala 2013:105) as she does not want to cause shock or distress or put people in an uncomfortable position. As the narration establishes her as someone who used to be quite open and talkative before, her silence is significant and her defensive stance that 'I am really not one for the telling' (Deraniyagala 2013:204) implies that grief is something to be kept to yourself. Of course, Deraniyagala, through publishing *Wave*, *did* tell her story and it is thus all the more interesting to look at how her narrated grief (i.e., her feelings and behaviours) is assessed by outsiders.

Public responses: social norms of grieving

In reviewing Deraniyagala's narration of loss, the online literary reviews on Goodreads almost inevitably contain normative assumptions about the emotion of grief. Specifically, they contain assumptions about how grief should be dealt with in private, the manner in which it should be outwardly expressed and finally, how it should be communicated through social interactions and through written means. Based on the qualitative content analysis of the 91 selected online reviews, our results yielded four general themes based on the existence of feeling rules, which were identifiable throughout our data pool. These are the following: (1) grief work and recovery, (2) deviant feelings and behaviour, (3) social class and the 'luxury of grief' as well as (4) the therapeutic narrative and literary genre. In the following subsections, we will expand on these categories.

Grief work and recovery

> The writer made me uncomfortable – it was like being caught up at a very, very long funeral, with intense remembrance going on forever.
>
> (M., March 04, 2013)

> This book was interesting, but I kept waiting for the author to figure out how to deal with her loss. I wanted some kind of closure for her at the end, but it just didn't happen.
>
> (D., March 07, 2013)

The online literary reviews reveal the presence of a strongly held belief that grief is something to be 'conquered' through the active management of emotions by the bereaved individual. The analysis reveals a focal point of mourning situated in the future, meaning that the objective of the bereaved lies on healing and on returning to a semblance of normality. Vital in the achievement of this goal is the transformation of negative emotions – like anger, sadness and confusion – into positive ones. Negative emotions are not desirable for the bereaved's recovery from grief, rather they are to be worked through and disposed of. However, in this regard, Sonali Deraniyagala's narration of grief veers off in a different direction. Her point of interest rests in the past, in recalling, with meticulous precision, the lives of her loved ones. Indeed, due to the majority of the memoir being exclusively devoted to her deceased family members, several reviews remark that the book itself may be viewed as an immortalization of her loved ones. Thus, almost solely reminiscing about times past, Deraniyagala's grief gives the appearance of being endless. Looking back, she is seen to be at an emotional standstill, in a passive state of not really doing anything productive to heal herself – or, to put it concisely, she is 'just' remembering. And, the reviews emphasize, she is clearly remembering *too* much and allowing her grief to continue on for *too* long:

> She can't get over it. Not that she should, but the end isn't an uplifting treatise on overcoming tragedy. . . . Someone else said 'grief porn'.
>
> (J., March 04, 2013)

Disappointment in Deraniyagala's autobiography also stems from the fact that the narrative abstains in providing the reader with a step-by-step guide on how to recover from a loss as intense as hers. She is not seen to take initiative or take charge of her life and of shedding her grief. Instead she is seen as trapped in her emotions and is thus unable to provide the reader with an example on how to overcome the multitude of emotions accompanying her grief:

> The other thing that stuck with me strongly was how much I wanted her to move on – not to forget her husband and children, but to open herself to life again, to move forward, to make space to love other people. It doesn't seem as if she has.
>
> (A., March 07, 2013)

> I kept waiting for her to explain how she was able to overcome her horrors and to slowly move on bit by bit to find solace in new relationships, perhaps an adopted child from the tsunami, or reconnecting with the people that were in Yala with her etc.
>
> (G., April 18, 2018)

The reviews also highlight the social dimension of grief – that is, they remark on the conception of grief as a social emotion (Jakoby 2012). The sociality of grief shows our connectedness to other people or, to be more precise, it shows, how the emotional reaction following the death of a significant other stems from the breaking of *social* bonds. And although the literary reviews recognize this loss of social bonds, they then emphasize the importance of establishing new bonds as an essential part of the process of recovery. And with this, it implies breaking bonds with the deceased somewhat, to dampen the social relationships one has had with the people one has lost. In short: to move on.

Deviant feelings and behaviour

The criticism of the author's lack of grief work and subsequent recovery from her grief strongly suggests that Deraniyagala's mourning is stretching the norm of what is considered to be an acceptable time frame to grieve in. Her grieving is deviant in the sense that it crosses the line separating socially accepted and even encouraged grief from so-called prolonged grief. The sheer quantity of narrated negative emotions, expected by the reader to decrease over time, instead of diminishing continues throughout the book, calling forth descriptions such as that the author is 'wallowing in sadness'. The length of her mourning thus delegitimizes her grief to a certain degree. However, it is not only the fact of her continuous grieving but also the way in which her grief becomes manifest – that is, her emotional reaction and behaviour – which is deemed inappropriate in the given situational context. The results show that especially her active grief responses – examples being her excessive drinking, stalking, self-injury and suicidal thoughts – are deemed to be unproductive and wrong ways of expressing her grief. These behaviours reflect badly on the author who is as a consequence labelled aggressive, cruel and cold or just generally deemed to be an unsympathetic person:

> I was shocked by some of the emotions the author had after almost dying in the Sri Lankan tsunami. The way she was in shock and unable to embrace others going through the same thing she was, her inability to overcome her grief even 6 years later, and her need to escape memory. . . . I do think she needed severe psychiatric counselling and group therapy with people suffering the same losses that she had to cope with.
>
> (G., April 18, 2018)

Her lack of communication or interest with people who have suffered similar losses as she has is also frequently remarked upon. The author is seen as self-involved and isolated in her grief. She does not reflect on the collective loss suffered but instead is lost in her own grief, unable to look past it to reflect or acknowledge the grief of other individuals. Once more, the importance of social bonds is brought to the forefront. The author's failure to establish social bonds with other bereaved people is seen as a missed step towards recovery and an inability to take advantage of the social resources available to her.

Social class and the 'luxury of grief'

The emotional and material lives are interconnected and cannot be analyzed separately. Yet social class and its link to bereavement and grief is a neglected field of research (Howarth 2007). Previous literature primarily focuses on working class responses to bereavement and has contrasted a 'working class stoicism' with a middle-class privileging of verbal communication of grief (Howarth 2007; Allen 2007). Working-class attitudes towards death and grief are associated with stoicism and nonverbal rituals, whereas the dominant model of grief privileges discourse (Howarth 2007:430). From a historical perspective, Tony Walter (1999) points out the class distinction of grieving in the Victorian Age. It was the upper and upper middle classes and in particular women of these classes who had the 'leisure' to obey mourning rituals and withdraw from social life for a certain period of time. With servants and material wealth at their disposal, they were excused from the responsibilities of day-to-day life (Walter 1999:35). The memoir *Wave* draws interesting and striking parallels with the previous point. The reviews evoke Deraniyagala's high social class in terms of family background, education and money as something that possibly delegitimizes her right to grief for as long as she does. The book's references to the author's material privilege – for example, the mention of nannies, cooks, drivers and personal security guards – made readers reevaluate and amend their perception of Deraniyagala's grief. The author, seen equipped with (material) resources many may not have, can thus be afforded with the time to grieve for as long as she wishes to:

> She was able to hide out in mourning for months and months. . . . Most people would have to pay bills and other mundane things, despite such heart-rending loss.
>
> (A., March 7, 2013)

Consequently, her grief is seen as a 'luxury' as it is unaffected by financial or social duties or the like. It is assumed that 'the cushioning of class' mediates trauma and loss. Her material privilege allows her to draw on coping mechanisms – such as taking trips around the world – not affordable to a vast majority of bereaved. Thus, equipped with many resources, the author's narration of grief is seen as atypical and not representative of the losses suffered by the collective majority of people afflicted by the 2004 Indian Ocean tsunami:

> I noted that at least one other person who appreciated some qualities in the book was also taken struck by the level and repeated representation of social privilege here that did not seem to be recognized as such by the author. It made me wonder what happens to those who had similar losses in this unimaginable disaster who were not able to take trips around the world that the author acknowledges was helpful in allowing her to get past her grief?
>
> (C., June 26, 2018)

However, the criticism of the reviewers does not only focus on her high social class but rests also on the fact that her privilege is recognized and remarked upon by the author. The social class barrier between reader and author is also an emotional one, as it affects the reader's ability to empathize and relate to the author and her grief. One reviewer explicitly links the lack of compassion felt for the author to her high material class status, seeing it as a kind of hitch or disturbance in the narration of grief:

> I did find myself tripping occasionally on the narrative, when Deraniyagala's class status inserted itself into the story . . . there is much cross-continent travel, vacations on the coast, a life of at least some ease and social

lubrication. . . . I did wonder (sociologically) about the other thousands upon thousands of victims of the tsunami, including those without homes in London, well-placed friends, economic resources, and the cushioning of class that, at least to some degree, mediates trauma and loss.

(M., March 09, 2013)

This finding sensitizes us to social inequalities because of the unequal distribution of coping resources such as time, privacy and money. The results suggest that one's social class (a) affects how grief is outwardly displayed (Hochschild 1983), (b) how it has to be inwardly dealt with, and (c) influences the empathic ability of members of different social classes to connect with the bereaved individual. The expression and social sanctioning of grief seems to be tightly connected to social class, with members of higher social classes being more harshly evaluated for their grief by the lower classes. To conclude, Walter's statement made about the Victorian time period that 'immersion in grief is a luxury only to be afforded by those with the requisite time and space' (Walter 1999:36) seems to hold true in present times as well. However, further research into the social class dimensions of grief is needed.

Therapeutic narrative and literary genre

'Therapeutic narrative' is a term coined by sociologist Eva Illouz (2008) and is characteristic for the genre of autobiographies. Therapeutic narratives, according to Illouz, should contain (a) an exposé; (b) specifications of time, space, situation and participants; (c) a sequence of events; (d) evaluation and assessment of events; and (e) closure. The therapeutic ideal is a healthy emotional state and subsequently also the goal towards which such narratives are oriented. Striving for this ideal is what brings forth stories of suffering, as the ideal of health and normality construes behaviours which are then in comparison deemed pathological or dysfunctional (Illouz 2008). Narratives in which suffering is foregrounded in this manner have led to such books being subsumed under the genres of 'mis lit' and 'misery memoirs', which are labels also found in online reviews to describe Deraniyagala's book. However, despite evoking the genre – the story's central focus resting on memory and on remembering pain and suffering – Deraniyagala's narrative of grief significantly deviates from the therapeutic narrative.[3] These deviations have evoked particularly negative reviews. One point of criticism is that the book does not provide the reader with a clear message, or some kind of insight or life lesson that the reader can take away from the memoir. There is no 'sense- or meaning-making', no reconstruction of a life of meaning (Neimeyer 2001). Furthermore, there is no elaboration on growing inner qualities and personal growth, no narrative of post-traumatic growth (Archer 1999):

The memoir read as self-indulgent . . . as a ruminating and depressing book rather than what it could have been: a look into how she still carries her family with her even though they are gone and it hurts everyday but she focuses on remembering them and honoring their life.

(A., May 14, 2018)

As a consequence of this, the reader is not given a sense of closure – that is, the narrative does not conform to the rules of so-called closure talk. The concept of closure 'provides a perfect framework for telling stories about pain and grief while providing a reassuring end' (Berns 2011:12). Due to the lack of closure and positive resolution to Deraniyagala's grief the reader is not left reassured but rather confronted with a feeling of uneasiness. According to Berns: 'If you leave people unresolved and adrift, it is not going to give the reader the sense that she can also take charge in her life' (Berns 2011:12). Thus the book is seen as depressing and discouraging to many reviewers.

A final point regarding the narration of grief, are the numerous comments remarking on Deraniyagala's honesty. The author's honesty in the portrayal of her grief is seen as a point of admiration but also one of criticism:

> Her unflinching honesty means that she also shows the darker sides of herself – and of grief. Like how she doesn't grieve her parents for a long time because of what she calls a pecking order to her grief. There's simply a limit to how many she can grieve over at one time. Or how she's not sure if a boy in an ambulance is her son or not. Or how she starts drinking and taking pills to cope. Or how for months she harass the family who buys her parents' home because she wants it back.
>
> (C., March 05, 2013)

Whilst some applaud the author's bravery in her 'unflinching' and 'raw' portrayal of her grief and the fact that she does not hold back or sugarcoat her emotions or reactions, others feel that this makes it read too personally, as a possibly useful therapeutic measure for the author herself but not something that should have been published. Rather, it is something that the author should have kept to herself, clearly deemed unfit for the eyes of the public. This would suggest that within the range of acceptable public discourse on grief, Deraniyagala's narration of loss falls short.

Conclusion

For Lyn H. Lofland (1985:181), grief is an emotion 'however much based in biological capacities, which touches directly on the mutual interdependence of selves and societies, of actors and others, of me and you'. The autobiography illuminates human vulnerability and frailty in the wake of significant relationship loss. It is not only the loss itself; death shakes the foundations on which the self of the survivor is constructed and known (Charmaz 1980). With its radicalness, the autobiography and its public responses reveal core features of human loss and grief. In this sense, the narrative offers an *ideal-type concept of bereavement* – that is, a representation of human loss and grief in a pure form. This analysis is significant because we can draw generalizations of the dominant features of loss and grief based on the overreaching particular experience, including:

1   The complexity of emotions and behaviours involved in grief (including the acknowledgement of 'deviant' forms as an integral part of bereavement).
2   The disruption of identity and the *loss of self* in the aftermath of a significant loss.
3   Ambivalences of closeness and distance of the dead (including ambivalences of memorialization in terms of avoidance or fear versus its potential as a core resource for 'recovery').
4   The idea of *distilled loss* in the aftermath of bereavement and *continuing bonds* with the deceased.
5   The importance of coping resources and the link to social inequality (time, money, social networks).

Furthermore, the autobiography sensitizes us to the social policing of grief and the various implicit and explicit feeling and display rules (Hochschild 1983). We find the medical perspective of grief to be very dominant in the reviews – that is, the notion that the grieving process of an individual should be aimed towards recovery. The author deviates from this in the sense that she is not looking forward, but backwards, and she is not relinquishing her social ties to the dead but rather continuing them on into the present. She is exploring her grief rather than overcoming it and thus, due to the lack of so called 'grief work', she is seen to be passive, her grieving continuing on for too long. The active responses that she does show – drinking, stalking, self-injury, suicidal thoughts and attempts – are seen to be unproductive and wrong ways of expressing her grief. There seems to be a clear consensus on how one should openly talk about grief and how it should or should not be framed. Thus, even if the length of her grieving and her behaviour and feelings are deemed to be justified, and legitimate, there still seems to be the idea that her 'abnormal' grief should have been kept private, it being of no benefit to the reader or teaching any kind of valuable lesson. Finally, concerning comments about the narration of grief, we find that the normative aim of recovery might actually be enhanced by storytelling conventions, which would have closure as an essential part of any good story.

Notes

1 www.youtube.com/watch?v=aX_bb_-2uEs (05.12.2017).
2 In research literature, there is also a current debate about how 'postmodern values' influence the dealings with loss and grief – for example, the prevalent notion of choice and self-determination in today's society (Walter 1994). However, this will not be further explicated here.
3 By contrast, a different narrative is offered by Nate Berkus, who also lost his partner in the 2014 tsunami. His story was told on *The Oprah Winfrey Show*. It fits the therapeutic narrative and includes references to thankfulness, the strength of surviving,

surviving for 'a reason' as well as ideas of spirituality (miracle, being part of 'something larger'). Eva Illouz (2008) uses *The Oprah Winfrey Show* to illustrate the core idea of the therapeutic narrative as it is exemplified in this particular genre: the talk show. See: 'Nate Berkus Finds Meaning After Surviving 2004 Tsunami', *The Oprah Winfrey Show* (2005), www.youtube.com/watch?v=eDj6MTVp9Vc (06.23.18).

References

Abels, Heinz (2010): *Identität [Identity]* (2nd Edition). Wiesbaden: V. S. Verlag.

Allen, Chris (2007): 'The Poverty of Death: Social Class, Urban Deprivation, and the Criminological Consequences of Sequestration of Death'. *Mortality*, 12:79–93.

Archer, John (1999): *The Nature of Grief: The Evolution and Psychology Reactions to Loss*. London: Routledge.

Àrnason, Arnar (2000): 'Biography, Bereavement, Story'. *Mortality*, 5:189–204.

Àrnason, Arnar (2007): 'Fall Apart and Put Yourself Back Together Again: The Anthropology of Death and Bereavement Counseling in Britain'. *Mortality*, 12:48–65.

Bamberg, Michael (2011): 'Who Am I? Narration and Its Contribution to Self and Identity'. *Theory & Psychology*, 21 (1):3–24.

Bandini, Julia (2015): 'The Medicalization of Bereavement: (Ab)normal Grief in the DSM-5'. *Death Studies*, 39:347–352.

Bauman, Zygmunt (1994): *Tod, Unsterblichkeit und andere Lebensstrategien [Mortality, Immortality and other Life Strategies]*. Frankfurt am Main: Fischer.

Berger, Peter L. and Thomas Luckmann (2004): *Die Gesellschaftliche Konstruktion der Wirklichkeit [The Social Construction of Reality]*. Frankfurt am Main: Fischer.

Berns, Nancy (2011): *Closure: The Rush to End Grief and What It Costs Us*. Philadelphia: Temple University Press.

Bradbury, Mary (1999): *Representations of Death: A Social Psychological Perspective*. London: Routledge.

Callero, Peter L. (2003): 'The Sociology of Self'. *Annual Review of Sociology*, 29:115–133.

Charmaz, Kathy (1980): *The Social Reality of Death*. Reading, MA: Addison-Wesley.

Charmaz, Kathy (1997): 'Grief and Loss of Self', in Kathy Charmaz, Glennys Howarth and Allan Kellehear (eds.): *The Unknown Country: Death in Australia, Britain and the USA*. London: Palgrave/Macmillan, pp. 229–241.

Charmaz, Kathy and Melinda Milligan (2006): 'Grief', in Jan E. Stets and Jonathan H. Turner (eds.): *Handbook of the Sociology of Emotions*. New York: Springer, pp. 516–538.

Deraniyagala, Sonali (2013): *Wave: A Memoir of Life After the Tsunami*. London: Virago Press.

Frost, Julia, Harriet Bradley, Ruth Levitas, Lindsay Smith and Jo Garcia (2007): 'The Loss of Possibility: Scientisation of Death and the Special Case of Early Miscarriage'. *Sociology of Health & Illness*, 29 (7):1003–1022.

Giddens, Anthony (1991): *Modernity and Self-Identity: Self and Society in the Late Modern Age*. Cambridge: Polity Press.

Goffman, Erving (1977): *Rahmen-Analyse: Ein Versuch über die Organisation von Alltagserfahrungen [Frame Analysis]*. Frankfurt am Main: Suhrkamp.

Goodrum, Sarah (2008): 'When the Management of Grief Becomes Everyday Life: The Aftermath of Murder'. *Symbolic Interaction*, 31 (4):422–442.

Granek, Leeat (2010): 'Grief as Pathology: The Evolution of Grief Theory in Psychology from Freud to the Present'. *History of Psychology*, 1:46–73.

Granek, Leeat and Meghan O'Rourke (2012): 'Is Mourning Madness? The Wrongheaded Movement to Classify Grief as a Mental Disorder'. *Slate Magazine*, March 12. Available online at: https://slate.com/human-interest/2012/03/complicated-grief-and-the-dsm-the-wrongheaded-movement-to-list-mourning-as-a-mental-disorder.html#comments.

Harris, Darcy (2009): 'Oppression of the Bereaved: A Critical Analysis of Grief in Western Society'. *Omega: Journal of Death & Dying*, 3:241–253.

Hochschild, Arlie R. (1979): 'Emotion Work, Feeling Rules and Social Structure'. *American Journal of Sociology*, 3:551–575.

Hochschild, Arlie R. (1983): *The Managed Heart: Commercialization of Human Feeling*. Berkeley, CA: University of California Press.

Howarth, Glennys (2007): 'Whatever Happened to Social Class? An Examination of the Neglect of Working Class Cultures in the Sociology of Death'. *Health Sociological Review*, 16:425–435.

Illouz, Eva (2008): *Saving the Modern Soul: Therapy, Emotions and the Culture of Self-Help*. Berkeley, CA: University of California Press.

Ironside, Virgina (1996): *You'll Get Over It: The Rage of Bereavement*. London: Penguin Books.

Jakoby, Nina R. (2012): 'Grief as a Social Emotion: Theoretical Perspectives'. *Death Studies*, 36:679–711.

Jakoby, Nina R. (2016): 'The Self and Significant Others: Toward a Sociology of Loss'. *Illness, Crisis & Loss*, 23:110–128.

Kauffman, Jeffrey (2008): 'What Is "No Recovery"?'. *Death Studies*, 32:74–83.

Klass, Dennis and Tony Walter (2007): 'Processes of Grief: How Bonds Are Continued', in Margaret S. Stroebe, Robert O. Hansson, Wolfgang Stroebe and Henk Schut (eds.): *Handbook of Bereavement Research: Consequences, Coping and Care*. Washington, DC: American Psychological Association, pp. 431–448.

Klass, Dennis, Phyllis R. Silverman and Steven L. Nickman (eds.) (1996): *Continuing Bonds: New Understandings of Grief*. New York: Taylor & Francis.

Lofland, Lyn H. (1982): 'Loss and Human Connection: An Exploration Into the Nature of the Social Bond', in William Ickes and Eric S. Knowles (eds.): *Personality, Roles and Social Behavior*. New York: Springer, pp. 219–242.

Lofland, Lyn H. (1985): 'The Social Shaping of Emotion: The Case of Grief'. *Symbolic Interaction*, 8:171–190.

Marris, Peter (1986): *Loss and Change*. London: Routledge and Kegan Paul.

Mayring, Peter (1997): *Qualitative Inhaltsanalyse: Grundlagen und Techniken*. Weinheim: Deutscher Studien Verlag.

McCarthy, Joan (2007): *Dennett and Ricoeur on the Narrative Self*. New York: Humanity Books.

McManus, Ruth, Tony Walter and Leon Claridge (2017): 'Restoration and Loss After Disaster: Applying the Dual-Process Model of Coping in Bereavement'. *Death Studies*, 42:405–412.

Neimeyer, Robert A. (2001): *Meaning Reconstruction and the Experience of Loss*. Washington DC: American Psychological Association.

Neimeyer, Robert A., Dennis Klass and Michael R. Dennis (2014): 'A Social Constructionist Account of Grief: Loss and the Narration of Meaning'. *Death Studies*, 38:485–498.

Parkes, Colin Murray and Holly G. Prigerson (2011): *Bereavement: Studies of Grief in Adult Life*. London: Routledge.

Power, Tamara, Debra Jackson, Rosyln Weaver, Lesley Wilkes and Bernie Carter (2012): 'Autobiography as Genre for Qualitative Data: A Reservoir of Experience for Nursing Research'. *Collegian*, 19:39–43.

Schütz, Alfred and Thomas Luckmann (1979): *Strukturen der Lebenswelt* (Volume 2). Frankfurt am Main: Suhrkamp.

Schwalm, Helga (2014): 'Autobiography', in Peter Hühn et al. (eds.): *The Living Handbook of Narratology*. Hamburg University. Available online at: www.lhn.uni-hamburg.de/article/autobiography.

Sofka, Carla J. (1997): 'Social Support 'Internetworks', Caskets for Sale, and More: Thanatology and the Information Superhighway'. *Death Studies*, 21:553–574.

Stearns, Peter N. and Carol Z. Stearns (1985): 'Clarifying the History of Emotions and Emotional Standards'. *American Historical Review*, 90:813–836.

Strauss, Anselm L. (1959): *Mirrors and Masks: The Search for Identity*. Glencoe, IL: Free Press.

Unruh, David R. (1983): 'Death and Personal History: Strategies of Identity Preservation'. *Social Problems*, 30 (3):340–351.

Walter, Tony (1994): *The Revival of Death*. London: Routledge.

Walter, Tony (1996): 'A New Model of Grief: Bereavement and Biography'. *Mortality*, 1:7–25.

Walter, Tony (1999): *On Bereavement: The Culture of Grief*. Maidenhead: Open University Press.

Wortman, Camille B. and Roxanne C. Silver (2007): 'The Myths of Coping with Loss Revisited', in Margaret S. Stroebe, Robert O. Hansson, Wolfgang Stroebe and Henk Schut (eds.): *Handbook of Bereavement Research: Consequences, Coping and Care*. Washington, DC: American Psychological Association, pp. 405–429.

6   Writing grief

The fraught work of mourning in fiction

Christian Riegel

Introduction

In writing about the modern elegy, Jahan Ramazani remarks that the 20th century presented challenges to the elegist: 'The poetry of mourning for the dead assumes in the modern period an extraordinary diversity' as it responds to the industrialization of warfare and mass death, the weakening of mourning rites and death being shifted to a taboo space (Ramazani 1994:1). Literary explorations of mourning for the dead are not restricted to poetry, as the cultural history of the 20th and early 21st centuries well demonstrates, for a rich tradition of addressing grief in fiction arose in the early-to-mid decades of the 20th century, including writers as varied as James Agee (1957), Virginia Woolf (1927), Truman Capote (1966) and Malcolm Lowry (1947). In the latter decades, figures such as Margaret Laurence (1966), Jonathan Safran Foer (2005), Graham Swift (1996) and Joy Kogawa (1981) explored the shifting world of uncertainty of meaning grieving individuals had to contend with. Mourning was recognized as operating counter to the certainty of consolation expressed in influential earlier examples in the literary tradition, such as John Milton's 'Lycidas' (1638) and Percy Bysshe Shelley's 'Adonais' (1821), and instead was refigured as complex psychic ground that required the grieving subject to negotiate a world that did not provide satisfying models to shape and support grief; moreover, the nature of loss was compounded by the sheer mass of traumatic experience the 20th century provided that individuals needed to contend with. Jacques Derrida expresses the challenges to mourning in this era when he states bluntly: 'Mourning is interminable. Inconsolable. Irreconcilable. . . . That is what whoever works at mourning knows' (Derrida 2001:143). For literary authors, then, the challenge has been how to create the space in their works for their characters to mourn, even when the prospects of consolation are dim, and how to create texts that will reach to a readership eager for models of mourning that are otherwise unavailable socially.

This chapter will examine how authors contend with the turbulent terrain of fraught grief of the late 20th and early 21st centuries by looking at two key novels, *Obasan* (1981), by Canadian author Joy Kogawa and *Extremely Loud & Incredibly Close* (2005), by American writer Jonathan Safran Foer. In writing loss, these authors explore mourning as a type of work or labour that unfolds as a process of mourning, and their resulting novels become products of that mourning, what one can deem an artefact of their work. Thus, these novels operate as memorial structures for their readers, enacting an ethical relationship so that readers engage with significant traumatic experiences of loss of the period, and learn about the nature of loss and about how to find in cultural expression useful models of coping. Kogawa's novel is interested in the intersection between her main character's traumatization at the hands of the Canadian government during the Second World War and the long legacy of the atomic bombings of Nagasaki and Hiroshima in terms of how these bombings shadow the 20th century. Her novel *Obasan* is particularly useful to examine in terms of mourning and memorializing as it is inherently interested in how individuals mourn privately and in how that private work of mourning is inextricably bound to a monumental and global trauma. Kogawa's fictional figuration of mourning and memorializing has the purpose of opening her readers to how grieving functions in individuals and then to how that grieving can serve as a memorial structure to readers so they can effectively commemorate a significant public loss which, in this case, is a key example of losses ascribed to a weapon of mass destruction. Similarly, Fore's novel *Extremely Loud & Incredibly Close* is exemplary in its articulation of the intersection of private grief and broader public and social needs to understand and process a global act of trauma which, in Foer's case, is the terrorist attack on the Twin Towers. Foer's main character performs a work of mourning in relation to his father, who died in the attack. The story that the main character tells, which is what readers encounter, is of how the main character attempts to process and understand how a global event has touched him so personally. Thus, readers are given insight into how a private work of mourning unfolds and how that private act relates to public commemoration. The text stands as a memorial structure to signal to readers how this traumatic act of terror can be remembered and understood. The discussion that follows in this chapter is established to elucidate how the work of mourning can be related to memorialising, and how this memorialising can serve as a memorial structure similar to conventional physician memorials and monuments, and then to use the novels by Kogawa and Foer to illustrate the theoretical framework.

The literary work of mourning and notions of memorial structures

Memorial structures might be more familiar in a social context as a monument in a public square, such as the ubiquitous structures that exist across Europe and North America, or as a memorial construction as is seen in the Vietnam Veterans Memorial in Washington, DC, or the Denkmal fuer die emordeten Juden (Memorial to the Murdered Jews) or the Sinti and Roma Denkmal (Sinti and Roma Memorial), both in Berlin. These structures and constructions serve as physical sites that one can visit: their presentation mediates the enormity of loss that they represent, and visitors are implicated in an active memorial practice through their engagement with the sites and their constructedness. In this chapter, I posit that a literary text, too, can serve a similar social function in relation to monumental public loss, engaging readers in its own enacted mourning and implicating its readers in complex acts of public recognition for the scope and impact of remembrance. While the novel has typically been seen to figure the private grief of its characters, the very fact of its publication and reception by readers shifts it into the public sphere, and the grief of its characters can be seen as reflecting the grief of its readers: when that grief is precipitated by a broadly social event (such as a genocide, an act of terrorism with numerous casualties, the atomic bombings in Japan, and the Second World War) then the text that enacts grief work also takes on a public and social function which can be likened to the kinds of socially oriented memorial structures we tend to be conventionally more familiar with. Novelists have used fiction to enact the fraught private grief of their characters, but because their grief is precipitated by a public event, the novels serve as a memorializing structure for their readers. Two novels that function within this paradigmatic understanding of the work of mourning and public memorialising are, as mentioned above, Kogawa's 1981 *Obasan* and Foer's 2005 *Extremely Loud & Incredibly Close*. *Obasan* examines the conflicted grief of Kogawa's protagonist, who suffers from the loss of her mother as a consequence of the atomic bombing of Nagasaki. The novel demonstrates how a work of mourning is affected by the politics of exclusion and racism, and how the monumental example of mass death caused by the atomic bombings can serve to refigure our understanding of grief as simultaneously private and public. In *Extremely Loud & Incredibly Close*, Foer articulates the tense nature of grief that results from the 9/11 terror attacks and how a work of mourning operates in a politicized manner even when it is deeply private in its impulses. Foer's protagonist struggles with the death of his father in the terror attacks, seeking to find means to engage in grief work while simultaneously being challenged by the public and global nature of the attacks, and as consequence his father's death. These novels demonstrate that grief in this era is tumultuous, its expression in fiction is ethical and monumental, and that the figuring of the work of mourning serves social and thus public ends.

A useful framework to understand literary expressions of mourning draws from the long literary tradition of mourning, sociological and psychological articulations of mourning, and geographical understandings of how grieving exists in relation to the physical world. In explorations of the two key novels of the last forty years published in English (United States and Canada), the work of mourning is seen as a physical act of traversing urban and rural landscapes and the act of textualising grief through fictional expression is posited as an act of mapping grief. That is, moving across and through geographical locations is for literary characters a means to work *at* their grief and is a way to create a memorial structure that textually serves as a monument for readers. Understanding further the physical sites of loss, as in Kogawa's exploration of Nagasaki and the British Columbia interior where Japanese-Canadians were interned and Foer's figuring of the Twin Towers and New York City, allows readers to engage with the grieving of the characters by 'travelling' through the landscapes to learn about how grief operates but also to have textual figuration of sites of loss serve as a form of memorial site. The novels can thus be seen to have a primarily social function:

they signal to their readers, a de facto community, the significance of the loss that is commemorated, and articulate possible ways in which one can mourn the difficult losses that permeate the 20th and 21st centuries.

Over the past fifty years or so, fictional production as a viable space for the enactment of grieving and texts as memorial constructions of that grieving have arisen out of the need in the middle of the 20th century to frame death and dying when social realms have failed. Geoffrey Gorer argued in 1955 in his seminal essay 'The Pornography of Death' that by the middle of the 20th century, death had become a taboo like sex was in the Victorian Age (Gorer 1955). Death and by extension grieving have shifted to the private realm and are no longer given social space for the grieving subject. The mid-to-late 20th century is a period where death is denied its place in society, according to Ernst Becker in *The Denial of Death* (Becker 1973). The social world contributes to the lack of public recognition for the pain of loss, and as a consequence the lack of social sanctioning for the expression of the emotions of grieving; public displays of emotion are seen as a 'loss of control . . . [and] often as a source of shame beyond even the guilt of survival' (Gilbert 2006:264). Fiction, as Kogawa and Foer demonstrate, is a form through which the conflicted nature of death in the social realm can be confronted. If death is socially forbidden – and by extension public displays of grieving – then the novel becomes in essence a social space where the work of mourning, the pain of loss and an ethics of mourning can be enacted.

Kogawa and Foer insert themselves into a continuum of literary engagement with death and mourning that reaches at least to the Greeks, such as Bion and Moschus, and flows through John Milton, Percy Bysshe Shelley and Matthew Arnold, amongst others. Central to an understanding of how mourning as work and its textual expression as memorial operate in the late 20th and early 21st centuries is to situate it in the literary tradition of the poetic and fictional expressions of mourning, which share the same cultural roots. In the English literary tradition, the elegy has a rich history, reaching to Milton's well-known elegy 'Lycidas' and the Greek tradition that he adapts. Milton's speaker seeks consolation in the act of singing to give presence to his dead friend. He articulates a close relationship between Lycidas's death by drowning on an imagined Greek sea, and their shared lives in a mythical Greek countryside: thus, the figurative is linked with the spatial and the spatial with the psychic (Milton 1637). This figurative practice is, notes Derrida (following Sigmund Freud) in *The Work of Mourning* (Derrida 2001), a response to the psychic disruption caused by loss and partakes of the work of mourning. For Freud, most cogently articulated in his 1917 essay 'Mourning and Melancholia', mourning is a kind of work that should be seen dually (Freud 1960). The German word for mourning, *Trauerarbeit*, reflects this meaning inherently: that mourning is work undertaken and also work that results from that undertaking – verb and noun, process and product. Freud's conception of mourning as work is particularly useful for explorations of literary representations of mourning and memorials for it allows for the idea that a text of mourning – such as an elegy or a fictional work – can figure as an active process of mourning (a *working at*) and to stand as the end result of that mourning: the elegaic text is thus a kind of memorial structure that signals its mourning process and serves for readers as a signalling object like a monument or other physical memorial might do. As Christian Riegel notes: 'For Freud, there is strong emphasis on the idea of working through and past grief, but for Derrida, the work of mourning is a multidimensional never-ending process that deeply involves and affects all aspects of the subject's life' (Riegel 2017:195), which fits appropriately with the fraught nature of mourning in the mid-to-late 20th and early 21st centuries:

> Work: that which makes for a work, for an *oeuvre*, indeed that which works – and works to open: *opus* and *opening*, *oeuvre*, and *ouverture*: the work or labor of the *oeuvre* insofar as it engenders, produces, and brings to light, but also labor or *travail* as suffering, as the engendering of force, as the pain of one who gives. Of the one who gives birth, who brings to the light of day and gives something to be seen, who enables or empowers, who gives the force to know and to be able to see – and all these are powers of the image, the pain of what is given and of the one who takes pains to help us see, read, and think.
>
> (Derrida 2001:142)

A Derridean 'work of mourning can do nothing to bring back the dead, doing no more than assert its own existence as the writing' of a literary text (Riegel 2017:196). For Derrida, mourning 'resists the closure that Freud signals as mourning in opposition to melancholia' (Riegel 2017:196), that is 'ungrieved loss, where the subject in the making has not been allowed to mourn a lost identification' (Taxidou 2004:90). This idea of resistant mourning is evident in Kogawa's and Foer's writing, for both invoke tropes of movement, travel across landscape and multitudinous engagement with reflections of grieving and dying: it is not so much that a labouring at mourning, as Freud would have it, leads to a cathartic and consolatory outcome, but rather that the acts of interaction with the landscape, memory and moving in and out of place and space involve active mourning that is engendered in figurative practice. The textual figuring of these acts, in turn, acts like a memorial structure or construction to readers.

This notion of the fictional figuration of a work of mourning as a memorial structure relates well to a multitudinous understanding of how memorials function socially. Critical discussion of memorials relating to war serves well to frame how a text can function as a memorial structure. For James E. Young, 'A memorial may be a day, a conference, or a space, but it need not be a monument' (Young 2006:4). That is, memorials can be seen as 'memory-sites' (Young 2006:4) and not just as installations in physical space. Jay Winter remarks about the personal and public functions of war memorials that '[they] were places where people grieved, both individually and collectively' (Winter 1995:79). While 'typically, we think of memorials as physical sites – monuments on public squares or in other publicly accessible locations, or as physical locations, such as a war site – the Thiepval Memorial to the Missing at the Somme, for example, or the Auschwitz-Birkenau camps, which are officially memorial sites' (Riegel 2017:191), textual memorials demonstrate that memorial status need not be fixed in place, that indeed language itself rendered in printed form can have a similar function to physically located memorials. Richard Boffey notes the distinction between physical spaces/sites and virtual ones in relation to memorials. While he does not explicitly consider literary texts as memorials in his consideration, he remarks that virtual 'memorials are much more accessible' (Boffey 2012:201). A novel that has monumental and memorial qualities has the advantages of access that a physical site does not. In such an equation between located memorials and virtual or textual ones, memorials should be seen 'as representations of history embedded within space and social contexts' and that 'remembrance does not take place in a vacuum but is, rather, an act of re-presenting the past in the present' (Boffey 2012:197). Memorials in all forms, then, function to provide context to acts of remembrance and commemoration, and context is elaborated in a social manner.

To James M. Mayo, this functional quality is key to understanding how a memorial operates in relation to its communities: 'The sentiments and the utilitarian purposes imposed on war memorials give them meaning. The choice of a particular sentiment and a particular purpose provides alternative possibilities for war remembrance' (Mayo 2007:62). This sense of multiple possibilities is what fiction writers offer in textual space: the working out of complex affective responses to losses on a mass scale presents readers with new views of loss that has affected them in broad ways. Bill Niven sees this as political in motivation, that the act of memorializing is inherently infused with political force, as he states when he writes that 'the cultural significance of memorials as reminders of past wars has always been . . . a political one' (Niven 2007:43). For novelists, then, such as the ones who form the focus of this chapter, their works of fiction provide the social and cultural space within which political and alternative notions of memorializing can be actualized.

The fraught act of figuring the dead is imagined alongside representations of place and space that become not only a backdrop for the emotionally affective engagement with loss, but also take on a memorial and monumental function through the process of textualization. That is, representation of place and space interrelate with the psychic work of mourning and form an elegiac-textual figuration – a work of mourning as noun – that stands as a monument or a literal structure of memorial to the lost one(s). Avril Maddrell links grief and geographies, and bodies and space, to cultural expressions of mourning. Maddrell is interested in how 'we can map the "invisible landscape" (Ryden 1993) of grief across multiple contiguous times-spaces and understand more of the spatialities of bereavement, mourning and remembrance' (Maddrell 2016:167). As Maddrell remarks: 'Bereavement, grief and mourning are experienced within space and can be both triggered and ameliorated in relation to particular places at particular times' (Maddrell 2016:169). Bondi (2005) argues that 'embodied emotions are intricately connected to specific sites and contexts' (cited by Maddrell 2016:169), and for Maddrell, 'the focus . . . is on understanding how bereavement mediates and influences the embodied and lived relationship to and with an assemblage of different spaces at any given time. The varied ways in which the experiences of grief and mourning intersect with different spaces and can be understood in "spatial" terms. . . . The landscape is a palimpsest not only of life, but also of the social relations and practices associated with death and remembrance' (Maddrell 2016:169–170). Physical place takes on a social function, as Karen Till notes: 'Places are never merely backdrops for action or containers for the past. They are fluid mosaics and moments of memory, matter, metaphor, scene, and experience which create and mediate social spaces and temporalities' (Till 2005:8). If the conventional memorial is located in a place that people visit to engage with the loss that is commemorated, then the textual memorial operates to figure place in its structure of language. In such a consideration, Foer's *Extremely Loud & Incredibly Close* brings to its readers the physical space of New York City and the Twin Towers in its attention to the peregrinations of its narrator across the city; and Kogawa's *Obasan* serves to render in text the forgotten sites of internment of Japanese-Canadians in British Columbia as well as the destroyed place that is Nagasaki immediately after the atomic bombing. In essence, these novels bring space and place to community, providing what can be defined as a 'socially shared' (Neimeyer et al. 2014:486) understanding of grief.

Fictional memorial structure: textuality and remembering the 9/11 terrorist attacks

In his 2005 novel, Foer takes up these notions of textualising grief for the purposes of memorializing when he explores the effects of the 9/11 terrorist acts in New York on a boy of 9, Oskar Schell, whose father was killed in the Twin Towers. While the novel presents the perspective of the boy as he comes first to understand the nature of grief, and second to learn how grieving might operate as an active engagement with the emotions, the novel is also more broadly interested in the intersection of this very personal loss with the communal sense of destruction that the terrorist acts wrought. Further, the novel presents a global scope to its consideration of human-created catastrophe and atrocity by invoking the Holocaust and the bombing of Dresden in World War II. As Ilka Saal notes, 'Bringing the trauma of 9/11 into conversation with other, older collective traumata suggests an attempt to engage the pain of others and to consider the myriad ways in which global power structures implicate one's own vulnerability in that of others' (Saal 2011:455). The novel is constructed with a memorial purpose, beginning with the boy's awareness of his father's death as he and his family travel to the father's funeral and ending with a set of pages that contain only slight variations of the same photograph, which, when flipped, show a person falling to his death from one of the towers. The novel signals dually to private mourning and to a socially constructed sense of how a set of losses permeates a whole society. As readers, we cannot help but be devastated by the inexorable path of the novel's narration to the closing pages, which drive home the difference between textualized mourning as a construct of language (the textual work of mourning) and the visual taken from the series of actual photos shot by the photographer Lyle Owerko. Conversely the front pages contain two photos that demonstrate the private: the first is a close-up of a keyhole, as if to suggest entry into the mind of Oskar, and the second is a grainy partial shot of a brick apartment building, which is ostensibly the apartment building that the narrator lives in, and that his dead father occupied. Much of the novel is concerned with how the 9-year-old boy mediates his own grief at the loss of his father to a public and traumatic event. He struggles to accommodate himself to find peace in death, instead imagining that his father jumped to his death, like so many victims. In its examination of the private grief of the narrator, *Extremely Loud &Incredibly Close* is interested in particular with the challenges of articulation, of finding language that will frame and shape an individual's grief. Bookended, then, by the private and the public the novel exemplifies a pattern of private mourning that simultaneously stands as public memorial structure.

Throughout *Extremely Loud & Incredibly Close*, Oskar is obsessed with writing and articulation through language. Near the beginning of the novel and shortly after his father's death, Oskar begins to write letters, primarily to famous people, which he sends out in the hope of receiving a reply: 'A few weeks after the worst day, I started writing lots of letters. I don't know why, but it is one of the few things that made my boots lighter' (Foer 2005:11). Over the course of the novel, Oskar writes copiously in a notebook that he titles 'Stuff that Happened to Me', and though 'it was completely full' (Foer 2005:325), writing gets him no closer to working through his grief. It is instead part of the circular process that Freud describes as melancholic (Freud 1960) and Derrida as a symptom of living (Derrida 2001:143). The notebook, however, does not lead to any sense of an active work of mourning that might lead to consolation, or at least understanding about the nature of his own grief and the death of his father. Eventually, to Oskar, the notebook takes on figurative value in relation to the burning of the Twin Towers; while paper, and the writing on it, has the potential for articulation in relation to the emotions of loss, it has failed and perhaps, to Oskar, this is because the primary fuel for the burning towers was paper itself. Oskar draws our attention to this characteristic of paper, when he muses, 'I read that it was the paper that kept the towers burning. All of those notepads, and Xeroxes, and printed e-mails, and photographs of kids, and books, and dollar bills in wallets, and documents in files . . . all of them were fuel' (Foer 2005:325). Paper as fuel, then, rather than as instrument of communication and of emotional outlet for the exploration of one's grief. Oskar concludes that if we existed in a truly digital realm, then his father would not be dead. That is, writing as it is currently deployed, is unable to fulfil his needs as grieving subject. As he notes: 'Maybe if we lived in a paperless society, which lots of scientists say we'll probably live in one day soon, Dad would still be alive. Maybe I shouldn't start a new volume' (Foer 2005:325). Language thus equals failure rather than tool for the work of mourning.

In the absence of knowledge of his father's death, Oskar is left in a liminal state that leaves him with only the powers of the imagination in his attempt at understanding. He tells his grandfather, 'I need to know how he died. . . . So I can stop inventing how he died. I'm always inventing' (Foer 2005:256). Not only does he not know how his father died, and thus must attempt invention as a substitute, there was also no body. Though a coffin is buried during a funeral service, no body is interred. Oskar is unable to imagine his father's body, and without that he struggles to figure his father's death in a positive light, and though he knows there is no body in the grave he becomes obsessed with the need to dig up the grave to open the coffin to verify this fact. And so, when he opens the coffin, he notes that 'I was surprised again, although again I shouldn't have been. I was surprised that Dad wasn't there. In my brain I knew that he wouldn't be, obviously, but I guess my heart believed something else. Or maybe I was surprised by how incredibly empty it was. I felt like I was looking into the dictionary definition of emptiness' (Foer 2005:321). In his poem 'Lycidas', Milton shifts the body of the subject of his grief from the horrific space of being drowned in the Irish Sea to imagining and figuring him in the poem laid out in a beautiful flower-covered funeral bier (Milton 1637). In the absence of a body, Oskar is left in a similar situation, but unlike Milton he is not able to draw on textual articulation as a way to refigure his father's death. A key challenge for Oskar is the public nature of the death, given that it was due to an act of terrorism that was not only witnessed by thousands firsthand, but was also witnessed by millions on television, and then tens of millions more via the Internet in the months that followed the event.

Oskar struggles with this idea that his private grief is open to worldwide knowledge. He focuses on the notion that his is a localized trauma, but that it has global implications. He find videos on foreign websites 'of bodies falling' (Foer 2005:256) from the buildings that are not available on American websites. Internationally, 'there were all sorts of stuff they weren't showing here, even though it happened here. Whenever I want to learn about how Dad died, I have to go to a translator program and find out how to say things in different languages' (Foer 2005:256). This notion of the public and private is difficult for Oskar to parse, for he cannot accept that something so personal can be in the public and social realms: 'It makes me incredibly angry that people all over the world can know things that I can't, because it happened *here*, and happened to *me*, so shouldn't it be *mine*?' (Foer 2005:256). Oskar breaks down one video, taken from a Portuguese website, and prints 'out the frames' with the goal to find his father's image: 'There's one body that could be him' (Foer 2005:257). However, in order to verify the identity of the body, he must magnify the still to the point that it becomes impossible: 'It's dressed like he was, and when I magnify it until the pixels are so big that it stops looking like a person, sometimes I can see glasses. Or I think I can. But I know I probably can't. It's just me wanting it to be him' (Foer 2005:257). For Oskar, the need to know how his father dies is linked to how he feels he might effectively grieve his death. To have certainty about his death would mean being able to find closure. As he notes: 'If I could know how he died, exactly how he died, I wouldn't have to invent him dying inside and elevator that was stuck between floors, which happened to some people, and I wouldn't have to imagine him trying to crawl down the outside of the building, which I saw a video of one person doing on a Polish site, or trying to use a tablecloth as a parachute. . . . There were so many different ways to die, and I just need to know which was his' (Foer 2005:257).

This lack of certainty is linked to his inability to give textual presence to his father, and pushes Oskar to overt consideration of the intersection of the private and the public as the novel draws to a close. In the absence of a body, and with the inability to imagine one that will help him to move towards consolation, Oskar looks to images of people falling from the Twin Towers. Oskar takes up a friendship with the man who has been his absent grandfather, whom he has never known, and who is not identified to him as his grandfather (a discussion of the role of the grandfather, who disappears immediately after the birth of his son, who is Oskar's father, and his trauma due to the bombing of Dresden is beyond the scope of this paper). In a key scene, he tells his grandfather that though he has been looking for answers for half a year, 'I don't know a single thing that I didn't know six months ago . . . *and* I miss my dad more now than when I started, even though the whole *point* was to *stop* missing him' (Foer 2005:255, italics in original). In the final pages of the novel, Oskar takes his notebook, which contains, as he writes, 'the whole world' (Foer 2005:325). He thus acknowledges that his trauma is connected with a global one. He looks at the pictures of the 'falling body' that he previously examined and wonders again whether or not it is his father:

Was it Dad?
Maybe.
Whoever it was, it was somebody.
(Foer 2005:325)

His final act in searching for his father is to reimagine his death as an apotheosis: his father isn't dying at all; he is rising up the building and returning in time to the final happy memory Oskar has of him, which is of him 'telling a story' that begins with 'Once upon a time' and ends with 'I love you' (Foer 2005:326). Oskar takes the still shots from the video and reorders them so that 'when I flipped through them, it looked like the man was floating up through the sky' (Foer 2005:325). While there are similarities with the apotheosis present in conventional elegies like 'Lycidas' and Shelley's 'Adonais', the rising up isn't to a triumphant heaven. Rather, it is a reversal of the very act that killed his father so that the final resting place is back in time, at home the evening before the terrorist attack where 'we would have been safe' (Foer 2005:325), as states Oskar.

The personal literary work of mourning as public memorial to the victims of the Nagasaki atomic bombing

Written several decades earlier than Foer's novel, Kogawa's 1981 *Obasan* has similarly as a key purpose to memorialize monumental loss and to have her text perform the social function of engaging readers with acts of remembrance. Kogawa explores the lost Japanese-Canadian communities that stem from the 1890s and had their apogee in the first four decades of the 20th century, centred in British Columbia's lower mainland, an area that abuts the Washington State border to the south and is bounded by the Pacific Ocean to the west. Kogawa uses the personal story of her protagonist and narrator, Naomi Nakane, to articulate a work of mourning relating to the loss of these communities at the hand of the Canadian government; this work of mourning signals its status as memorial text to readers, serving as an artifactual structure where none exist in the landscape. Bound up in this national context is how Kogawa uses the text to stand as memorial to the broader resonances of the dropping of the atomic bombs in Hiroshima and Nagasaki, shifting this Canadian story of loss into a global space of remembrance. *Obasan* has heretofore been read as a specifically Canadian story that addresses a Canadian injustice, as well as the lack of public recognition of the losses that are associated with that injustice (Amoko 2000; Beedham 1999; Gottlieb 1986; Howells 1987; Kambourelli 2000; Karpinski 2006; Verduyn 1998; Yamada 1996), and while this reading is viable it does not take into account the global resonances of the figuring of the atomic bombing of Hirsohima and Nagasaki that forms the climactic moment of the novel. This global reach gives the novel a broadly memorial status and signals how an immensely private grief becomes inseparable from the shadow of the human-made nuclear catastrophe that plagued the latter part of the 20th century.

The Canadian history of Japanese-Canadian exclusion that Kogawa treats in *Obasan* begins with the bombing of Pearl Harbor in December of 1941; the Canadian government created a 'protected zone' along the British Columbia coast that banned Japanese-Canadians (the majority of whom were Canadian-born citizens) from the zone. Just over 22,000 Japanese-Canadians were sent initially to internment camps and then relocated primarily to the interior of the province for the duration of the war, while some were sent further east to Alberta and beyond to labour in work camps. Property was confiscated, never to be returned, and after the war Japanese-Canadians were not allowed to go back to the British Columbia coastal areas that formed the heart of the community, as the Canadian government maintained restrictions of movement until 1949. Many were repatriated to Japan, despite having been born in Canada, and it was only in 1988 that the Canadian government offered an official apology and redress. As a consequence of the government's actions in the 1940s, the well-established community was disrupted and dispersed. Naomi speaks of the immediate postwar period, when the government forced impossible choices on its Japanese-Canadian citizens, the essence of the Japanese-Canadian community was wrecked: 'The fact is that families already fractured and separated were permanently destroyed. The choice to go east off the Rockies or to Japan was presented without for consultation with separated parents and children. Failure to choose was labelled non-cooperation' (Kogawa 1981:163). Kogawa explores these historical events from the perspective of a 35-year-old woman, Naomi Nakane, who is descended from Japanese-Canadians and living in Alberta, where she had been relocated after the war. Naomi's mother returned to Japan during the war to take care of her elderly mother and ultimately perished as a consequence of the Nagasaki atomic bombing: the fate of her mother has not been revealed to Naomi at the opening of the novel, some 30 years after its occurrence, and remains a shadowy loss that she is unable to process.

When the novel opens, Naomi is dealing with the death of her uncle (simply named Uncle), who along with his wife, raised Naomi. While *Obasan* is ostensibly about how Naomi deals with his death, she as a consequence revisits her own troubled past and comes to grieve the loss of her mother and father. However, *Obasan* has broader ambitions to chronicle and memorialize the history of loss that permeates the Japanese-Canadian community as well as the sense of loss, globally, that is felt in relation to the perpetration of weapons of mass destruction. Written and published well before there was widespread interest across the Canadian nation in the fate of the Japanese-Canadians, *Obasan* serves to fulfil the need in the community for overt acts of remembrance to occur and for those acts to be made concrete through textualization. Naomi's Aunt Emily, who is her mother's sister, has spent much of the postwar years fighting for the rights of Japanese-Canadians, but has not, as Naomi notes, found the right form to effectively express the deep and abiding loss she feels: 'All of Aunt Emily's words, all her papers, the telegrams and petitions are like scratchings in the barnyard, the evidence of much activity. . . . But what good they do, I do not know – these little black typewritten words – rain words, cloud droppings. . . . The words are not made flesh. Trains do not carry us home, Ships do not return again. All my prayers disappear into space' (Kogawa 1981:168–169). Language is disordered and unstructured, is not able to provide a restorative function, cannot make up for loss, and thus it does not contribute to a work of mourning. By extension it is not able to provide a memorial function.

Naomi notes this lack of any signs of commemoration for the experiences and losses of the Japanese-Canadians when she and her two aunts return to British Columbia's interior, where they had been housed in a formerly abandoned mining town. They find that there is nary a trace of their time spent there. As Naomi narrates, 'The first ghosts were still there, the miners, people of the woods, their white bones deep beneath the pine needle floor, their flesh turned to earth, turned to air. Their buildings – hotels, abandoned mines, log cabins – still stood marking their stay. But what of the second wave? What remains of our time there?' (Kogawa 1981:101). The forced internment of the Japanese-Canadians is erased on the landscape as it is in the popular consciousness. The range of habitations that Naomi and her fellows occupied during the war years are simply not found in any literal sense:

> We looked for the evidence of our having been in Bayfarm, in Lemon Creek, in Popoff. Bayfarm and Popoff were farmlands in Slocan before the tar-paper huts sprang up. Lemon Creek was a camp seven miles away carved out of the wilderness. Tashme – formed from the names of Taylor, Shirras, and Meads, men on the B.C. Security Commission – also arose overnight, fourteen miles from Hope, and as quickly disappeared. Where on the map or on the road was there any sign? Not a mark was left.
>
> (Kogawa 1981:101)

If the signs of their communal losses are either muted or nonexistent or appear in forms (such as Aunt Emily's documents) where they are not effective, then Naomi has as a task to find her own modes of expression for her grief. Her story of loss, which comprises the bulk of the novel, and by extension the story of her community, will have to find other expression. Through her narrator, then, Kogawa fictionally tracks a historical record that is only dim in the broader consciousness. Her novel follows Naomi as she reconstructs her past by examining a series of documents – historical, public and personal – that her aunt has left with her. She combines these with her childhood memories to weave together a narrative that tells her story from before her mother disappeared to Japan to the present moment.

Deeply implicated in Naomi's narrative is when her mother travels to Japan to take care of her own mother, never to return; for the young Naomi her absence is only known as a disappearance that has no explanation. Even decades later when she is an adult, Uncle refuses to answer her questions about what happened to her mother. 'Too young,' he tells her, 'still too young' (Kogawa 1981:5). Her mother's demise after the Nagasaki bombings is deemed too traumatic to be passed on, and while this act of protection on the art of Uncle hinders Naomi's ability to grieve her mother, it also serves metonymically to signal the fraught nature of memory work in the 20th century. If the trauma of loss is of such a magnitude and horror that it cannot easily be imagined, witnessed, and processed, then it is perhaps impossible to reconcile the traumatic with consolation, Kogawa suggests. Naomi is left in a liminal state, unable to process the possibility even of her mother's death: 'The stillness is so much with me that it takes the form of a shadow which grows and surrounds me like air. Time solidifies, ossifies the waiting into molecules of stone, dark microscopic planets that swirl through the universe of my body waiting for light and morning' (Kogawa 1981:59). The fact of the text that Kogawa constructs, however, points to the possibility of memorialising and that textuality can create a memorial space and become a structure for readers to frame their feelings of loss in relation to a monumental event.

Obasan begins with a specific reference to the date that Nagasaki was bombed in a scene where Uncle commemorates the losses but does not disclose to Naomi the significance of the date. By beginning the novel with this distinct historical reference to what is unquestioningly one of the singularly traumatic events of the 20th century, both in Japan and in the public imagination, Kogawa contextualizes her consideration of the Japanese-Canadian experience during and after the Second World War. The dropping of the bomb is indelibly linked to the political actions of the Canadian government given that Canadian citizens, like Naomi's mother, were unable to return to Canada during the war years despite their inalienable constitutional rights. Racist government policies are thus complicit in the death of a Canadian citizen caused by the bombing. Kogawa can, therefore, be seen to memorialize in her novel the intertwined elements of the treatment of the Japanese-Canadians in Canada and the deaths due to the atomic bombings of the war.

Just as for Naomi, the date of the dropping of the Nagasaki bomb is confusing, so too for readers of Kogawa's is the invocation of this date as a moment of memory confusing. Though some readers will, naturally, recognize the date, they will not be able to situate its significance in terms of the novel's narrative arc until it is linked in *Obasan*'s climactic revelation of Naomi's mother's victimization due to the bomb close to the end. In the climactic chapter of the novel, letters from Naomi's grandmother Kato are read aloud to Naomi so she can learn what her mother's experiences of the war had been. As Naomi learns about the bombing, so too do Kogawa's readers about the horrors of the bombing and its aftermath. Readers are thus put in the position of being witnesses to nearly unimaginable trauma, and the novel's articulation of this trauma takes on a monumental and thus memorial function: textuality serves social, political and historical functions of remembrance. Naomi's mother and grandmother, survivors of the bombing, are described as having the 'visible evidence of horror written on their skin, in their blood, carved in every mirror they passed, felt in every step they took' (Kogawa 1981:210), and Kogawa's readers are opened to the visible trauma of the aftereffects of atomic bombs.

The idea that trauma is inscribed on the bodies of her characters reinforces the sense of memorializing that Kogawa underscores. Shifting the horrific effects of the bombings on humans into a narrative gives them textual presence, and organizing these details into a coherent narrative reinforces the commemorative nature of her text. Kogawa spares none of the horrific details, as if to ensure that her readers take on their roles as ethical witnesses: 'Men, women, in many cases indistinguishable by sex, hairless, half-clothed, hobbled past. Skin hung from their bodies like tattered rags. One man held his bowels in with the stump of one hand' (Kogawa 1981:213–214). Grandmother Kato is a direct witness to the horror, mass death and aftermath of the atomic bombing, and through her letter she transmits her knowledge to others. Naomi and, by extension, Kogawa's readers, become de facto witnesses to grandmother Kato's and Naomi's mother's experience. This view into the traumatic opens readers to the horrific but also to the need to recognize, remember and ultimately memorialize the losses incurred: 'What she saw was incomprehensible. Almost all the buildings were flattened or in flames for as far as she could see. . . . Tall columns of fire rose through the haze and everywhere the dying and the wounded crawled, fled, stumbled like ghosts among the ruins. Voices screamed, calling the names of children, fathers, mothers, calling for help, calling for water' (Kogawa 1981:213).

While the details of the horror are raw, blunt and traumatic for readers to process, they can be seen to operate in similar ways to the effects of experiencing more conventional memorial sites. The explicit details conveyed in the United States Holocaust Memorial Museum, for example, have similar effects on those who experience the exhibits. The details of loss are not spared for visitors, as is the case with Naomi's readers. The personal and private emotional engagement of Kogawa's characters thus contextualizes the memorial function of the novel. For example, when Naomi learns of how her grandmother discovers the damaged body of her family member, as well as the terrible disfigurement of her mother, readers are made aware of the severity of her loss and it is, within the construct of a fictional text, presented as a wholly private event: 'Beneath the wreckage, she saw first the broken arm, then the writhing body of her niece, her head bent back, her hair singed, both her eye sockets blown out. In a weak and delirious voice, she was calling Tomio. Grandma Kato touched her niece's leg and the skin

peeled off and stuck to the palm of her hand' (Kogawa 1981:213); 'The woman
was utterly disfigured. Her nose and one cheek were almost gone. Great wounds
and pustules covered her entire face and body. She was completely bald. She sat
in a cloud of flies and maggots wriggled among her wounds. As Grandma watched
her, the woman gave her a vacant gaze, then let out a cry. It was my mother'
(Kogawa 1981:215). Yet, by the presence in a novel published for public consumption of these intimate details readers are made witnesses to the horror of the
mass destruction of the atomic bomb. This witnessing is similar to Naomi's act of
witnessing in that the sheer awfulness of the material places readers in a position
of affective response: we cannot avoid the resonances of the implications of death
on such a large scale and its human face. For Naomi, to learn about her mother's
injuries and death is to be brought to a place of recognition and remembrance –
'Gentle mother, we were lost together in our silences. Our wordlessness was our
mutual destruction' (Kogawa 1981:219) – which is to say that to be worded is to
be engaged in acts of memory. Eva C. Karpinski deems this process 'testimony',
arguing that *Obasan* 'has a power to perform the pedagogical and ethical work
of unsettling its readers' (Karpinski 2006:47). Reading the novel becomes a work
of memory, and an obligation to remember, recognize and valorize – to engage in
testimony: the textual articulation of the horror takes on the monumental role of
a constructed memorial.

Conclusion

Fiction writers engage the communal, and thus the social, in ways similar to how
James E. Young conceives of the social function of memorials in *The Texture of
Memory*. 'Memorials,' he argues, 'provide the sites where groups of people gather
to create a common past for themselves, places where they tell constitutive narratives, their 'shared' stories of the past. They become communities precisely by
having shared (if only vicariously) the experiences of their neighbors' (Young
1993/2006:6–7). A fictional text as memorial, as Jonathan Safran Foer and Joy
Kogawa illustrate in their novels, becomes a social site where a 'shared memory'
and 'the sense of a shared past' (Young 1993/2006:6) can be enacted. In writing
about Holocaust memorials, Young notes that often the 'essentially public dimension of their performance' (Young 1993/2006:11) is ignored. Novels as memorials
serve as reminders that textual memorials can only have a public function through
the fact of their publication and reception in the public sphere, what Young defines
as a 'conflation of private and public memory' (Young 1993/2006:15). This notion
of the private and the public can be seen to be wholly social in its construction, as
Robert A. Neimeyer, Dennis Klass and Michael Robert Dennis remark: 'Far from
being a private and dispassionate cognitive process, contending with the meaning
of loss and the meaning of our lives in the wake of it is typically deeply emotional,
intricately social, and inevitably constructed and sometimes contested in broader
linguistic and cultural contexts' (Neimeyer et al., 2014:486).

By creating their novels as memorial constructs, Joy Kogawa in *Obasan* and
Jonathan Safran Foer in *Extremely Loud & Incredibly Close* bring the wide range

of society into contact with deaths suffered on a large scale and demonstrate the reality of what it means to grieve in the face of human-made catastrophes of aggression. By figuring the grief of their characters as they attempt to come to grips with the nearly unimaginable scope of death that the loss of their loved ones has intersected, these novelists provide readers with fictional texts that serve as memorial structures to help frame, contextualize and give ethical space to acts of remembrance in the face of the fraught terrain of grieving in the 20th and 21st centuries. As Kogawa and Foer show in their fictional approaches to writing grief and constructing memorial texts, literary expression is well-suited to the social and public functions conventionally attributed to the kinds of memorials and monuments we typically see in public spaces. The novel, too, they show, is a construction for public consumption and interaction, and thus shares many of the qualities of conventional memorials. Fiction proves to be well-suited for this purpose as it bridges the private and personal and the public and social. Research in this particular configuration of the understanding of mourning and memorializing is in its infancy (see Riegel 2017), but the connections between mourning and memorializing in literary texts, and in particular in fiction, should become fruitful ground for further investigation given the proliferation of novels that deal with mourning and memorializing in the latter part of the 20th century and the first decades of the 21st. This chapter points in the direction of future studies of fiction and its social functions in mourning and memorializing, which should prove to be a growing area of investigation.

References

Agee, James (1957): *A Death in the Family*. New York: Vintage Books (Reprinted 1998).

Amoko, Apollo O. (2000): 'Resilient ImagiNations: *No-No Boy, Obasan*, and the Limits of Minority Discourse'. *Mosaic: An Interdisciplinary Critical Journal*, 33 (3):35–55.

Becker, Ernst (1973): *The Denial of Death*. New York: Free Press.

Beedham, Matthew (1999): '*Obasan* and Hybridity: Necessary Cultural Strategies', in Katherine B. Payant and Toby Rose (eds.): *The Immigrant Experience in North American Literature*, e. Westport: Greenwood, pp. 139–149.

Boffey, Richard (2012): 'Review of Anderson and Doss'. *Museum and Society*, 10 (3):197–207.

Bondi, Liz (2005): 'Making Connections and Thinking Through Emotions: Between Geography and Psychotherapy'. *Transactions of the Institute for British Geographers*, 30:433–448.

Capote, Truman (1966): *In Cold Blood*. New York: Vintage Press (Reprinted 1994).

Derrida, Jacques (2001): *The Work of Mourning*. Chicago: University of Chicago Press.

Foer, Jonathan Safran (2005): *Extremely Loud & Incredibly Close*. Boston & New York: Mariner Books.

Freud, Sigmund (1960): *A Metapsychology: The Theory of Psychoanalysis (The Standard Edition of the Complete Works of Sigmund Freud* Volume XVII). London: Hogarth Press.

Gilbert, Sandra M. (2006): *Death's Door: Modern Dying and the Ways We Grieve: A Cultural Study*. New York: W. W. Norton.

Gorer, Geoffrey (1955): 'The Pornography of Death', in Geoffrey Gorer (ed.): *Death, Grief, and Mourning*. New York: Doubleday, pp. 192–199.

Gottlieb, Erika (1986): 'The Riddle of Concentric Worlds in Obasan'. *Canadian Literature*, 109:34–53.

Howells, Coral Ann (1987): *Private and Fictional Worlds: Canadian Women Novelists of the 1970s and 1980s*. London: Methuen.

Kambourelli, Smaro (2000): *Scandalous Bodies: Diasporic Literature in English Canada*. Toronto: Oxford University Press.

Karpinski, Eva C. (2006): 'The Book as (Anti)National Heroine: Trauma and Witnessing in Joy Kogawa's *Obasan'*. *Studies in Canadian Literature, 31 (2):46–65*.

Kogawa, Joy (1981): *Obasan*. Toronto: Penguin (Reprinted 2017).

Laurence, Margaret (1966): *A Jest of God*. Toronto: Penguin (Reprinted 2018).

Lowry, Malcolm (1947): *Under the Volcano*. New York: Harper Perennial (Reprinted 2007).

Maddrell, Avril (2016): 'Mapping Grief: A Conceptual Framework for Understanding the Spatial Dimensions of Bereavement, Mourning and Remembrance'. *Social & Cultural Geography*, 17 (2):166–188.

Mayo, James M. (2007): 'War Memorials as Political Memory'. *Geographical Review*, 78 (1):62–75.

Milton, John (1637). 'Lycidas'. *The Major Works*. Oxford University Press (Reprinted 2008).

Neimeyer, Robert A., Dennis Klass and Michael Robert Dennis (2014): 'A Social Constructionist Account of Grief: Loss and the Narration of Meaning'. *Death Studies*, 38 (8):485–498.

Niven, Bill (2007): 'War Memorials at the Intersection of Politics, Culture and Memory'. *Journal of War & Culture Studies*, 1 (1):39–45.

Ramazani, Jahan (1994): *Poetry of Mourning: The Modern Elegy from Hardy to Heaney*. Chicago: University of Chicago Press.

Riegel, Christian (2017): 'Mourning, Memorial and the Yizkor Books in Eli Mandel's Out of Place'. *Mosaic: An Interdisciplinary Critical Journal*, 50 (2):187–204.

Ryden, K. C. (1993): *Mapping the Invisible Landscape: Folklore, Writing and the Sense of Place*. Iowa: University of Iowa Press.

Saal, Ilka (2011): 'Regarding the Pain of Self and Other: Trauma Transfer and Narrative Framing in Jonathan Safran Foer's Extremely Loud & Incredibly Close'. *Modern Fiction Studies*, 57 (3):451–476.

Shelley, Percy Bysshe (1821): 'Adonais', in *The Major Works*. New York: Oxford University Press (Reprinted 2009).

Swift, Graham (1996): *Last Orders*. Toronto: Vintage Editions (Reprinted 2005).

Taxidou, Olga (2004): *Tragedy, Modernity and Mourning*. Edinburgh: Edinburgh University Press.

Till, Karen (2005): *The New Berlin: Memory, Politics, Place*. Minneapolis: University of Minnesota Press.

Verduyn, Christl (1998): 'Reconstructing Canadian Literature: The Role of Race and Gender', in Veronica Strong-Boag, Sherill Grace and Avigail Grace (eds.): *Painting the Maple: Essays on Race, Gender and the Construction of Canada*. Vancouver: University of British Columbia Press, pp. 231–242.

Winter, Jay (1995): *Sites of Memory, Sites of Mourning: The Great War in European and Cultural History*. Cambridge: Cambridge University Press.

Woolf, Virginia (1927): *To the Lighthouse*. Boston: Mariner Books (Reprinted 2004).

Yamada, Mitsuye (1996): 'Experiential Approaches to Teaching Joy Kogawa's Obasan', in John R. Maitano and David Peck (eds.): *Teaching American Ethnic Literature: Nineteen Essays*. Albuquerque: University of New Mexico Press, pp. 293–311.

Young, James E. (1993/2006): *The Texture of Memory: Holocaust Memorials and Meaning*. New Haven: Yale University Press.

Part III
Forms of grief

7 The denial of grief

Reflections from a decade of
anthropological research on
parental bereavement and
child death

Mary Ellen Macdonald

Introduction

Do we live in a 'death-denying' society, where death is a 'taboo' topic? From the vantage point of clinical literature, it has been argued that the answer is 'yes'. In the biomedical context, palliative care advocates have expressed concerns about serious repercussions of death denial – namely, that dying patients are being over-treated, and patients and families are being given false hope about curative care. This reality has implications for those working against what they feel is an over-emphasis on curative medicine for patients with terminal illnesses and their families (Zimmermann and Rodin 2004).

According to sociological literature, however, the death-denial thesis is over-stated (Walter 1991; Kellehear 1984; Armstrong 1987). Some scholars have even suggested that, on the contrary, we are obsessed with, and fascinated by, the dead body, and that death, the corpse, and forensic science make up the backbone of much of contemporary entertainment (Penfold-Mounce 2016).

Death denial – or not? Such a question requests a yes/no binary response. A few decades ago, Allan Kellehear posed a more sociological version of the question: What is the theoretical and practical explanatory value of the death-denial thesis (Kellehear 1984)? Kellehear's conclusion then was that this thesis has little socio-logical value.

I have been doing anthropological research on parental bereavement for over a decade. When I started in this field, I felt the death-denial thesis irresistible and I admit to reproducing it unsophisticatedly in my own work. Over ten years later, I am in the Kellehear camp, no longer believing the thesis holds theoretical or practical explanatory utility. Worse, however, I think it distracts public as well as academic conversations from what is a much more urgent phenomenon. What I have seen in my work and feel compelled now to address is a societal *denial of grief*.[1]

The *grief-denial* thesis I will advance in this chapter begins from the observa-tion that, in the Western sociocultural context, death is not taboo. On the contrary, we are saturated with images of the dead body via our nightly news, television shows and movies, and video games. The fictitious death, the military death, the educational death, the Hollywood death are marketed for public consumption (e.g., from *Law and Order* to *Body Worlds*). This ubiquitous phenomenon is not only happening with public death and dying; within more private, individualized clinical contexts, dying also seems to be 'having a moment' (Hayasaki 2013). Clinical research agendas are responding to the aging of society by helping patients come to terms with debilitating chronic illnesses and their resultant deteriorating bodies over their senior years. Families are being encouraged to talk collectively about advance directives. In Canada, the recent legalization of Medical Assistance in Dying (MAID) has opened new conversations and priorities for improving palliative care, including both clinical services as well as advancing public discussions about private dying (e.g., talk radio shows, death cafes, and death salons).

Is death hyper-medicalized, hyper-popularized, having a moment, or not? I do not intend to engage these debates in this chapter. Regardless of where one stands on these questions, for me it is undeniable that there is an important sequellae of death that is rarely addressed in any public or clinical context: that is, the social reality of those left behind after a death, the grievers. There continues to be little public appetite for grief. Grief is not sexy, grief is not entertaining, grief does not sell Netflix dramas. Our responses to grief are not simply indifference, either; we actually seem to be afraid of grief. This fear is perhaps intuitive: grief is uncontrollable, uncontainable, messy. Social responses to a grieving person seem especially awkward when the death controverts a normative master narrative or cultural script: child death, death by suicide, or murder. If there is an important taboo to be addressed, it is a *grief taboo* not a death taboo.

The following chapter contributes to the sociology of sorrow by drawing on empirical and theoretical research on grief (especially but not only parental bereavement after the death of a child) to look at what I am calling *grief denial*. It asks: What is *grief denial*? What does it do, and what is at stake for the bereaved? To begin to answer these questions, I pull at the following threads.

To start, I reflect on what our discourses on grief suggest about how we define and respond to it. In English, there are no words for capturing the social relationship that is challenged by child death, and so we rely on terms such as bereaved parent/grandparent/sibling. Our lack of language reflects and reproduces stigmatizing societal responses to child death. Further, the psychological language used to characterize grief draws on metaphors of work and productivity, management and containment (e.g., grief work, tasks of grieving, managing grief, coping with loss, stages of grieving). I am especially concerned with how these metaphors merge with neoliberal discourses that frame grief as a threat to productivity and thus something that must be resolved quickly. We want grief to go away, and thus our discourses try to contain, control, and deny its existence. My work has queried how grievers live these discourses.

Next, I address what many scholars have argued to be the biomedicalization of grief and how this contributes to frameworks that reinforce the social denial of grief. The models these frameworks produce approach the construct of grief through a scientific paradigm that locates grief within an individual griever, parsing grief responses into normal and pathological categories. Critiques of this 'colonization' (see, e.g., Jacobsen and Petersen in this volume) uncover the social hierarchies of grief, and the resultant taboo and stigmatization that is created, supported, and reinforced through these frameworks. Many grievers respond to the social stigma by isolating themselves from what are lived as harsh social judgments.

Finally, I will suggest that current bereavement models are epistemologically unified as they frame grief within an empiricist postpositivist paradigm. As such, they deny the ontological possibility and importance of the other ways of living grief that are present in the stories of bereaved people. My own work has used the theory of 'absent presence' (Bille et al. 2010) to imagine how bereaved parents live with the embodied absence of their loved ones (Macdonald 2018a). In closing, I reflect on what is at stake for the bereaved when grief denial erases their dead, followed by suggestions of future directions for researching the social denial of grief.

The discursive construction of grief

How does our language reflect and shape social understandings of grief? In English, we have multiple words used interchangeably for the emotional experienced of a death: loss, grief/grieving, mourning, bereft/bereavement. In lay contexts, the boundaries among these terms are often blurred. An examination of 'persistent lay discourses' (Breen and O'Connor 2007) about grief reveals the common assumptions undergirding them. Social 'myths' paint grief as a consistent entity: grief follows a distinct pattern; is short-term and finite; is quasi-linear with stages, tasks, or phases; is a process that needs to be 'worked through'; requires that the bereaved find meaning in the death; culminates in the detachment from the deceased; and is possibly pathological if continued (Breen and O'Connor 2007:201). While research has refuted many of these homogenizing, decontextualized assumptions, even professionals who work with the bereaved often uncritically rely on these myths (Breen and O'Connor 2007). Within these 'persistent lay discourses', certain terms and metaphors recur: 'work', 'stages', 'tasks', 'coping', 'management'. These terms reinforce the idea of the timeline of grief, and the possibility – indeed responsibility – that grief can and should be contained, completed, and resolved.

Loss

'Loss' is a word commonly paired with 'grief'. We often hear said to a bereaved individual: 'I'm sorry for your loss'. A recent parliamentary motion in Canada opened a process to imagine better supporting parents whose child had died, under the banner: M-110, Supporting Families after the Loss of an Infant Child. This motion was put forward by the Government of Canada's Standing Committee on Human Resources, Skills and Social Development and the Status of Persons with Disabilities and was described as 'a study of the impact on parents who have suffered the loss of an infant child' (Blake Richards 2019).

Euphemisms often are used to respond to uncomfortable and tabooed topics. While the dead are no longer physically present, they can remain present in their loved ones' lives in new, transformed ways. As such, they are not lost. Using 'loss' replays the myth that the deceased – and thus, our relationship with them – are lost, finished, over, and the griever must sever ties and detach from them. Testimony from bereaved parents supporting this parliamentary motion clearly resisted this conceptualization: their children were deceased, yes, but not 'lost' to them. Bereaved parents struggle against the sentiment of loss, struggle expressly to keep the deceased child present in their social community. Saying the child's name, for example, keeps them present, as does maintaining the child's bedroom, and creating legacy projects (e.g., scholarships in the child's name). Resorting to the euphemistic language of loss prevents theorizing what is lost and what is transformed; further, it blinds us to the efforts bereaved parents make as they continue parenting their deceased children.[2]

Bereaved parent

Another discursive location for scrutiny is the labels used to describe those who experience a death. Grief challenges many normative cultural scripts – for example, turning a conception of time on its heads when children die before parents. Socially sanctioned labels mark the new social position created by death: a child whose parents die becomes an orphan; the death of a spouse produces a widow/widower. We have not evolved an English word to describe a parent whose child has died; this gap is particularly fraught for those whose child died before being born. 'Bereaved parent' is the label used by many to signal the parent of a child who has died. This awkward phrasing reflects and reproduces the troubling and often stigmatizing social response to child death, and especially so in the realm of stillbirth and perinatal death. In our research on online memorial sites after child death, we observed that the phrase 'angel mommy' was commonly used to capture the new role a mother cultivated with her deceased child (Mitchell et al. 2012). Angel mommy resists the descriptive term 'bereaved parent': 'bereaved parent' signals a lack of child whereas 'angel mommy' embeds the deceased child (as angel) into the kinterm. This term then affords the possibility to continue actively parenting the now-deceased child.[3]

Bereavement leave

In an effort to better understand the material constraints experienced as a result of bereavement, I led a team to review how grief is accommodated in workplace contexts. To do so, we descriptively and discursively reviewed labour standards across industrialized countries. We found that the term 'bereavement leave' is also euphemistic. Without an exception, within each labour policy across the multiple jurisdictions there was something akin to 'bereavement leave'; however, in no location did this leave attend to a phenomenological concern for grieving employees. Across all jurisdictions, the leave provided a discrete managerial response to accommodating a worker to plan and/or attend a ceremony to commemorate the deceased. This requirement was commonly interpreted as needing two to three days of protected time, with or without pay depending on the jurisdiction. Bereavement was thus cast as a generic, time-limited process involving instrumental tasks that could be resolved within a discrete activity and time frame (Macdonald et al. 2014). While euphemistic, 'bereavement leave' exerts real power over the lives of grieving employees as it manages their grieving.

A discursive examination of the language in these policies demonstrated remarkable congruence in the values undergirding the international documents. Birth, family life, caregiving, and religious practices were clearly celebrated through policies such as maternity and family leave, compassionate care benefits, and the allowance of time for funeral preparation. Workplace safety, efficiency, and economic salience were also primary concerns. Hierarchies of grief were suggested in some jurisdictions where certain kinds of deaths (e.g., murder) could elicit extra support. In no document was perinatal death considered worthy of bereavement leave, although it was considered under maternity leave in a few jurisdictions. The value of employee loyalty was demonstrated in some programs through which an employee could access more generous leave based upon their years of service; in other words, they could earn an enhanced right to grieve. What was entirely missing across all the documents was any positive effort *to authentically care* for an employee who experience a death (Macdonald et al. 2014).

Illness, trauma, or tragedy?

A query we raised in this review of labour standards was how employees could find support beyond the time allotted for ceremonial events. Perhaps unsurprising, bereavement leave was often paired with sick leave: the only way to get extended protected leave was by seeking physicians' services, which then enabled access to sick leave policies. The idea of responding to grief by medicalizing it via sick leave was also clearly present in the parliamentary proceedings mentioned above.

My concerns with this managerial response include the following: First, family physicians often have little training in grief support. In research interviews with bereaved parents, I have heard many suggest that family physicians can turn to pharmaceutical solutions quite quickly. Many bereaved parents are not comfortable with this approach, instead seeking a kind of support that family physicians do not have the training to offer. Second, while some grief reactions will benefit from medical and pharmaceutical solutions, the research in public health suggests that the majority of grievers do not need specialized medical care (Aoun et al. 2015). Moreover, there is concern in the literature about the possibility of harm caused when bereavement therapy is not tailored carefully to the individual client's needs and desires (Bonanno and Lilienfeld 2008).[4]

Metaphors and models have the power to beget action and confer meaning. In his juxtaposition of the language of trauma versus sorrow to conceptual grief, Dennis Klass (2013) has opened an important discussion. Trauma has become a common metaphor used in grief therapy, embedding grief into discourses of individual injury. As an injury, service providers are compelled to intervene when they see grief. The frame of trauma as injury compels an optimism: if grief is an injury, it can perhaps be cured. Klass posits that shifting the metaphor from trauma to tragedy forces a more existential, contemplative comprehension of grief, one that resists a need to cure and instead allows the bereaved to 'dwell in their sorrow' as they adapt to their forever-changed selves in a forever-changed world. Tragedy as a metaphor of a social experience obliges accompaniment and supportive presence, not cure. Once does not 'recover' from tragedy in the way implied by the language of trauma.[5]

Neoliberalism

A final reflection on our grief language is how the discursive constructions of grief merge – with surprising ease – with neoliberal discourses. Grief is troublesome within a neoliberal society: it prevents people from working, slows down production, and reduces an individual's ability to make rational choices. This emotional state compromises the ideal workplace through absenteeism, presenteeism, and increased expenditure in sick days. Further, the presence of a bereft employee casts an awkwardness on the workplace when coworkers do not know how to be with their colleague's grief. Persuasive arguments are made in documents such as *Grief Index: The 'Hidden' Annual Costs of Grief in America's Workplace* (James et al. 2003), in which metrics calculate the threat of grief to business's bottom line. Interestingly, the clinical and lay language used to characterize grief draws on metaphors of work and productivity – for example, grief work, tasks of grieving, managing grief. As a threat to productivity and workplace safety, our language helps to contain and manage grief, pushing to resolve it quickly – preferably in the three days allowed for bereavement leave (Macdonald et al. 2014).

Our high-speed neoliberal society is perhaps an exact antithesis of the grieving body. The grieving body aches and emotes; it can be slow, unsteady, unpredictable, emotional, and irrational. As my team has theorized elsewhere (Macdonald et al. 2014), grief is not necessarily akin to sickness, chronic illness, or disability. There is neither a predictable course to bereavement, nor a wheelchair ramp–type accommodation that can attend to a grieving employee. Further, the employee who returns after the death of a love one is not the same person who left; grief leaves the self forever changed. The social isolation that can results during time away from the workforce can be exactly what a bereaved person *does not need*; having work tasks and social opportunities in the workplace can be helpful for some. However, these tasks and engagements have to suit the bereaved person's new sense of time, ability, and pace. Unfortunately, many work environments do not know how to respond to a bereaved employee; coworkers do not know what to say, and managers do not know how to reschedule and adapt tasks. Back in 1991, Tony Walter wrote: 'Today then, the dying and bereaved become uniquely isolated, lepers even, because they highlight the Achilles heel of the modern individual' (Walter 1991:306). Two-and-a-half decades later, the bereaved are even further antithetical to the neoliberal subject.

What do grief-denying discourses do?

Examining grief-denying discourses should not be simply an academic exercise; these discourses have real repercussions for the bereaved. To begin, they create and reinforce social hierarchies of grief: Who has a right to grieve? How long should they grieve? In what manor (private or public) must they grieve? The answers to these questions are all socially arbitrated. Patricia Robson and Tony Walter have theorized this social process, and in so doing, challenged Kenneth J. Doka's binary disenfranchised grief theory (Doka 1989) with more sophisticated reflections of the social construction of normative grieving (Robson and Walter 2013). These hierarchies are at play, for example, when biomedical language erases the 'baby-ness' of a baby and dehumanizes a stillborn child with terms like 'nonviable fetus'. Claudia Malacrida's analysis of the social economy of perinatal death demonstrates how the *nongestures* that follow a perinatal death (e.g., *the lack of* gifts, flowers, cards, offers of meals and financial assistance, and *the absence of* supportive employment policies) affect parents as they grieve (Malacrida 1999). The silence that follows when a fetus is not interpreted to be a baby and the adults are not seen to be parents leaves the grievers alone – unsupported emotionally as well as financially – as they grieve.

These hierarchies also help explain a social world in which non-grievers feel and act repelled by the bereaved. Grief is experienced by non-grievers as more than a taboo, and more than pitiable. Grief is experienced as something to be avoided for deeper, personal reasons. There is a 'There but for the grace of God go I' dimension to how non-grievers interact with the bereaved. Through this interaction, bereaved parents feel stigmatized by a grief that is perceived as if socially contagious: it is as if non-grieving parents fear they could catch what bereaved parents are living, that their child could die, too. As bereaved parents watch neighbours cross the street to avoid having to speak with them, feel judged for maintaining their deceased child's bedroom, are confronted by platitudes such as, 'Well, at least you can always have more children', they respond by isolating themselves away from a world that wants to arbitrate how they live with their memories and their nonliving child.

Well-meaning yet uninformed responses to grief can do more harm than good. I was one of three social researchers called to deliver remarks during the Canadian parliamentary proceedings mentioned above. While impressed that parental grief was being taken seriously by a parliamentary motion, and that grief was being acknowledged as something our federal system should better recognize and support, we three were troubled by the potential of any resultant legislation to further vulnerabilize grievers. Collectively, our testimonies addressed the hierarchies of grief embedded in the motion as it singled out infant death over all other kinds of child and non-child death, thus perpetuating the idea that some kinds of grief are more worthy than others (Cadell 2018; Joy 2018; Macdonald 2018b).[6] Further, missing in the motion was an awareness of the ripple effect of grief; only parents were included as the legitimate grievers when an infant dies. Grief is, by definition, a lonely experience; by excluding these other grievers from social support and employment protection, the motion risked reinforcing the vulnerability many are already living.

It is worth reflecting on how grief entered the political sphere in this example. Private members bills in Canada are sponsored by individual Members of Parliament (MPs) and thus are ostensibly nonpartisan. However, the voting process for moving motions forward is, of course, subject to the political allegiance of the voting members. In this case, the MP sponsoring the motion was from the official opposition party (the Conservative Party of Canada). Compounding the politics, the proceedings were held on the run-up to a federal election, and the meetings were truncated as a result. No doubt related, shortly after the process was completed a Conservative request to amend a bill before Parliament (C-86) to allow parents 12 weeks of leave following the death of a child (including perinatal death) was defeated by the ruling Liberal party.

Another interesting component of this political process was its location within the Government of Canada's Standing Committee on Human Resources, Skills and Social Development and the Status of Persons with Disabilities. As such, the lion's share of the testimony and the tenor of the final report (May 2019) was focused on employment-related issues. The issue of public education was raised in our session, however, and a Committee member requested follow-up:

MR. ROBERT MORRISSEY (EGMONT, LIB.): You referenced public education. We hear that a lot. My question would be simply this: Where and when? Where do you see the public education piece beginning? Is it in academics? Is it at schools? Who does it involve – the young, the old? Who?

DR. SUSAN CADELL: What pops into my head is [putting educational messages on] bus shelters and buses. We need to be talking about this at all ages. I think buses and public transportation and of course social media – those two follow one another – are places where we can start a conversation. When people are talking about death and dying, we benefit from that as a society.

(HUMA 2018)

I reproduce this exchange because it underscores the enormity of the challenge of normalizing grief through a political process. The question from the Committee member is coming from an assumption that grief education needs a rarefied model of expertise. The response from Cadell, a social work researcher and educator, is rooted in a community empowerment model that sees grief as simply part and parcel of being human. Unfortunately but not surprisingly, this grassroots version of the public education of grief is not referenced in the final report of the Committee (May 2019).[7]

Ghosts: challenging the *-izations* of grief

Many scholars have written about what I will call the *-izations* of grief: medicalization, psychiatrization, psychologization, professionalization, colonization, and so on. These discourses all contribute to producing a social denial of grief; even the term 'denial' pulls upon psychologising discourses. These *-izations* have much in common. For example, they locate their notions of grief within an individual griever through which clinical terminology parses grief responses – and thus the grievers – into normal and pathological categories.

Every framework, through its discursive production, produces and reproduces ways of seeing the world. In so doing, they will metaphorically, perhaps literally, obscure other ways of seeing and knowing. These *-izations* of grief emerge from a postpositivist scientific paradigm of knowledge production. Historically, the lineage of this paradigm traces to the natural sciences where a universal, natural world is only discernible through empirical (i.e., sensory) objective methods. While the postpositivist paradigm helps greatly in the understanding of phenomena such as gravitational pull or global warming, many social researchers are concerned that health phenomena are not amenable to this paradigm (Taylor 1987).

The scientific framework through which we have constructed grief begets the methods needed to produce knowledge; these methods favour the empirical. Postpositivist science is 'hyper-visual' (Gordon 2008), with a bias towards an 'ocular, visual epistemology' (Denzin 1997:182). In other words, in this version of knowledge production, we need to see it to believe it. As such, there is little to no place for the subjective, for intuition, for the metaphysical in grief theory. In so doing, the *-izations* prevent us from other ways of knowing grief. From studying grief experiences, I now believe that the bereaved live important phenomena that cannot be empirically verified (Macdonald 2018a). For example, many bereaved parents live within a paradigm that enables the embodied presence of the absented deceased. Mikkel Bille and colleagues have theorized the 'absent presence' left behind after death, asking:

> How are objects, people and phenomena 'there' from an experiential perspective, even though they are 'not there' from a positivist perspective? How are losses presented in the everyday lives of the bereaved? How are religious ideals of transcendence materialized? How are past events, histories or future expectations materially manifested in the present?
>
> (Bille et al. 2010)

In prior work, I have suggested that what the bereaved have left after death is the 'presence of absence' of their loved one; that is, they have their ghosts (Macdonald 2018a). By 'ghost', I am proposing a metonymic connection between the living and the dead. Some may read this as playful; others as irreverent or sacrilegious. In popular imagery, 'ghosts' conjure ideas of paranormal activities, spurred on by horror film technologies which render them scary and evil, with plotlines in which they seek vengeance for earthly deeds or complete unfinished business. A revision was 'Casper the friendly ghost', which began as a cartoon in the 1940s and morphed into series still popular today. In religious imagery, ghosts can be positive or negative, and often connote spirit or soul. The ultimate benevolent spirit in Christianity is the Holy Ghost; another extreme requires exorcisms to rid bodies of evil.

In using the term 'ghost', I mean neither the fearful, nor the playful nor the religious. I am using the term to create a placeholder *to think with* about something which we have yet to define: the absent presence of the deceased. In bereavement theory, this space has yet to be theorized outside the *-ization* science. I want to challenge us to imagine an ontological construct; a new epistemology is required to think it respectfully. Gordon's sociology of haunting is useful to think about 'ghostly matters' as signifiers of what is missing and what must be examined (Gordon 2008). I depart from Avery F. Gordon, and Lois Tonkin's (2012) uptake of her work in the field of child death, in that I am not focused on haunting. It is the ghosts themselves who are of interest to me, and especially their presence in the holes left behind by those absented, the deceased.

Ghosts are a productive metaphor. Our normative grief models, with the biases emergent from an ocular epistemology, try to force the bereaved to give up these ghosts. We really do need to see them to believe them; and ghosts, we believe, we cannot see. What harm may be done when we delegitimize what our frameworks will not allow us to see? Through our positivist lens, these ghosts must be explained away as, for example, attachment bonds, or pathologized into different kinds and stages of grieving. In so doing, these ghosts are erased and silenced.

Yet, research shows how the bereaved are comforted when they keep their ghosts nearby. Joan Didion wrote that, after her husband's sudden death, she resisted throwing out his shoes because he might need them when he came back (Didion 2007). Interviews with bereaved parents demonstrate how they endeavour to keep their deceased children present in their daily lives. In one of my studies, a mother described that the rabbit who looked through her back window was her deceased son checking on her (Macdonald and Mikaela 2010). Further, our work shows how parents continue parenting their deceased children. In our Internet-based research, bereaved parents used the technologies of Web 2.0 to create virtual neighbourhoods in which they could use electronic messaging capabilities to set up playdates for children in heaven, and through which they could implore their deceased children to wear warmer clothing when the seasons changed (Mitchell et al. 2012; Macdonald 2018a).

Harm is done when the *-ization* models epistemologically deny the ontological possibility and importance of embodied absence, when we delegitimize what these frameworks will not allow us to 'see'. This epistemological clash further stigmatizes and isolates grievers. If our current modalities for understanding grief do not allow us to see what is empirically not there, this means discounting, forgetting, erasing the dead from the embodied experience of the bereaved. Their ghosts cannot cohabitate with current bereavement models.

Mikkel Bille and colleagues are concerned that our theories of meaning are limited by their focus on what is present. They argue we must also look for what is absent. What is absent – in this case, the dead – also contains its own meaning: 'Absences are cultural, physical, and social phenomena that powerfully influence people's conceptualizations of themselves and the world they engage' (Bille et al. 2010:4). The dead, in other words, have their own meaning; their meaning bumps up against – and thereby challenges and transforms – the meaning of being bereaved.

Conceptualising bereavement as involving a relationship between the living and the deceased affords the dead what Floris Tomasini theorizes as 'residual subjectivity' (Tomasini 2009). Tomasini writes about a scandal at the Alder Hey Children's Hospital in the United Kingdom, where, in the 1990s, organs of deceased children had been retained without parental permission (Tomasini 2009). Tomasini's work pushes thinking beyond the idea of the dead as nonexistent persons by showing how the parents experience the deceased as an 'existential absence'. Within this 'existential absence' the dead maintain a 'residual subjectivity and identity'. Elements of personhood were coproduced through the relationship between parents and their child, which did not end with death. As subjects, however, the dead become at risk for what Tomasini calls 'post-mortem harm' when not treated with the dignity and respect normally afforded subjects (e.g., by not getting the expected burial, by disrupting bodily integrity, by removing organs). Two quotations stand out from Tomasini's work:

> From the parents of Christopher (5.5 years) oral testimony: After Christopher's death and during the post-mortem process his parents were assured he would be cared for. Christopher was as precious in death as he was in life. His parents can never forgive or erase the memory of what happened to him following his death.
>
> (Tomasini 2009:443)

> For example, from the mother of Alexandra (stillborn) oral testimony: The third and most compelling reason for her emotion as a parent is that she would have done anything to protect her child. That was what she was there to do, even more so in death because it was the only thing she could do for her child at that stage. . . . There was only one thing she could do and that was to protect her in death and she did not do it and she has to live with that.
>
> (Tomasini 2009:446)

Tomasini's phenomenon of postmortem harm was present in interviews I conducted with bereaved parents about their decisions regarding an autopsy request after their child's death in an intensive care unit. After his daughter died following numerous surgeries and interventions, a father told me that he refused the autopsy request because: 'She's been through enough' (Macdonald et al., 2006).

Grieving with the body

The deceased – when living – had a material body that filled an embodied space in their social world. Absent presence allows us to *think with* the material body about how what is now absent affects present living. Increasingly, narratives in academic and social media are showing how the material body is at work in grief and grieving. For example, seeing and holding the deceased child, including after an induced abortion for fetal anomalies in the second trimester (Mitchell 2016), is being encouraged in paediatric contexts. Some hospices have temperature-controlled rooms to allow parents, as one parent described, 'to spend time with [the child] whenever we felt the need' (Todorović 2016). An extreme example from a British hospital was reported in a tabloid under the headline: 'Grieving mother spends FIFTEEN days bonding with body of her stillborn son as she changes his nappy, rocks him and reads to him before finally saying goodbye' (Hull 2016). This article was shared almost 7,000 times on social media, and commented on almost 700 times.

Constructing images and memories of the deceased child are also becoming normative activities after a death. Memory boxes (e.g., with handprints and footprints, photos, and hair clippings) have become standard practice in paediatric palliative care (Harris and Douma 2010). The mission of the Now I Lay Me Down to Sleep charity is 'to introduce remembrance photography to parents suffering the loss of a baby with a free gift of professional portraiture'. Their website claims to have 'gifted more than 40,000 complementary portrait sessions since 2005' across 40 countries.[8] The techniques of *remembrance photography* use sepia tones and other technologies to remove the trappings of the child's medicalized life and death (e.g., removing breathing tubes, changing blue skin to pink) from the photograph. This process re-sentimentalizes the dead body into an innocent sleeping child, producing a normative ideal of what death should look like.

Conclusion

After writing these reflections on my own and others work in the realm of death, dying, and bereavement, I am left with a growing conviction that an as yet untheorized location from which to ponder grief and its social denial is in the responses of non-grievers to the bereaved. In focusing on non-grievers, it becomes clearer how our society is repelled by grief. As a researcher who studies grief, even I provoke this response in people. After explaining what kind of research I do, a common 'stranger at a dinner party' response is: 'Oh, I could never do that – that must be so sad!' followed quickly by a change in topic to the weather or the menu.

An additional area from which we can better understand this phenomenon I am calling *grief denial* is through uncovering and theorizing sites of resistance. Working with a team in Canada led by Susan Cadell (quoted above), we are coming to understand how memorial tattoos are a productive place to theorize both how the body is finding a way into normative models of grieving, as well as how the body is itself a site through which grievers resist the denial of their grief. Memorial tattoos are much more common than we realized when we started the project. They privately (in some cases) and publicly (in others) convey complex messages about bereavement (Cadell et al. 2018). The tattooed body is both a body in mourning while also a body physically integrating into its skin – and thereby its self – an indelible representation of the deceased.

Our project to date involves collecting images of memorial tattoos, displayed in whatever way the participant is comfortable. We are listening to the bereaved narrate stories about tattooing decisions, including the process of choosing the image, the bodily location, and the tattoo artist, and about the legacy of the resultant tattoo. In the collection to date, we have a vast range of images (e.g., names, dates, signatures, fingerprints, animals, insects, faces) located across private and public body zones. Stories point to themes of remembrance, sadness, heartbreak, hope, fondness, and advocacy (e.g., explicitly encouraging public conversations about suicide).

Given what is at stake for the bereaved living the social denial of their grief, I am compelled forward with these future research directions. I hope the next decade sees many other social scientists taking up and advancing some of the reflections I have offered.

Notes

1 Further agreeing with Kellehear, I am ambivent about this label, as it uses 'psychological concepts to fit sociological problems' (Kellehear 1984:714).
2 This paragraph is based upon my remarks to the Canadian Parliamentary Committee addressing Motion 110: *Supporting Families after the Loss of an Infant Child* (Macdonald 2018b). My testimony can be found at: www.ourcommons.ca/DocumentViewer/en/42-1/HUMA/meeting-125/evidence.
3 I first developed these ideas in my Keynote Address: *An overview of sociocultural trends in thinking about child death*, delivered at the First National Pediatric Palliative Care Symposium, October 30, 2013, in Ottawa, Canada.
4 This paragraph is based upon my remarks to the Canadian Parliamentary Committee addressing Motion 110: *Supporting Families after the Loss of an Infant Child* (Macdonald 2018b). My testimony can be found at: www.ourcommons.ca/DocumentViewer/en/42-1/HUMA/meeting-125/evidence.
5 These ideas were originally developed in my plenary talk: *Giving up the ghost? How the dead remain socially present in our worlds*, delivered at the 21st International Congress on Palliative Care, October 18, 2016, in Montreal, Canada.
6 See full testimony at: www.ourcommons.ca/DocumentViewer/en/42-1/HUMA/meeting-125/evidence.
7 The final report of the parliamentary committee was released February 2019. it can be found at: www.ourcommons.ca/Content/Committee/421/HUMA/Reports/RP10295739/humarp14/humarp14-e.pdf.
8 www.nowilaymedowntosleep.org.

References

Aoun, Samar M., Lauren J. Breen, Denise A. Howting, Bruce Rumbold, Beverley McNamara and Desley Hegney (2015): 'Who Needs Bereavement Support? A Population Based Survey of Bereavement Risk and Support Need'. *PloS One*, 10 (3).
Armstrong, David (1987): 'Silence and Truth in Death and Dying'. *Social Science & Medicine*, 24 (8):651–657.
Bille, Mikkel, Frida Hastrup and Tim Flohr Sørensen (2010): 'Introduction: An Anthropology of Absence', in Mikkel Bille, Frida Hastrup and Tim Flohr Sørensen (eds.): *An Anthropology of Absence: Materializations of Transcendence and Loss*. New York: Springer, pp. 3–22.
Blake Richards (2019): 'Blake Richards, Member of Parliament, Banff-Airdrie'. Available online at: www.blakerichards.ca/motion-110/motion-110-text/.
Bonanno, George A. and Scott O. Lilienfeld (2008): 'Let's Be Realistic: When Grief Counseling is Effective and When it's Not'. *Professional Psychology: Research and Practice*, 39 (3):377.

Breen, Lauren J. and Moira O'Connor (2007): 'The Fundamental Paradox in the Grief Literature: A Critical Reflection'. *Omega – Journal of Death and Dying*,55 (3):199–218.

Cadell, Susan (2018): 'Witness Testimony'. *Motion 110: Supporting Families After the Loss of a Child*, Ottawa, ON: Government of Canada.

Cadell, Susan, Melissa Reid Lambert, Mary Ellen Macdonald, Deborah Davidson, Marcel O'Gorman and Melanie Baljko (2018): "The Pain of the Tattoo Was a Relief": Advancing a Theory of Embodied Pain in a Study of Memorial Tattoos'. *Journal of Pain and Symptom Management*, 56 (6).

Denzin, Norman K. (1997): *Interpretive Ethnography: Ethnographic Practices for the 21st Century*. Thousand Oaks, CA: Sage Publications.

Didion, Joan (2007): *The Year of Magical Thinking*. New York: Vintage Books.

Doka, Kenneth J. (1989): *Disenfranchised Grief: Recognizing Hidden Sorrow*. Lanham, MD: Lexington.

Gordon, Avery F. (2008): *Ghostly Matters: Haunting and the Sociological Imagination*. Minnesota: University of Minnesota Press.

Harris, Leslie L. and Caryn Douma (2010): 'End-of-Life Care in the NICU: A Family-Centered Approach'. *NeoReviews*, 11 (4):194–199. Available online at: https://neoreviews.aappublications.org/content/11/4/e194.

Hayasaki, Erika (2013): 'Death is Having a Moment.' *The Atlantic*, 25, October, 2013. Available online at: www.theatlantic.com/health/archive/2013/10/death-is-having-a-moment/280777/.

Hull, Liz (2016): 'Grieving Mother Spends FIFTEEN Days Bonding with Body of Her Stillborn Son as She Changes His Nappy, Rocks Him and Reads to Him Before Finally Saying Goodbye'. *The Daily Mail*, 20, July. Available online at; www.dailymail.co.uk/news/article-3700040/Grieving-mother-nearly-died-giving-birth-spent-15-days-bonding-stillborn-son-saying-goodbye.html#ixzz4F2PWsmNg.

HUMA (Standing Committee on Human Resources Skills and Social Development and the Status of Persons with Disabilities) (2018). 'Evidence, Tuesday, November 20, 2018'. *Motion 110: Supporting Families after the Loss of a Child*. Ottawa, ON: Government of Canada.

James, John W., Russell Friedman and Eric Cline (2003): *Grief Index: The 'Hidden' Annual Costs of Grief in America's Workplace*. Sherman Oaks, CA: Grief Recovery Institute Educational Foundation Inc.

Joy, Karima (2018): 'Witness Testimony'. *Motion 110: Supporting Families after the Loss of a Child*. Ottawa, ON: Government of Canada.

Kellehear, Allan (1984): 'Are We a 'Death-Denying' Society? A Sociological Review'. *Social Science & Medicine*, 18 (9):713–721.

Klass, Dennis (2013): 'Sorrow and Solace: Neglected Areas in Bereavement Research'. *Death Studies*, 37 (7):597–616.

Macdonald, Mary Ellen (2018a): 'Why Should the Bereaved Give Up Their Ghosts?'. *Discover Society*, 6, February.

Macdonald, Mary Ellen (2018b): 'Witness Testimony'. *Motion 110: Supporting Families after the Loss of a Child*, Ottawa, ON: Government of Canada.

Macdonald, Mary Ellen and Mikaela Knot (2010): 'Bunnies, Butterflies and Lawn Mowing: How Deceased Children Stay Present in Parents' Lives'. *Canadian Anthropological Association Annual Conference*, Montreal, QC.

Macdonald, Mary Ellen, Kimberly Kennedy, Sandra Moll, Carolina Pineda, Lisa M. Mitchell, Peter H. Stephenson and Susan Cadell (2014): 'Excluding Parental Grief: A Critical

Discourse Analysis of Bereavement Accommodation in Canadian Labour Standards'. *Work: A Journal of Prevention, Assessment and Rehabilitation*, 50:511–526.

Macdonald, Mary Ellen, Stephen Liben and S. Robin Cohen (2006): 'Truth and Consequences: Parental Perspectives on Autopsy after the Death of a Child'. *Pediatr Intensive Care Nursing*, 7 (1):6–15.

Malacrida, Claudia (1999): 'Complicating Mourning: The Social Economy of Perinatal Death'. *Qualitative Health Research*, 9 (4):504–519.

May, Bryan (2019): 'Supporting Families af the Loss of a Child', in *Report of the Standing Committee on Human Researouces, Skills and Social Development and the Status of Persons with Disabilities*. Ottawa, ON: Government of Canada.

Mitchell, Lisa M. (2016). "Time with Babe': Seeing Fetal Remains After Pregnancy Termination for Impairment'. *Medical Anthropology Quarterly*, 30 (2):168–185.

Mitchell, Lisa M., Peter H. Stephenson, Susan Cadell and Mary Ellen Macdonald (2012): 'Death and Grief On-Line: Virtual Memorialization and Changing Concepts of Childhood Death and Parental Bereavement on the Internet'. *Health Sociology Review*, 21 (4):413–431.

Penfold-Mounce, Ruth (2016): 'Corpses, Popular Culture and Forensic Science: Public Obsession with Death'. *Mortality*, 21 (1):19–35.

Robson, Patricia and Tony Walter (2013): 'Hierarchies of Loss: A Critique of Disenfranchised Grief'. *Omega – Journal of Death and Dying*, 66 (2):97–119.

Taylor, Charles (1987): 'Interpretation and the Sciences of Man', in Paul Rabinow and William M. Sullivan (eds.): *Interpretive Social Science: A Second Look*. Berkeley, CA: University of California Press, pp. 33–81.

Todorović, Ana (2016): 'Nadia's Story: It is a Decision That No Parent Should Have to Make: Should We Let Our Very Sick Baby Die Before She Was Born?'. *Aeon.co*. Available online at: https://aeon.co/users/ana-todorovic.

Tomasini, Floris (2009): 'Is Post-Mortem Harm Possible? Understanding Death Harm and Grief'. *Bioethics*, 23 (8):441–449.

Tonkin, Lois (2012): 'Haunted by a 'Present Absence''. *Studies in the Maternal*, 4 (1):1–17.

Walter, Tony (1991): 'Modern Death: Taboo or Not Taboo?'. *Sociology*, 25 (2):293–310.

Zimmermann, Camilla and Gary Rodin (2004): 'The Denial of Death Thesis: Sociological Critique and Implications for Palliative Care'. *Palliative Medicine*, 18 (2):121–128.

8   Public mourning

Displays of grief and grievance

Jack Santino

Introduction

On January 7, 2015, two men entered the Paris office of a satirical newspaper called *Charlie Hebdo* and opened fire on those present. Twelve people were killed and 11 others were injured. Among the dead were the some of the principal artists and editors of the weekly publication, which consists primarily of cartoons. Among the killed was an already wounded police officer named Ahmet Merabet. The two intruders, brothers, were members of Al-Quaida who were punishing *Charlie Hebdo* for publishing drawings of the Prophet Muhammed. The forces of order responded with a massive manhunt; meanwhile, there were other attacks over the following days. At a kosher supermarket, a gunman held 19 people hostage, killing four of them, all Jewish. The brothers were eventually killed by police.

Charlie Hebdo is a publication that pushes the boundaries of good taste. It routinely presents cartoon images which can only be called extreme stereotypes, and these include images of Black people, Jews, lesbians, and Catholic priests. The rendering of the Prophet was not flattering, and it was certainly not in accord with a general Muslim ban on depicting him at all. These attacks and killings were met with nationwide shock and horror, and were widely viewed as an attack on freedom of expression in a country that prides itself on the separation of church and state – what is called *la laïcité*. Along with the intense manhunt, on January 11 approximately two million people filled the streets of Paris, including 40 world leaders, in a ceremony of memorialization, mutual support, and condemnation of the attacks, and their insistence on the continued strength of traditional French values.

I was in Paris shortly thereafter, attending a scholarly conference on carnival and conducting research. Attending Paris' revitalized *boeuf gras* carnival parade to la Place de la République, I found myself confronting a vast site of public mourning, public grief mixed with patriotism and condemnation of the terrorist acts. The central statue of Marianne, the iconic symbol of France, was surrounded with wreaths, flowers, candles, flags, and other items. Moreover, the statue itself was covered with drawings and messages. Portraits of the deceased cartoonists, drawn in cartoon style, were seen around the base of the statue. Because the attack was on a newspaper, and thus on the value of free expression, drawings and cartoons were prevalent. Moreover, pens and pencils – drawing implements – were common, both in representations and actual objects left at the site.

Further, the plaza itself was being used as a canvas. People were painting and had painted messages on the stone floor of the plaza itself, all honouring victims, condemning attacks, and insisting that the terrorists would not succeed in deterring liberty of expression. People were still lighting candles and laying wreaths, now weeks after the attacks. This outpouring of public grief coupled with outrage was not confine to the Place de la République

The next day I went to the *Charlie Hebdo* headquarters. Upon leaving the nearest Metro station, I saw that both sides of the boulevard had also become the sites of more of this public mourning, what I refer to as 'spontaneous shrines' – unofficial assemblages of objects related to victims of violent or untimely deaths. At the Metro stop, there was one such shrine dedicated to the Muslim police officer who lost his life.

The *Charlie Hebdo* offices were closed and guarded by an armed soldier, but the intersection at the end of the street was filled with mourning materials. Street signs were covered by signs that declared the area a *Place de la Liberté d'Expression*. Among the flowers, wreaths, candles, notes, drawings, were pens and pencils in abundance. Clearly, along with the slogan '*je Suis Charlie*', the drawing tools had become a central symbol for this particular tragic event. The scene was not vacant – people were present, still leaving tokens of their sense of connection to the event, and those killed in it.

While this was my first encounter with the *Charlie Hebdo* memorialization, it was not my first encounter with this phenomenon of public grieving or public memorialization of death. Nevertheless, I find such 'spontaneous shrines' invariably moving; encountering them is always, for me, an emotional experience.

In the following chapter, my main interests include the emergence of a new kind of public ritual expression of grief and grievance. I will suggest that the public memorialization of death almost always addresses social issues while utilizing familiar funereal symbols and tropes to commemorate deceased individuals. I have termed such phenomena 'spontaneous shrines', and in this chapter I examine the implications and appropriateness of this term. Spontaneous shrines have emerged in the late 20th century to mark a certain type of death – violent, untimely, or unnecessary. The causes of such deaths are themselves matters of public concern, and range from driving fatalities to terrorism. I have conducted extensive research on these phenomena in Northern Ireland, France, and the United States, and I draw on my own and others' research in my analysis. As in the case of the *Charlie Hebdo* killings outlined above, I have visited the sites described and spent time discussing the shrines with people who have helped create them, developing knowledge as to the reasons these shrines are important to those who participate in their construction.

The phenomenon of spontaneous shrines

As alluded to above, this public mourning in Paris, in this case after the very public killings, is an example of a phenomenon I have referred to as 'spontaneous

shrines' (Santino 1992, 2006). I see these as spontaneous in that they are not official memorials; indeed, often they might obstruct public walkways or otherwise
intrude in public and private space and be frowned upon by the officials. However,
people seem to feel a need to sacralize spaces where a violent death occurred, as
well as spaces which are in some way associated with the deceased – symboli-
cally, territorially, personally. Unlike the permanent memorials constructed by
official institutions, they are ephemeral. People do not ask permission to leave
their items; these are actions of individuals acting in consort to create an assemblage of materials that communicates to a broad spectatorship (Santino 1986).
People are doing more than memorializing the deceased, however. As suggested
above, people express outrage at the causes of the untimely, usually unnecessary
deaths. This aspect moves the artefacts into the realms of the social and political.

This duality – the personal memorialization of the particular deceased individuals, and a critique (implied or stated) of the social and political contexts which
allowed, or caused, these deaths to occur, is a unique feature of spontaneous
shrines. Further, they mark a specific type of death: deaths which are untimely,
usually violent, unnecessary, preventable. In many ways, they are an emergent
ritual response for a type of death for which no such popular ritual response fully
existed. For example, when John F. Kennedy was assassinated in 1963, in Dallas,
Texas, despite the enormous outpouring of grief and shock that followed, the area
where he was killed was not sacralized as a shrine by ordinary people. In contrast,
when, decades later, his son, John F. Kennedy Jr. was lost in a private plane crash,
JFK Jr's apartment building façade in New York was covered with notes, flowers,
and candles. In the generation between the two untimely deaths, the tradition had
developed.

In my research on similar materials in Northern Ireland and elsewhere, I have
found that people often say that the reason they choose to leave flowers or something else at the place where the deaths occurred is because this is the last place
the person was alive (Santino 2001:75–97). Because of the death, the place has
become sacred, taboo, a place that requires some kind of ritual response. Often
at such places, one will find messages to the deceased, as well as, in some cases,
messages written as though from the deceased (see Zeitlin 2006; see also Fraenkel 2002). In this way, these sacred sites are portals, places where one can communicate more directly with the deceased. It is for this reason that I see them
as having the qualities of a shrine. Thus, 'spontaneous' is used to indicate the
unofficial nature and personal motivations of those who contribute to such sites,
and 'shrine' suggests that, while they serve to memorialize, they are also more
actively addressing social issues, they have a spiritual dimension (which will vary
in definition and understanding according to individuals), and they are frequently
felt to be a point of access to said spiritual quality.

My own early research concerning this phenomenon took place in Northern Ireland at a time when frequent paramilitary 'tit-for-tat' killings were unfortunately
a fact of everyday life. In 1991 I provided the text for an exhibit of photographs
taken by Michael McCaughan in Belfast. In the article for the catalogue accompanying the exhibition, I first used the term 'spontaneous shrines' to characterize this

emerging mourning tradition (Santino 1992) and continued to conduct research in Northern Ireland because I saw the shrines as an important alternative voice to the general discourses on the 'Troubles' – whether paramilitary or even academic. This research resulted in the 2001 publication of *Signs of War and Peace: Social Conflict and the Uses of Symbols in Public*. The particular context of long-standing social conflict in Ireland informed my initial interest and the further development of theoretical perspectives on the materials. Other important scholarly works have addressed, and been perhaps inspired by, similar but different materials. Road-side crosses, which represent a tradition which most likely parented the wider use of memorial materials at sites of untimely death nationally and internationally, received careful study by Holly Everett (2002); while the collapse and resulting student deaths of a bonfire structure led to Sylvia Grider's (2001, 2006, 2007) important early publications. The massive response to the death of Lady Diana is the subject of numerous studies (see Kear and Steinberg 1999; Walter 1999); and the equally massive responses to the attacks of September 11, 2001, in the United States (New York, Washington, DC, and Pennsylvania) has also inspired a great deal of scholarly interest in the subject, as the work of Beatrice Fraenkel (2002) and many of the articles in Santino (2006) attest. Such large-scale attacks continue, and the responses continue to involve people expressing their grief, their torment, and their anger publicly, by means of spontaneous shrines. On March 11, 2003, a commuter railway was bombed in Madrid. Folklorist Cristina Sánchez-Carretero began a photo-documentation project of the shrines; this project led to a permanent collection and archives of both photographs and the materials themselves, called 'El Archivo del Duelo' (Sánchez-Carretero 2011). In another important publication, Sánchez-Carretero and coeditor Peter Jan Margry suggest 'grassroots memorials' as a more appropriate term (2011). While debate continues on academic terminology, the disruptive deaths continue to rent society, and people continue the mourning ritual, so much so that we can view it as having become a standardized, rather than emergent, tradition.

In British North America, in the 17th century, epitaphs on tombstones were sometimes written in the voice of the deceased: 'Where you are now, I once was; where I am now, you will be'. Clearly, these messages reminded the spectators of their own mortality and the fleeting nature of life, reflecting the particular worldview of Puritanism. However, one also sees here a sense of two-way communication between the quick and the dead, due to the presence of the remains. That is, the final resting place of the deceased would appear to be a place where this world and the next are connected and porous; where not only can the living send their thoughts to the deceased, but the deceased can communicate with the living as well. We find similar ideas, or beliefs, reflected in earlier English, Scottish, and Scandinavian traditional ballads such as 'The Unquiet Grave' (Child 1882–1898/1965; Ballad #78) in which the spirit of the deceased tells a mourning lover that excessive mourning is hindering the spirit from continuing on to fully enter the otherworld. Indeed, one can find instances of such beliefs in traditional materials throughout the Western world. These beliefs are consistent with the idea that the soul inhabits the body, that it becomes autonomous upon death (or shortly thereafter), and that the place of interment is a material point of transition and a portal to the spirit world.

Spontaneous shrines resemble graves. Both (generally) utilize flowers and candles as means of memorialization, and even the notes left at spontaneous shrines are similar to notes left at shrines of saints and healers, both official statuary and unofficial places of folk healing. Below I will argue that spontaneous shrines represent a popular attempt to control the means of mourning, placing the memorabilia in public thoroughfares and commercial properties. However, a major distinction between gravesites and spontaneous shrines centres on the remains of the deceased. When bodies are disposed of by burial, one retains a sense that what was once the person is still present beneath the earth where one prays, cries, celebrates birthdays and holidays, and so on. With spontaneous shrines, the remains are not present. Significantly, it is the act of dying rather than the body of the deceased that is paramount; time and again, people testify that the site of the death is significant because it is the last place the person was alive on earth. It is the point of (sudden, violent) exit; the place where one's last breath was taken. And while I believe the shrines address the societal ills that have contributed to the death, it is also true that this shift from bodily resting place to site of dying represents a major development in the social thinking about death.

The same ideas regarding communication with the deceased, the porous nature of this world and the next, the site as portal, that we saw with graves are relevant here. Significantly, the presence of the body is not necessary. With the emphasis on the final breath, with honouring the last place the individual was alive, the emphasis shifts to life, not the eternal sleep. The two mourning traditions are not incompatible – most often, families will carry out traditional burial or cremation practices in addition to the presence of shrines. Often, different groups are involved – friends and a more distant public may maintain the shrines (in part because of the element of social protest against the cause of death, such as drunk driving, police brutality, gang violence, etc.), while the family carries on more private traditions. And while all deaths require ritual attention, only a certain type of death requires the spontaneous shrine. Nevertheless, the shift in emphasis may represent a shift in social and religious belief concerning the body and the afterlife.

History

The spontaneous shrine as we see it today has become a common, almost reflexive popular response to untimely death. The practice of leaving items that signify one's relationship to someone who is deceased, as well as items that signify traditional mourning practices and ritual, such as candles and flowers, is seen by some as having begun after the completion of the Vietnam Veterans Memorial on the National Mall in Washington, DC (Hass 1998). While no one connected to the Vietnam War actually died on this spot, many of the commemorated soldiers died in Southeast Asia, a place unattainable for most friends and families. The memorial itself was revolutionary. It consists of two long granite walls meeting at one end to form a V-shape. The terrain slopes down as one approaches the nexus of the V, and the names of every individual who died is etched into the granite. Previous war memorials often named only generals and commanding officers, according to rank; here, names were listed according to date of death. In its way, it resembles a traditional granite tombstone. The plans were met with disdain when first revealed, many veterans preferring something more conventional. In fact, a representational statue was later added to the memorial. However, to the surprise of almost everyone, the Vietnam Veterans Memorial was astoundingly successful. It was designed to allow people to find the names of their beloved on the stone; people did rubbings of those names. But soon people began to interact with the monument in other ways. Old friends left tokens of esteem such as 'dog tags' (metal identification numbers), as well as items such as cigarettes and beer. Soon it became a national phenomenon, so much so that the National Park Service put in place a program to gather and preserve the offerings.

Various large-scale tragic events brought attention to the abovementioned practice both nationally and internationally. Some people point to the outpouring of emotion in London after the death of Lady Diana in Paris; others to New York after September 11, 2001, and the attacks on the New York World Trade Center, as early, possibly foundational events that established the marking of sudden, violent death in this public, ritualistic way. There are many precedents, however, including roadside memorials indicating automobile fatalities. Items, most often crosses, are often seen in this capacity and seem to be traceable to the Spanish Catholic influence in what is now the American Southwest (Everett 2002). In addition, roadside crosses are known in many European countries, including Ireland and Greece, though these are usually government-sponsored and serve different purposes. Nevertheless, we can say that folk traditions deriving from European and indigenous practices in North America led to the spread of informal marking of tragic death sites with memorabilia, often religious, such as crosses, and this in turn has influenced a tradition, widely dispersed by media, of ritually responding to certain deaths in a very public, spectacular manner. Now international in scope, spontaneous shrines have become a standard public response. Nevertheless, they remain unusual – they call attention to themselves; the communication is immediately understood (someone died here, in a bad way); and as public and visual as they are, they are also a medium for personal grief and the expression of private thoughts.

Of course, the spontaneous shrine, as we know it today, commemorates death. However, as we have seen, it corresponds to a certain kind of death – death which is public (of a public figure, or which takes place in public space, or which is the result of some controversial social situation). These deaths are usually untimely and often violent – shootings, car collisions, police brutality, gang fighting, and so on. Usually there is a sense that the deaths need not have happened – they are the results of drunk driving, political extremism, drug overdoses, poor city design, and so on. In other words, they were preventable, and the cause of death corresponds to a social problem, an issue that could be addressed. Thus, the spontaneous shrines, while memorialising a specific individual or individuals, also comment on a social issue. Importantly, they suggest ways of viewing that issue, in the context of these particular deaths. A teenager's high school jacket at a scene of an fatal accident where residents have been requesting traffic lights be installed; a letter written by a grief-stricken daughter to her father shot by paramilitaries in Northern Ireland and posted for all the world to see; a 'ghost bike' (a bicycle painted white and left at the place where a bicyclist was killed by a motorist) – all these and more are public statements asking, and causing, a public audience to pressure a local government into action, to consider their attitudes towards war, or to call attention to the problem of drinking and driving.

Spontaneous shrines both commemorate the dead but also speak to social and political issues, to a greater or lesser degree on a continuum from commemoration to social commentary. Nevertheless, both dynamics are usually evident in most examples. Because of the social nature of the reasons for the deaths, the ritual response is also public. Certainly, these individuals have been privately mourned and their deaths attended to privately by family and friends, according to their own traditions. But the spontaneous shrine coexists with these. It serves a different purpose. It does different work.

In the mass-mediated world on the 21st century, we have seen the rise internationally of this ritualized response to horrific events – in Great Britain, as we have seen; in Russia after a school shooting; in Spain, after the commuter train bombings of March 11, 2004. In other countries, including Ireland and Romania, the local culture resists this international trend. Still, we can view these phenomena as a mass cultural, but still popular cultural, movement that allows a secularized, or at least ecumenical, ritual response to a particular type of death, to turn one's private grief into popular public action. That is, due especially to the spectacular nature of the shrines – they are meant to be seen, to catch people's attention – they are commonly depicted in media reports and through these disseminated widely. But they are not the creation of mass media. They are popular in the first sense, meaning 'of the people'. In this sense, we could term them 'folk rituals'; in this case, the terms 'folk' and 'popular' are interchangeable.

In creating spontaneous shrines, people are recapturing control over their death beliefs and mourning customs. In today's cemeteries (in the United States, at least), people are not allowed to leave objects or plant flowers. Mourning is tightly regulated. The teddy bears one sees on the site of a driving collision are forbidden in the cemetery. With spontaneous shrines, people decide for themselves what is appropriate and what is acceptable.

Moreover, in the United States, the burial site has gone from the home to the church to the suburban cemetery-as-park. Spontaneous shrines, which are analogous to graves in many ways, are found in the heart of daily life. Curbsides, parking lots, apartment buildings – where a death occurred, people seize proprietorship of space both public and private and place their non-condoned mourning materials there.

As for belief, as mentioned above, people often have suggested to me that this place where the loved one died is important because that is where they were last alive. This is where they took leave of this world. It has also been suggested to me that, in the context of Christianity, as the doctrine of the resurrection of the body in the final days recedes, popular emphasis has shifted to the place of death, not the place of interment. In all these ways, we can see that the spontaneous shrines are proactive, and performative, popular developments.

Performative commemoratives

The linguist John L. Austin (1962) has given us a concept of performativity based on his research on speech acts he terms 'performative utterances'. He describes performative utterances as speech acts that, in being said, have direct social effects, that it is the act of saying them that causes the desired condition to come into being. We often find examples of performative utterances in various rites of passage, as when one takes marriage vows, or swears to tell the truth in a court of law, or when a president is inaugurated. 'I now pronounce you . . .' for instance, or 'I do solemnly swear . . .' are situations in which the saying is the doing. Thus, Austin has expanded the idea of performativity from referring to actions or genres of performance, to referring to actions – here utterances – that cause a direct change in status or the social milieu.

I would suggest that very often, public memorializations of death are performative in a similar fashion. That is to say, rarely are such public displays restricted to expressions of grief alone. In addition, they reference a social issue, a social problem, and they take an explicit or implicit attitude towards it. Beyond the spontaneous shrines, for instance, we see the dead memorialized in war protests, in the AIDS Memorial Quilt project, and in Holocaust memorials, where names are read aloud or combat boots displayed publicly; where individuals who died of a disease are memorialized in individual pieces of cloth but the resulting, enormous quilt is displayed to show the magnitude of the problem; where individuals lost to genocide are remembered by engraved cobblestones in roadways. In all these cases, the memorialization of individuals is a means of personalising a larger, more abstract or distant situation. This personalization is also found in spontaneous shrines. In Northern Ireland, a place plagued until recently by sectarian killings, the spontaneous shrines feature notes to the deceased from brokenhearted family members and cast the deceased in domestic terms: 'Daddy' or 'Grandpa' (Santino 2001:82). The paramilitary organizations are not addressed, neither is vengeance called for. The critique of the paramilitary discourse and ethos is implicit: How does killing my father help me or this land?

In these and similar cases, there is a persuasive element within the memorials. This war is questionable; we have to do something about AIDS; demonizing a race is never acceptable. Real people, with names and loved ones, die as a result of these situations, and we can do something about them. It is this intention, implicit within public memorializations of death, that I see as performative. The intention is to cause a change in the minds and hearts of spectators, and through them, society at large. I would categorize spontaneous shrines and other public memorializations of death as 'performative commemoratives', extending Austin's idea from verbal utterances to public performances (Santino 2006:5–15). As such, spontaneous shrines are always political. That is, they are involved in social issues, they take a position on them, and they are meant to persuade others to that position. In Northern Ireland, mentions of the paramilitary groups responsible for the deaths are virtually nonexistent in the actual shrine materials. However, these same materials cast the deceased as innocent victims; they are described in domestic terms rather than militaristic; prayers for peace and an end to violence accompany obituaries of the deceased. There is no overt condemnation of paramilitary groups, or religious/ethnic groups, but the point is made: The paramilitary actions are destroying families, and by extension, society.

One may also see in these phenomena a kind of emergent ritual. The spontaneous shrines correspond to a certain type of death; they provide a particular ritual response to particular conditions where there were none before. Symbolic actions which are considered by the participants to be instrumental – socially effective rather than entirely expressive or only symbolic – resemble more structured, traditional ritual in that they too are symbolic actions considered instrumental by believers, and are felt to have social (as well as spiritual) power. Rites of passage show this most directly – there is a change in status from before to after the ritual. With performative commemoratives, the change is a desired one. In this way, I see many public actions as 'ritualesque' (Santino 2011). Due to the public nature of these phenomena, they rely on a vocabulary of visual and auditory symbolism that is shared with more formal ritual. Here I am looking specifically at events which have as an explicit goal the addressing of a public issue with the purpose of rousing spectators to take some action or to adopt the point of view being expressed.

Due to their unofficial nature, spontaneous shrines can be viewed as an emergent folk tradition. Others might prefer to view them as an example of popular culture, if by 'popular culture' we mean actual traditions of people acting, rather than the mass media. In either case, spontaneous shrines are a fact of contemporary life. The public understands their communication; they represent death memorialization as people desire it. This may evoke sneers or disapproval in many quarters – often, the shrines look like trash scattered on the ground – but at a time when formal death rituals are increasingly regulated, spontaneous shrines show people reclaiming agency over their own traditions. Also, people reclaim public and commercial space – whether it is on the side of the highway or in the McDonald's parking lot. There is an authenticity displayed. Often, as in the case of the *Charlie Hebdo* example I opened this chapter with, the experience of seeing, reading, participating in these created environments can be quite moving, even overwhelming. The grief is there, along with moral outrage over deaths that didn't need to happen. When Princess Diana died after being pursued by paparazzi in Paris, the resulting outpouring of grief, as expressed in vast shrines in London, forced the Queen to break protocol and change her and her family's public behaviour. Spontaneous shrines represent the voice of the people, as expressed through this emergent tradition of personal grief and public censure; of personal beliefs and communal action. When I was viewing the *Charlie Hebdo* site, I was, as I stated, quite moved by it. Intellectually, I noted the use of pencils as a primary symbol, and thought of how each such event has its own particularity. Particular symbols, event-specific symbols, often emerge and lend specificity to the site. The emphasis is on *liberté d'expression*, the multitude of tributes, the heterogeneity of them: some emphasized Judaism, others mourned the Muslim police officer who was slain trying to help; a display of the creativity of all the different tributes at stake. Each, in its own way, represented an understanding of the participant's relationship to the deceased and to the event. And, while not everyone appreciates the appearance of these (materials are piled in layers and are not arranged in an orderly way; walls, posts, stairways, all are adorned), I myself, along with many others, find them very communicative, very emotional, very moving. While they are the net result of numerous individual actions, they are a true communal creation. There is a range of ideas expressed, but the range is consistent with a condemnation of violence as a means to an end, and a higher value placed on freedom of expression than on a sensitivity to a group's religion. This latter leads to the unspoken question of anti-Muslim sentiment and Islamophobia, which is unfortunately beyond the scope of this chapter.

While I viewed these materials, and was so moved by them, I found myself think of Carnival. An unlikely connection, I realized, but there are similarities in that Carnival allows for the expression of otherwise taboo social critiques. Still, spontaneous shrines, while involving ritual actions, are largely material culture, and Carnival is a performance genre. And Carnival, despite its social critique and political parody, is a joyous celebration (with some exceptions; see Ladurie 1979; Bercé 1977.) However, carnival has been defined as an excess, or overabundance of signifiers, with its costumes, music, processions, and so on. And what was overwhelming about the *Charlui Hebdo* shrine (and I dare say, the 9/11 and Princess Diana shrines) was the sheer enormity of it, the multitudinousness of it. All those symbolic objects, each with its own set of associations, were juxtaposed to others. Still the expression was of grief, not joyful liberation. I thought, though, that perhaps we are witnessing the development of something that might be called 'carnivals of grief' or 'carnivals of grievance'.

I would argue that we are witnessing the increasing use of death memorials as social protest. We see it in the AIDS Memorial Quilt project. We see it in anti-war protests at which deceased combatants are individually named, as with a roll call; I have seen public displays countering domestic violence with, again, the display of the names, images, or memorabilia of individual victims. In parts of South America, women carry portraits of their children who have been 'disappeared' by the government'. In all these cases and others, we see the bringing together of personal grief, particular deaths, with public statements of grievance and protest, and of politics. In all cases the intent is to make something happen, to effect change, or to persuade a public to a certain position. In most, if not all, cases the power dynamic is imbalanced – the public displays of grief and grievance are themselves representative of a population lacking direct power to change the conditions of the deaths; often these populations are what Judith Butler (2015) terms 'precarious'. Perhaps the rise of spectacular displays of grieving in protest is related to the mediated nature of contemporary society; perhaps it helps that these reflect both individual but also group sentiments – there is (political) strength in numbers.

Spontaneous shrines are a ubiquitous example. As I have stated, some are more overtly addressed to a social problem than others. A roadside memorial, for instance, may or may not be intended as a warning to motorists by those who maintain it, though in my research I would say it usually is; while a police shooting of an unarmed member of a minority culture will result in a more politically pointed expression of grief and outrage. The *Charlie Hebdo* shrines described at the beginning of this chapter, a result of international terrorism, were equal parts memorialization for the deceased (whom the public did not know personally); outrage at the attacks; declarations of solidarity and nationalism; and condemnation of the perpetrators and their means to their end.

The public memorialization of death is not restricted to the spontaneous shrines. It is seen in phenomena such as the AIDS Memorial Quilt, Holocaust memorials, and anti-war demonstrations. The names of people killed are publicized with the goal persuading the public to a particular point of view – AIDS kills our loved ones; we need to do more about it. This war is wrong; all these people died needlessly (or, inversely, this war is right; don't let these warriors have died in vain). The Holocaust – we must never forget. In all these cases and more, the emphasis of the public displays is more heavily weighted towards the political or social end of the continuum.

While there is often religious symbolism and iconography found in such displays, I argue that these are essentially secular rituals. There are precedents for the shrines, as we have seen, but the concatenation of elements in this particular way has emerged in the late 20th century and continues to evolve in the 21st. Perhaps it is due in part to the spectacular nature of the shrines and memorials referred to above and throughout this chapter – they are visual; they call attention to themselves. As such, they are picked up by media outlets and used to represent reports visually and dramatically. In turn, the widespread distribution of these images on television or the Internet contributes to the diffusion of the custom internationally, in a way not unlike the role print played in earlier societies (Anderson 1991).

Conclusion

Public mourning takes many forms. In this chapter we have examined 'spontaneous shrines' as an emergent ritual. Along with other public displays of grief and grievance, spontaneous shrines combine the memorialization of deceased individuals with a stance on the causes of their deaths. Spontaneous shrines and other public memorials of death seek to directly impact the public, to persuade spectators by framing the deaths as preventable or by condemning the ideologies apparent in the causes of death. These represent, I feel, a true popular culture – not popular culture defined as mass media or corporately controlled entertainment, but popular culture as the actions and behaviours of people asserting agency. Spontaneous shrines are by definition not officially sanctioned, though they may serve as an impetus for further official memorialization. Indeed, spontaneous shrines are often seen on commercial properties such as restaurant parking lots, or on public properties such as national highways or state university campuses. These are not always welcomed. They may be viewed as a deterrent to business. With spontaneous shrines we witness people reclaiming public space and asserting the right to mourn where and how they choose.

Like all symbolic and ritual materials, spontaneous shrines are polysemic. It is fair to say that each individual creates particular meanings for themselves, using culturally traditional paradigms. We make no claim to essentialism in this chapter; spontaneous shrines do not mean any single thing for all people. Nevertheless, we can fairly describe the phenomena as referencing violent and untimely deaths, and serving a dual purpose of mourning and protest (Senie 2006).

References

Anderson, Benedict (1991): *Imagined Communities: Reflections on the Origin and Spread of Nationalism*. London: Verso

Austin, John L. (1962): *How To Do Things With Words*. Cambridge, MA: Harvard University Press.

Bercé, Yves-Marie (1977): *Fête et Révolte: Des Mentalité Populaires de XVIe au XVIIIe Siecle*. Paris: Hacette.

Butler, Judith (2015): *Notes Toward a Performative Theory of Assembly*. Cambridge, MA: Harvard University Press.

Child, Francis James (1882–1898/1965): *The English and Scottish Popular Ballads*. New York: Dover Books.

Everett, Holly (2002): *Roadside Crosses in Contemporary Memorial Culture*. Denton, TX: University of North Texas Press.

Fraenkel, Beatrice (2002): *Les Écrits de Septembre*. Paris: Textuel.

Grider, Sylvia (2001): 'Spontaneous Shrines: A Modern Response to Tragedy and Disaster'. *New Directions in Folklore*, 5. Available online at: http//www.temple.edu/isllc/newfol/shrines.html.

Grider, Sylvia (2006): 'Twelve Aggie Angels: Content Analysis of the Spontaneous Shrines Following the 1999 Bonfire Collapse at Texas A&M University', in Jack Santino (ed.): *Spontaneous Shrines and the Public Memorialization of Death*. New York: Palgrave/Macmillan, pp. 215–232.

Grider, Sylvia (2007): 'Collection and Documentation of Artefacts Associated with Roadside Memorials and Spontaneous Shrines', in Jennifer Clark (ed.): *Roadside Memorials: A Multidisciplinary Approach*. Armidale: EMU Press, pp. 41–55.

Hass, Kristen (1998): *Carried to the Wall: American Memory and the Vietnam Veterans Memorial*. Berkeley, CA: University of California Press.

Kear, Adrian and Deborah Lynn Steinberg (eds.) (1999): *Mourning Diana*. London: Routledge.

Ladurie, Emmanuel Le Roy (1979): *Carnival in Romans*. New York: Braziller.

Margry, Peter J. and Cristina Sánchez-Carretero (eds.) (2011): *Grassroots Memorials: The Politics of Memorializing Traumatic Death*. New York: Berghahn.

Sánchez-Carretero, Cristina (2011): *El Archivo del Duelo*. Madrid: CSIC

Santino, Jack (1986): 'The Folk Assemblage of Autumn: Tradition and Creativity in Halloween Folk Art', in John Michael Vlach and Simon Bronner (eds.): *Folk Art and Art Worlds*. Ann Arbor, MI: UMI Research Press.

Santino, Jack (1992): "Not An Unimportant Failure': Rituals of Death and Politics in Northern Ireland', in Michael McCaughan (ed.): *Displayed in Mortal Light*. Antrim, NI: Antrim Arts Council.

Santino, Jack (2001): *Signs of War and Peace: Social Conflict and the Use of Public Symbols in Northern Ireland*. London: Palgrave/Macmillan.

Santino, Jack (ed.) (2006): *Spontaneous Shrines and the Public Memorialization of Death*. London: Palgrave/Macmillan.

Santino, Jack (2011): 'The Carnivalesque and the Ritualesque'. *Journal of American Folklore*, 124 (491):61–73.

Senie, Harriet F. (2006): 'Mourning in Protest: Spontaneous Memorials and the Sacralization of Public Space', in Jack Santino (ed.): *Spontaneous Shrines and the Public Memorialization of Death*. London: Palgrave/Macmillan, pp. 41–56.

Walter, Tony (ed.) (1999): *The Mourning for Diana*. New York: Berg.

Zeitlin, Steve (2006): 'Oh Did You See the Ashes Come Thickly Falling Down? Poems Posted in the Wake of 9–11', in Jack Santino (ed.): *Spontaneous Shrines and the Public Memorialization of Death*. London: Palgrave/Macmillan, pp. 99–117.

9 Grief in human and companion-animal loss, bonding, and dividual pet-personhood

Douglas J. Davies

Introduction

Who is it who grieves – who experiences sorrow? To answer this apparently simple question is to involve complex issues of both personhood and of loss through death. These will be explored here through two models of identity, one focused on 'the individual' and the other on 'dividual personhood', and through currently influential grief theories, all set within the context of human-pet relationships and the death of those companion animals. By means of a theoretical schema dealing with the interplay of ideas, emotions, values, identity, and destiny this will generate the notion of pet-personhood while also furnishing one sociological approach to the notion of sorrow.

Adopting the familiar anthropological idiom of Claude Lévi-Strauss that certain phenomena are 'good to think', and his allied idea that 'the animal world is . . . thought of in terms of the social world', will allow us to pursue two aspects of grief; one concerning the impact of one human being's death upon a fellow human being, and the other the impact of a pet's death upon its human companion (Lévi-Strauss 1964:81, 89). Certainly, grief can strike hard when someone loses a loved person, and strike hard, too, when someone loses a loved pet, and while many find this parallel entirely understandable, some simply cannot equate human and animal losses. Still, even these people may find some interest in the privileged positions accorded to pets in many individuals' lives and homes, and in how human-animal grief may offer an opportune context in which to ponder human-human grief theories and notions of sorrow. To foster such interests, this chapter will integrate a variety of methods and materials, including a limited amount of social survey data concentrated in section four but relevant throughout the chapter.

Theoretical alignments

Disciplinary interests are, unfortunately, such that many psychological studies of emotions often ignore the issue of grief while studies of grief often ignore the psychology of emotions, a situation rather repeated in sociology. Yet, within life's ordinary complexity, this single term – 'grief' – embraces many points on the wide spectrum of emotions. Similarly, 'grief' attracts an enormous literature on human-to-human loss but relatively little on how the loss of animals impacts upon their associated humans. However, this double background of emotions and grief on the one hand, and the human-human and human-animal grief on the other, sets the scene for this chapter's concern with the pragmatic fact that the death of companion-animals touches the emotions of millions of human beings, and that this carries potential theoretical benefits for critical analysis of grief theories.

Accordingly, after considering key influential theories of grief over human-human loss I will develop a discussion of human-animal loss grounded in terms of personhood and the observation that most contemporary Western theories of grief start from the concept of the individual and of relationships between such individuals. While this seems perfectly 'natural', it is, of course, a perspective deeply shaped by particular cultural pressures. By drawing upon some theoretical ideas derived from different societies, largely but not exclusively 'non-Western', I will propose a different emphasis on grief, one rooted in the concept of dividual and not individual personhood (see Davies 2017:53–78). This relatively unfamiliar notion of dividual or complex personhood will require some explanation, as in the section 'Dividual Grief, Pet-Personhood' below, especially since I want to make dividual the basis of an idea that we might call 'pet-personhood'. This approach has the wider benefit of enhancing how animals are understood and valued as fellow creatures, how they contribute to human identity, and how their loss affects that identity.

Naming relationships

While acknowledging contemporary discourse-correctness over using the terms 'pet' or 'companion animal' I will, for brevity and familiarity's sake, mostly speak of 'pets' and of 'owning' and 'ownership', alert to the importance of respect 'owners' pay to 'pets'. However, this is done while decrying any objectification or subjugation of animals to human wills. This highlights the deep significance reflected in the common notion of pets as family members rather than as property. Moreover, such honorary kinship undergirds our approach to a pet's identity and could, through an analysis of dividuality and the pet-personhood of the 'owner', be taken further than this chapter allows, or than it is in some sociological texts concerning 'animal selves' (Peggs 2012:30–32, 76–78). Donna Haraway, however, has drawn close to dividual notions of what I describe here as pet-personhood when she spoke of 'composing persons' and of 'more than human persons' (Haraway 2016:102, 217). She invoked Marylin Strathern's anthropological work, which, as we will see later, applied to Melanesian situations the notion of 'dividual' or 'divisible' persons initially discussed by MacKim Marriott for 'South Asian theories of the person' (Strathern 1988:348). Both Marriott and Strathern have been influential on my own thinking on personhood, identity, and death (Davies 2017:75–77).

Emotional interactive index

All such discussion of identity involves the complex dynamism of emotions given that ideas of grief are, themselves, embedded in emotion, and since animal companionship exists at a high level of emotional interaction even without verbal 'talk'. Human conversation, utterances, inner monologues, and dialogues are, by partial contrast, all grounded as much in idea-play and imaginative reflection on past and future events as they are in allied moods and emotional flurries. While any or all of these options may be directed towards one's pets, which may often make responsive or initiatory sounds interpreted by humans as auditory communication, it is the emotionally embodied mode of animal behaviours that carries most communicative material. This dynamic emotionality merits emphasis as the look of the eyes, mouth, tongue, teeth, tilt of the head, position of the ears, paws, back-arching, tail and body, together with leaping, walking, body-rubbing, back-lying, and other characteristics attractive to the human owner.

This suggests that some kind of emotional interactive index of pets and persons might be useful when considering human-animal relationships and their intensity, an index, we may assume, that reaches higher than that of gardeners and their plants, though even that assumption cannot be guaranteed. I say this as an avid gardener who often speaks to plants and who, as a cactus fan, has some kind of relationship with especially long-lived specimens. Dan Miller's London ethnography of domestic spaces alluded to one such situation when 'Simon . . . insisted on planting something new right on top of . . . one of his favourite plants . . . that he had cultivated for twelve years . . . when it died . . . [he was] sure that there would be some re-birth' (Miller 2008:51). Indeed, to think like this is to appreciate that the whole world of horticulture 'and tending gardens' awaits deeper analysis in terms of identity, longevity, replacement, and loss, all as part of 'an urge to engage with the natural world' (Bradshaw 2018:20). However, whether with animals or plants, we are seldom far removed from philosophical question of identity, loss, and sorrow.

Emotion transformation process

One means of engaging with these questions in terms of pets can be drawn from a shorthand approach to relating emotions to ideas, values, identity, and destiny (see Davies 2017:5–8, 2019:249–252). This proposes that while the world is full of 'ideas' it is only when an idea becomes pervaded by an emotion that it becomes a 'value'. If such a value then contributes to a person's sense of identity, we may think of it as a belief, albeit with no religious designation. Some such beliefs, however, are appropriated to substantiate a person's sense of destiny and, in that case, it makes sense to speak of religious beliefs. In traditional religious worldviews such destiny factors commonly offer some ultimate status through or beyond death. Still, some do hold ideological or philosophical positions that confer a sense of destiny without any such traditionally religious base. For many in what is often designated as secular societies, the transformation from idea to identity-conferring value accomplishes all that is required within the meaning-making processes of life, and it may well be that the contemporary use of the notion of being 'spiritual', or being 'spiritual but not religious', relates precisely to this position.

'Grief' exemplifies this process, in that we may simply acquire the word when young, but only when we experience emotions of loss does 'grief' becomes a 'value' to us. If, in time, this value becomes part of our sense of identity, then it serves as a belief. For many traditional religious believers, participation in rites often contextualize these 'religious beliefs' to generate a sense of destiny, through various aspects of suffering and death, whether of saviour, saint, or martyr, or in their personal life. Among relevant comments related to such issues, Pittu Laungani and Bill Young have spoken of Westerners as learning 'of death in the abstract' as 'cognitive awareness' but of being kept in that 'distanced' state through professional services and the medicalization of death (Laungani and Young 1997:220). Still, I think they underplay the impact of grief even in such contexts of bereavement. But what of pets and their deaths? For here, too, human companions may experience emotions of loss, especially if an animal has helped constitute something of a person's identity. Some older teenagers, for example, will have grown up alongside a long-lived pet whose death touches them deeply, and it is precisely to account for how companion animals may enter into a person's emergent or ongoing identity that I speak of 'pet-personhood'. In such cases, relationships with a 'pet' takes the word 'pet' into the domain of being a value, and perhaps even further to marking a belief-like element, but whether or not we can speak in terms of 'destiny' is an argument taken up below.

Grief theories: attachment, bonding, and pets

Taking these ideas forward in the light of this volume's accounts of grief and sorrow in their long and complex history, I now pinpoint key elements of Western notions of attachment and loss theories on the one hand (Parkes et al. 1991) and of continuing bonds and narrative theories on the other (Klass and Steffen 2018; Walter 1996). These carry deep complementary relevance for this chapter, and will be carried forward in the section on pet-personhood and grief.

Attachment theory

Attachment theory, albeit often focused on human-human relationships, holds a significant place for pet death because the nature of the relationship between pet and owner is, precisely, one of deep attachment. The aetiology of attachment theory owes a great deal to ideas of animal behaviour and the power of attachment of one creature to another in the process of survival. The adaptive value of attachment is especially obvious for human beings and their evolution given the long duration of infancy that demands extensive parental and community support. The emergence of fond bonding between parent and child, especially in Western thinking between mother and child, has occasioned a great deal of psychological and psychiatric research (Bowlby 1969, 1973, 1980). Similarly the loss of one who has been our succour has been rightly captured in ideas that grief is the price paid for love (Parkes 2006). The ease with which a pet may become a vicarious child cannot be ignored in this context, and not simply in terms of 'love', for the underlying import of protection inherent in a child's dependence upon its parent must not overshadow the longer-term protection that a child may bring to its parent and community workforce. Though in many cultures the old and potentially decrepit need the protection of their adult offspring, we should not ignore the psychological 'protection' and social status that having a child brings both to women and men, something that is highly desired in some Western contexts, too. It is against that background that pet ownership and loss also needs pondering in terms of its own complexity of protection. At one end of a spectrum stands the guard-dog as security against harm, and at the other end the cuddled lapdog feeds a sense of meaningfulness into its adoring carer's life. While 'meaning' is a complex notion, it includes the emotional sense of a life having purpose and practical significance, one form of which lies in a pet – the care and attention given to it and its responsive attitude to its owner (Davies 1984). Nurturing can be its own reward. The death of that pet easily removes one dynamic element in a person's sense of meaning in life, and to their personhood as such. In this sensitive area not many would now dare to agree with that voice from ancient Rome recorded by Plutarch:

> The emperor Augustus once caught sight of some wealthy foreigners in Rome carrying about young monkeys and puppies in their arms and caressing them with a great show of affection. He asked whether women in those countries did not bear children, thus rebuking in truly imperial fashion those who squander upon animals that capacity for love and affection which in the natural order of things should be reserved for our fellow men.
>
> (Plutarch 1960:165)

One British journalist recently touched a certain popular ambivalence in this area noting the extensive social media portrayal of cute pets and how he dressed up his own dog in a Christmas cap, as well as recent complaints made to the Royal Society for the Protection of Animals regarding buskers' dogs being exploited as a means of extracting cash from a sympathetic London public. His conclusion was that 'we ultimately need to live in a mature and humane society where the sight of a dog in a Father Christmas outfit is not considered adorable. Until then it's kind of adorable' (Maher 2018). In fact, dogs are an ordinary daily presence in social media, much more than cats, and this is without any discussion of the darker domain of animals within human sexual fantasy and 'visual perversity', and what that implies for notions of personhood (Malamud 2012:94).

Thinking more positively, theoretically, and within a 21st-century context, when ordinary language talks of being 'attached to', or even being 'devoted to' our pet, it echoes the technical understanding of attachment theory, even though some research shows differences in the nature of the 'affection' shown to pets as opposed to one's children (Bradshaw 2018:98). Still, in such loss contexts, the death of a pet relates to attachment theory's view of loss manifest in the emotions of grief, with the degree of attachment varying from a single person whose pet has been the major focus of daily attention to the loss of a pet within a family context where one individual possesses numerous foci of attention – on other family members, occupation, leisure, and so on. In this, the whole interplay of dependency on the one hand and caregiving on the other is complex (Bradshaw 2018:135). Today, there appears to be an increasing number of single people, whether older or younger adults, who own a pet on which they shower enormous attention, with flourishing commercial enterprises providing varieties of food, clothing, toys, jewellery, and veterinary insurance. So it is that pet death often involves loss following attachment, bringing its own forms of grief, though whether 'sorrow' is applicable here is questionable and will be discussed later.

Continuing bonds

Continuing our descriptive analysis of grief theory reveals a contemporary scene that focuses less on loss in relation to severe attachment and more on continuing bonds that maintain the relation with the departed. Dennis Klass and Edith Maria Steffen (2018) strongly emphasize the paradigm-style shift from attachment-loss theories to the continuing bonds perspective and note the variety of thinkers contributing, sometimes independently, to its emergence. The narrative base of personal reflection has also played a significant part in this general perspective (Walter 1996; Valentine 2008). This shift often reflects the preferences of sociology rather than psychiatry, partly because the latter tends to deal with pathological cases and sociology with ordinary life situations and contexts, as well as memories held of the dead and stories told about them. This ongoing narrative of the dead also applies to pets, with many people able to recall their first pet or those predating their current companion. It is a curiously interesting social fact that contemporary information technology sometimes prompts reminders of usernames with 'name of first pet', assuming its continuing presence in memory.

Continuity is especially telling when choosing a dog of the same breed to replace a dead pet, reaching its extreme in cases of owners spending large sums of money in getting a pet cloned (Bradshaw 2018:61–62). But, even in ordinary 'replacements', there can be a sense of one animal carrying on the identity of its predecessor, even given some temperamental differences. Here continuing bonds are manifest in continuing similarity to an animal. Speaking personally, as time went on, I found the breed similarity between our first Airedale terrier, Angus, and his successor, Luke, involved a complex overlap. Twenty years later I find it hard to differentiate between them unless telling a story of what Angus or Luke once did, thus reinforcing the significance of narrative in separating what is otherwise conflated.

What, then, of the emotions of loss? Even if we speak of active memories of our pets, we also speak of our sense of their loss when they died. Here attachment and loss theory remains significant for feeling sadness at their death and absence, that inward awareness of personal depletion, and sometimes the tears that can be similar for pet or human loss. The human sensorium, that dynamic totality of emotions, is activated at distinctive moments and for distinctive periods, albeit of brief duration. This is not to say that subsequent reflection on the different significance of a dog's or grandparent's death will not lead to major differences even if the immediate impact of loss may be similar.

Attachment critiqued

Having sketched the broad themes of attachment-loss and continuing-narrative bonds it is also important to consider contemporary criticism of attachment theory drawn not from the death studies but child-rearing practices. While significant in itself this also reinforces what I will say about dividual or complex personhood in relation to grief, for the anthropological materials informing these notions offer their own valuable criticism of an overly Westernized notion of the radically individualized self. This is especially important because one significant development in social scientific studies of attachment theory within human socialization criticizes just this individualist approach as 'a theory that has become so boxed in by its own predetermined concepts that its practitioners do not ask critical questions about the validity of these concepts' (Quinn 2013:233). Further openness to diverse experiential forms of human attachment as advocated, for example, by Naomi Quinn and Jeanette Marie Mageo (2013) in the context of human socialization, is of considerable value when applied to bereavement and death. By contrast some evolutionary-grounded thinkers have seen the keeping of pets and grieving at their death as an outmoded form of bonding behaviour that might once have aided survival but is now outmoded: 'Somehow evolution has so far failed to connect our conscious ability to conceive of the finality of death with the much more primitive system that generates the distress of separation' (Bradshaw 2018:270).

One earlier stream of sociological research by Basil Bernstein (1971), though now somewhat forgotten, still offers similar creative opportunities in its differentiation between more individualistic and more collectivist modes of identity generation. He distinguished between varieties of 'linguistic codes' that reflected modes of children's socialization in different British social classes and, by extension, patterns of social relationships. He captured a certain middle-class pattern of life in the notion of the 'elaborate' linguistic code that fostered an individualistic and autonomous focus of identity, contrasting it with the 'restricted code' of certain working-class groups, which emphasize shared, communal forms of identity. Theoretically speaking, these descriptions are not far removed from the individual and dividual modes of personhood that I am pursuing within contemporary funerary rites and will detail below. These have not, as far as I am aware, been researched in terms of modes of bereavement and grief, but I include them as supportive of the dividual personhood, soon to be documented below.

Echoing grief

With these thoughts in mind, and almost as a cameo-interlude in our theorizing over major grief theories, I now pinpoint one of many factors arising from pet loss that concerns the interplay of companion animal death and the human response once typified as 'echoing grief' (Davies 1997:172–174, 2017:217–219).

Take the case of two married people whose companionship with each other and their dog was shared for many years, and then the husband dies. He is mourned by the widow, whose feelings reveal some of the features associated with grief's emotional kaleidoscope, yet, at home, she finds a sense of support in talking to the dog and from the dog's responsive and proactive behaviour. In public, she also receives some support from others when walking the dog and engaging in activities once shared when her husband. Then, one day, the dog suddenly dies or, worse still, gets sick, leaving her with the decision of having her 'animal companion' 'put it to sleep'. Then with the pet's death, a double wave of emotion follows, one for the dog, and another for her previously dead and partially mourned husband.

My proposal here is that part of her lifetime bond with her husband was retained in and through their dog. Part of her husband did not 'die' but was retained in her relationship with the dog as well as within her own embodied sense of memory of him. The dog was, in effect, a significant part of both the loss of her attachment to her husband and of her 'continuing bond' with him. It is only now, with the death of 'their' dog that she also loses another significant 'part' of her husband even though, in another sense, her husband is 'retained' as part her widow's dividual personhood with him. Though there is no simplicity in such an existential situation we can still speak of echoing grief, in that the emotions she feels at the death of the dog prompt an echo of the grief she felt when the husband died. Whether 'echo' is the correct word is disputable: what is actually intended is a complex idea seeking to capture and combine and to assume an intensification of emotion occasioned by the dog's death. This case illustrates the value both of attachment-loss and continuing bonds approaches, while also inviting the further perspective now being increasingly introduced into this chapter through the notion of 'dividual grief'. But before focusing directly on this concept, it will be useful to consider some empirical research on pet death in order to provide illustrative materials for the overall personhood dimension of this chapter.

Empirical profiles of pet loss

One research source of particular significance for this chapter lies in Betty J. Carmack and Wendy Packman's account of pet loss. They garner a significant body of existing data on emotional responses to pet loss while also adding their own detailed material on some 33 persons, presumably from the United States, all framed in terms of continuing bonds theory. They highlight the fact that, to date, 'the concept of continuing bonds (CB) has not been labelled as such in the pet bereavement literature'; they do so and add to it the notion of CBE, or continuing bonds expression. This captures their research program of seeking to 'examine and quantify' emotions of pet loss and associated issues of trauma and grief (Carmack and Packman 2011:274–275). Before reviewing some of this material and then their study as a prime example of why I think the continuing bonds approach needs critical analysis, I will sketch some results of an early 1990s project spearheaded by Laura Lee and Martyn Lee, which involved myself in some questionnaire design and analysis on pet loss, in which nearly a thousand self-selected pet owners responded to questionnaires placed in one UK national broadsheet and one dog-focused magazine (Lee and Lee 1992; Davies 1992, 2017:214–222).

Briefly, and with relevance for this chapter, that work reported emotions of loss, presented here as approximate percentages for dog (first number) and cat owners (second number). The emotions in the questionnaire included the following: Sadness (56–47), Relief (44–36), Guilt (28–32), Shock (28–27), Numbness (22–22), Release (6–2); additionally, approximately 70–75% of both dog and cat owners reported a sense of devastation (Lee and Lee 1992:133). Such feelings pinpoint an overall impact on life and its ordinary flow, reflected, for example, in the 10% of owners who contacted their family doctor because of their loss. Of these, some three-quarters of the dog owners, and about half of the cat owners reckoned their doctor was sympathetic, with about 49% of the dog owners and 22% of the cat owners thinking that the doctor had actually helped them. Interestingly some 13% of the dog owners and 18% of cat owners also said they had taken time off work because of the loss. Certainly, in terms of how the loss had affected their way of life, nearly half the dog owners (47%) and just over a third of cat owners (38%) said they had been affected, a difference probably reflecting the role of walking the dog and the difference its death had made to such activity. Also, in terms of life significance, approximately 80% of dog and 75% of cat owners saw the death as a shifting 'chapter' in their life. For both, some three-quarters saw the death as having 'revived memories of previous bereavements, both human and animal', reflecting this chapter's reference to 'echoing grief' (Lee and Lee 1992:134).

In a 234-person subset of the above survey, 92% being female, a significant gender divide in this response, 29% said they were members of a religious group, and 67% were not. Even so, 60% reckoned they believed in an afterlife for humans, 15% did not, and 24% were unsure. That profile was roughly matched by their belief, or not, in an afterlife for animals: 56% believed in one, 15% did not, and 28% were unsure of it. A separate question asked whether they thought that animals have souls: 77% thought they did, 6% did not, and 15% were unsure. These interesting responses invite a variety of interpretations, not least that having a 'soul' symbolizes a certain depth and personal authenticity to a creature. Yet, as in many surveys that reduce complex notions to simply tick-boxes, we observe here that while 77% of owners might regard their pet as 'having a soul' only 56% clearly thought in terms of their having an afterlife, though, in fairness, the ample 28% who were unsure might well accommodate the remainder. Still, these responses probably suggest that 'soul' language may symbolize the depth of a creature and its relationships as much as any property of afterlife. Perhaps this was also reflected, again in the 234-person subset, when people were asked whether they 'thought that people can come back as animals'. Some 15% thought they could do so, 49% did not, but some 35% were unsure; perhaps this also reflects aspects of a person's relationship with an animal that has uncertain qualities of depth and possibility, properties far removed from relating to some 'mere' animal or mechanistic entity. Indeed, relationships take very many forms, often evident in remarkable events relating to pets, some depicted as miraculous (Skiff 2012). Others even referred to séances in which the medium speaks of the dog awaiting the arrival of its owner in the afterlife (Wood 2012:237–239). Carmack and Packman also include material on people who 'had thoughts about being reunited in some way with their animal', citing one person who sensed that 'her cat was 'still in my heart – that's been a revelation to me' (Carmack and Packman 2011:281, 277).

Of many familiar accounts, one known to me personally that has also been published, an 'owner' promised her dog, Holly, at the time of her final visit to the vet's for euthanasia, that 'we would be together again someday'; the woman says that the dog 'continues to inspire me on a daily basis . . . she will always be with me in spirit' (Winton 2013:190–191). In the Lee/Davies survey, some results reflect how long it took respondents to adjust to the pet's death. Winton's quote was written 32 days after Holly's death, while the Lee/Davies survey suggests the following time of adjustment to their loss. Here again percentage rates for dog owners come first and cat owners second. In terms of length of time until 'acceptance of death', owners responded as follows: Days (12–15); Weeks (14–15); Months (42–47); Years (23–27). This, of course, reflects a variety of factors, but the great majority spoke of months, and then of years. Acceptance, of course, is one thing, while ongoing memory is another, and it is that element of 'memory' that I would see as constituting the influence of the pet on or within the sense of personhood of the owner. Carmack and Packman note that 'the most frequently endorsed CDEs about pet death were recalling fond memories (85%), holding onto or using belongings (79%), reminiscing with others (79%), and lessons learned and/or positive influences (76%) (Carmack and Packman 2011:276).

Matters of identity and relationship pervade all these issues and involve issues such as pet funerals, pet crematoria, and cemeteries now found across the United Kingdom with appropriate facilities for owners to bring their pets and be treated with suitable sympathy (Davies 2017:209–212). These facilities should now, perhaps, be added to the growing notion of 'deathscapes', a concept that has, hitherto, tended to be restricted to human remains (Maddrell and Sidaway 2010). These issues of pet death, funerals, and grief move us towards the notion of pet-personhood, where the pet seems to have become partly internalized and helps constitute the human companion's identity.

And this, crucially, brings me to my analysis of Carmack and Packman and this chapter's concern with pet-personhood. For their chapter offers a prime example of the unquestioned assumption of the 'individual' a priori in understanding personhood. They follow the conventional 'Western' assumption of the individual and individual relationships underlying attachment theory even as they move to a strong preference for continuing bond theory; abandoning the strong emphasis on the 'loss' element in attachment and loss theorizing in the process. My theoretical proposition would be to encourage the further theoretical shift to dividual, complex, or composite personhood to arrive at the dividually rooted notion of pet-personhood to which we now, finally, turn.

Dividual grief, pet-personhood

In advocating the rationale, provenance, and value of the notion of dividuality as a framework for the notion of pet-personhood, we begin with McKim Marriott's original anthropological work in India. He argued that an in-depth understanding of Indian-rooted societies needed to start not from the concept of the individual, but what he called 'dividual personhood' (Marriott 1976). This will appear strange to many Western-based thinkers for whom *the* individual and individualism lies at the root of much philosophy, theology, and social science (see Allport 1950). Dividual personhood, by contrast, locates its foundational dynamics in the complex integration of interpersonal relationships of family, wider kin-group, village, community, or other associations, all now cohering within a person's composite identity. Other anthropologists, including Marylin Strathern (1988), Sabine Hess (2006), Mark Mosco (2010), and Benjamin Smith (2016) have developed this approach for other parts of the world. Arnar Arnason (2012), too, has amply criticized the undue emphasis placed on relationships *between* the roles people are reckoned to occupy, rather than how relationships enter into the very nature of a person. In Strathern's words: 'Persons are frequently constructed as the plural and composite site of the relationships that produced them' (Strathern 1988:13). The stress lies less on the relationships *between* persons and more on the dynamic presence and effect of those relationships *within* a person. Though apparently slight, this change of emphasis not only carries a significant shift in itself but also has consequences for other issues, such as how we think about memory or grief. Even our manner of speech concerning these perspectives is instructive. The individualist stance, for example, leads us to speak of our having a memory *of* someone, or of grieving *for* someone, with the stress lying on one individual's thoughts about or emotions concerning another individual. While, on one, common sense level this seems obvious, on another it is not, for the dividualist perspective has 'the other' already built into someone's personhood. This carries consequences that are far beyond this chapter for how we analyze both memory and grief: in essence 'memory of' another is its own kind of self-reflected narrative.

Here my consideration of dividual personhood allows much greater purchase for the concept of embodiment, especially in the form of 'pet-personhood', a term I have alluded to elsewhere but expand on in this chapter (Davies 2017). Here, we can return to our opening caveats on the notions of ownership and companionship for, in pet-personhood the emphasis falls neither on ownership nor yet on the nature of a relationship between human and animal – as valuable as each is – but on the significance of the animal within the identity of the 'owner'. The pet has become part of the human self: in technical terms one might say that ontology has changed. When English cultural convention speaks of someone as a 'dog person' or a 'cat person' it approximates to this notion of pets within dividual personhood. 'Dog person' depicts an internalized phenomenon involving an underlying affinity towards the animal that develops in and through the time they spend together as well as through their mutual behaviours.

One of Marriott's technical terms furthers this analysis. It concerns 'substance codes', certain entities or phenomena that enter into identity-formation, with 'dividual persons' being 'always composites of the substance codes that they take in' (Marriott 1976:111). Here I propose that pets constitute their own substance code and can be identified as such through the tactile, auditory, visual, and olfactory stimuli of the dog towards its owner, all frequently aligned with affectionate care and discussed earlier. One remarkable 1891 article in the once popular *Strand Magazine* described the 'admirable qualities' of dogs as 'frank, friendly, and faithful', despite the article being devoted to cats and their relatively recent popularity in England (Cobban 1891:131). The notion of substance codes is valuable in many ways, not least for those currently fostering the notions of 'lived experience' and 'material culture', for an animal companion is part of one's lived experience of the material culture of pet spas, from food and clothing to cleaning up excrement deposited in public places.

Pet-personhood, then, betokens a form of dividual, composite, or complex personhood involving a transformed incorporation of an animal within human identity as such. And this bears consequences for pet death. Just as human personhood can come to exist dividually, as 'another person' becomes part of oneself, with that person's death involving a potentially seismic reaction within the dividuality of the griever, so too can this be the case with the death of a pet. Pet death causes emotional waves within pet-personhood. In other words, both a human bereaved of another human and a human experiencing the death of a pet expereince some degree of inner transformation of identity. Quite a different question, albeit not pursued here, is whether domestication of an animal is its own form of 'dividuality' for that animal.

Certainly, pet loss involves a change in the owner and may influence many emotional dimensions, not least that of all trust, notably in the case of canine companionship. One eminent anthropologist proposed that 'everyone is affected by the quality of trust around him or her', and while she spoke largely of humans this also applies, for example, to dogs (Douglas 1986:1; see Fukuyama 1996). While the notion of unconditional love is frequently invoked for the attitude of many dog owners to their companion-animal, much as of a mother to her child, the notion of trust should not be ignored. The nature of human and companion-animal relationships is extensively dependent upon what we so easily describe as trust. To lose a trusted companion is to involve a depletion of dividual personhood. Potential anthropomorphism and extrapolation of animal companionship to human and social domains cannot be ignored in all this and can, indeed, prompt wider creative ideas as, for example, between trust and betrayal, for we might argue that trust assumes the absence of betrayal or even the potential for betrayal. And since it is highly likely that a certain level of social self-consciousness is demanded before betrayal is even possible, I assume that a dog cannot betray its human companion, something that is not the case in the reverse. This betrayal motif is sometimes adopted by people feeling guilty about having their dog 'put down'. They speak of betraying their companion animal, betrayal being one of the foundational social experiences of social life or, in the theoretical terms of this chapter, of intra-inter-personal or dividual living.

Conclusion: deutero-emotion, sorrow and destiny

These considerations of grief, loss, and bonding bring us to the encompassing theme of sorrow, prompting the questions of whether sorrow and grief are similar? Do they belong to the same logical type and bear some family resemblance, and might this differ for human-human as opposed to human-animal relationships? My basic response is negative. Grief and sorrow are not necessarily co-terminus, for reasons grounded in my previous analysis of ideas, emotions, values, identity, and, especially, destiny.

Sorrow floods world literature, touching most of us when a sense of identity depletion and lapse of hope pervades life events. Sorrow's overarching property highlights the oscillating vitality-mortality dynamic embodied in the animated phenomena populating our lives, whether humans, pets, plants, or our own stories. And, indeed, it is story and not narrative that predominates, for story's intimacies touch areas of life that more abstract 'narratives' cannot reach. Moreover, it is here that pets carry a double load of significance. First in their unspoken yet sounded emotions of tactile and visible greeting and presence – with presence being a defining feature of animal companionship and its absence a cause of grief, and second because of Claude Lévi-Strauss' odd idiom of some phenomena being 'good to think'. For companion animals allow us not only 'to think' abstract notions of commitment, devotion, care, and unconditional love, but to experience them during life and in the concomitant loss at their death.

As for being 'good to think', and for pondering the grief-sorrow boundary, let me rehearse one story from my own infancy, first told to me by my father, and still apt for emotional reflection. For Gellert, that most faithful hound of the Welsh Prince Llewellyn, also my father's name, was left at home to guard the prince's baby son. On returning he found the baby's cradle upturned and blood on his dog's jaws. Fearing the worst he took his sword and killed Gellert, only then finding the baby safe, asleep, but near a great wolf that Gellert had vanquished in defence of the child. To this day, we can visit Beddgelert, the eponymous village of Gellert's grave in North Wales and can only but sympathize with Prince Llewellyn's heartache, especially if the tale is told by an ardent dog lover.

Though less mythical, many have their tales to tell, often entwined with family emotions of pet-loss, with grief pivoting around life's influential hopefulness and death's de-spiriting fragility, dynamics that take their own form when framed within dividually understood pet-personhood. This form of personhood, itself a form of the human animal's intrinsic sociability, offers one potential starting point for a sociology of sorrow.

Sorrow is, in this sense, a higher order of culturally conceived emotions of grief. While, theoretically, all emotions are to be understood as the cultural naming of feeling-states (Davies 2011), there is something more to be said about classifying the case of sorrow as a higher order, meta-level, account of emotions. This treats sorrow on the existing model of second-order or deutero-truths evident in ordinary meaning-making processes, as it is exemplified by anthropologist Roy Rappaport in the development of his ideas of 'deutero-learning' (Rappaport

1999:304–312). Such second-order ideas, such as 'fair play', 'human rights' or 'kindness to animals', capture the outcome of implicit, pervasive, and culturally shared experiences with a speech community's members knowing what each term 'means' until, perhaps, asked to provide sharp definitions. For deutero-truths operate as a cultural shorthand allowing many to communicate and engage with each other over essentially complex, and perhaps even undefinable, issues. 'Deutero-truths are assumptions about the nature of things' yet may appear to be 'low in specificity, or are even downright vague' (Rappaport 1999:306). So it may be with sorrow if, in alignment with the idea-emotion-value-identity-destiny schema proposed earlier, sorrow is to be set within the frame of destiny: only destiny-grounded phenomena may occasion sorrow. And perhaps we might take this even further and say that it is only on and through a narrated reflection that sorrow arises. It does not belong in the moment of grief.

Accordingly, if grief at a pet's death falls within the identity boundaries of dividual personhood then, by my proposed approach, it would be grounded in grief. Sorrow is best invoked only when embodied emotion is evoked through the reflective narrative frame of destiny. But, again in terms of the transformation schema, there will be some for whom the impact of a companion animal's loss is so co-constitutive of their sense both of dividual identity and destiny as to invite the category of sorrow.

While much of this is but playing with words to stimulate imaginative analysis, I conclude with the more pragmatic wish to keep both loss and ongoing bond as pertinent idioms of and for the internal dynamics of dividual pet-personhood. Within the theoretical understanding of continuing bonds, the 'loss' of a pet can be interpreted as the relocation of its dynamic influence within the identity of the owner, for dividual personhood involves dynamic change over time, and what may appear as either grief or sorrow at one period of life may not be so at another. Sorrow, even when described in relation to a notion of destiny, is likely to be an ontological variable for even a sense of destiny is also likely to be experienced only periodically and in conducive contexts. In conclusion, our opening question of who grieves and who experiences sorrow depends on those who, at critical times, have their identity shaken or notion of destiny disturbed.

References

Allport, Gordon W. (1950): *The Individual and His Religion*. New York: The Macmillan Company.

Arnason, Arnar (2012): 'Individuals and Relationships: On the Possibilities and Impossibilities of Presence', in Douglas J. Davies and Chang-Won Park (eds.): *Emotion, Identity and Death: Mortality across Disciplines*. Farnham: Ashgate,. pp. 59–70.

Bernstein, Basil (1971): *Class, Codes and Control*. London: Routledge and Kegan Paul.

Bowlby, John (1969): *Attachment*. London: Basic Books

Bowlby, John (1973): *Separation*. London: Basic Books.

Bowlby, John (1980): *Loss; Sadness and Depression*. London: Basic Books

Bradshaw, John (2018): *The Animals among Us: The New Science of Anthrozoology*. London: Penguin Books.

Carmack, Betty J. and Wendy Packman (2011): 'Pet Loss: The Interface of Continuing Bonds Research and Practice', in Robert A. Neimeyer, Darcy Harris, Howard R. Winokuer and Gardon F. Thornton (eds.): *Grief and Bereavement in Contemporary Society*. New York: Routledge, pp. 273–284.

Cobban, J. Maclaren (1891): 'Cats'. *The Strand Magazine*, July-December, pp. 131–140. London: Burleigh Street, Strand.

Davies, Douglas J. (1984): *Meaning and Salvation in Religious Studies*. Leiden: Brill.

Davies, Douglas J. (1992): 'Appendix 1: Pet Loss – The Facts', in Laura Lee and Martyn Lee (eds.): *Absent Friend: Coping with the Loss of a Treasured Pet*. High Wycombe: Henston, pp. 132–135.

Davies, Douglas J. (1997): *Death, Ritual and Belief*. London: Cassell.

Davies, Douglas J. (2011): *Emotion, Identity, and Religion: Hope, Reciprocity and Otherness*. Oxford: Oxford University Press.

Davies, Douglas J. (2017): *Death, Ritual and Belief: The Rhetoric of Funerary Rites* (3rd. Revised Edition). London: Bloomsbury.

Davies, Douglas J. (2019): 'The Death Turn: Interdisciplinarity, Mourning and Material Culture', in Zahra Newby and Ruth E. Touson (eds.): *The Materiality of Mourning: Cross-Disciplinary Perspectives*. London: Routledge, pp. 245–259.

Douglas, Mary (1986): *How Institutions Think*. London: Routledge and Kegan Paul.

Fukuyama, Francis (1996): *Trust, the Social Virtues and the Creation of Prosperity*. London: Penguin Books.

Haraway, Donna J. (2016): *Staying with the Trouble: Making Kin in the Chthulucene*. Durham: Duke University Press.

Hess, Sabine (2006): 'Strathern's Melanesian 'Dividual' and the Christian 'Individual': A Perspective from Vanua Lava, Vanuatu'. *Oceania*, 76 (3):285–296.

Klass, Dennis and Edith Maria Steffen (2018): *Continuing Bonds in Bereavement*. London: Routledge.

Laungani, Pittu and Bill Young (1997): 'Conclusions 1', in Colin Murray Parkes, Pittu Laungani and Bill Young (eds.): *Death and Bereavement across Cultures*. London: Routledge, pp. 218–232.

Lee, Laura and Martyn Lee (eds.) (1992): *Absent Friend: Coping with the Loss of a Treasured Pet*. High Wycombe: Henston.

Lévi-Strauss, Claude (1964): *Totemism*. London: Merlin Press.

Maddrell, Avril and James D. Sidaway (2010): *Deathscapes: Spaces for Death, Dying, Mourning and Remembering*. Farnham: Ashgate.

Maher, Kevin (2018): 'Dressing Up Dogs is Cruel – Also My Mutt is Too Big for My Hoodies'. *The Times*, 2, December, Times 2, p. 3.

Malamud, Randy (2012): *An Introduction to Animals and Visual Culture*. Basingstoke: Palgrave/Macmillan.

Marriott, McKim (1976): 'Hindu transactions: Diversity without dualism', in Bruce Kapferer (ed.), m. In *Transaction and Meaning: Directions in the Anthropology of Exchange and Symbolic Behavior*. Philadelphia: Institute for Study of Human Issues, pp. 109–142.

Miller, Daniel (2008): *The Comfort of Things*. Cambridge: Polity Press.

Mosco, Mark (2010): 'Partible Penitents: Dividual Personhood and Christian Practice in Melanesia and the West'. *Journal of the Royal Anthropological Institute* (New Series), 16:215–240.

Parkes, Colin Murray (2006): *Love and Loss: The Roots of Grief and its Complications*. London: Routledge.

Parkes, Colin Murray, Joan Stevenson-Hinde and Pater Marris (1991): *Attachment across the Life Cycle*. London: Routledge.

Peggs, Kay (2012): *Animals and Sociology*. Basingstoke: Palgrave/Macmillan.

Plutarch (1960): *The Rise and Fall of Athens, Nine Greek Lives*. Harmondsworth: Penguin Books.

Quinn, Naomi (2013): 'Adult Attachment Cross-Culturally: A Reanalysis of the Ifaluk Emotion *Fago*', in Naomi Quinn and Jeanette Marie Mageo (eds.): *Attachment Reconsidered: Cultural Perspectives on a Western Theory*. New York: Palgrave/Macmillan, pp. 215–239.

Quinn, Naomi and Jeanette Marie Mageo (eds.) (2013): *Attachment Reconsidered: Cultural Perspectives on a Western Theory*. New York: Palgrave/Macmillan.

Rappaport, Roy A. (1999): *Ritual and Religion in the Making of Humanity*. Cambridge: Cambridge University Press.

Skiff, Jennifer (2012): *The Divinity of Dogs: True Stories of Miracles Inspired by Man's Best Friend*. London: Hay House.

Smith, Benjamin R. (2016): 'Sorcery and the Dividual in Australia'. *Journal of the Royal Anthropological Institute*, 22 (3):670–687.

Strathern, Marylin (1988): *The Gender of the Gift*. Cambridge: Cambridge University Press.

Valentine, Christine (2008): *Bereavement Narratives: Continuing Bonds in the Twenty-First Century*. London: Routledge.

Walter, Tony (1996): 'Bereavement and Biography'. *Mortality*, 1 (1):7–25.

Winton, Lesley (2013): *Holly the Mahogany Girl*. London: J & H Publications.

Wood, Steve (2012): 'He'll be Waiting for You', in Jennifer Skiff (ed.): *The Divinity of Dogs: True Stories of Miracles Inspired by Man's Best Friend*. London: Hay House, pp. 235–236.

Part IV
Grief and social critique

10 The medicalization of grief

Allan V. Horwitz

Introduction

Medicalization is the process by which traits or conditions become defined and treated as medical problems. The growth of medical jurisdiction is 'one of the most potent transformations of the last half of the twentieth century in the West' (Clarke et al. 2003:161). Although occasional cases of demedicalization exist, such as masturbation or homosexuality, medicalization far more commonly involves the movement of phenomena that were previously seen as nonmedical into medical jurisdiction.

This chapter places the medicalization of grief in the latest version of the American Psychiatric Association's *Diagnostic and Statistical Manual, fifth edition* (DSM-5) in historical and evolutionary context. It begins by outlining an age-old tradition of medical and literary work that recognized the normality of intense suffering after the death of a loved one. It then summarizes a large literature that shows how grief is a naturally selected response that developed over the course of evolution. The chapter then turns to the treatment of grief in the diagnoses of Major Depressive Disorder (MDD) in the DSM-III (1980). The MDD criteria considered all depressive conditions with at least five specific symptoms that endured for two weeks as cases of MDD. However, bereavement was the sole exception to conditions that otherwise met the symptom-based criteria. The DSM-III recognized: 'A full depressive syndrome frequently is a normal reaction to [the death of a loved one]' (American Psychiatric Association 1980:333). The next edition of the DSM specified that even bereaved conditions that in other respects met the criteria for MDD should not be considered as disorders unless they featured especially severe symptoms of 'morbid preoccupation with worthlessness, suicidal ideation, marked functional impairment or psychomotor retardation or prolonged duration' (American Psychiatric Association 1986:222; American Psychiatric Association 1994:327).

The DSM criteria thus embodied the universal realization that patients would not receive a diagnosis of depression if their symptoms were due to what the DSM defined as 'uncomplicated grief'. Yet, they also recognized that – while most bereaved people who would otherwise meet the criteria for MDD do not have mental disorders – in some cases bereavement could 'go wrong' and indicate a disorder. This occurred when the grieving process lasted for at least two months (instead of two weeks) and involved at least one especially severe symptom.

The chapter concludes with a discussion of how the last remaining holdout to the medicalization of distress – grief – finally succumbed to the pressures to treat intense suffering as a medical problem. The latest edition of the DSM, the DSM-5 (American Psychiatric Association 2013), abandoned the bereavement exclusion so that grief is no longer an exception to the MDD criteria. Even bereaved conditions that do not have especially serious symptoms and that endure for two weeks now fit the diagnostic criteria for a depressive disorder. The controversy over the medicalization of grief illuminates some central issues about the dynamics pushing towards an ever-growing tendency for psychiatry to define normal distress as mental pathology, to encourage professional help for natural loss events, and to expand drug treatments to a growing range of experiences. It also suggests a new factor related to medicalization: the fear of the consequences that might stem from *demedicalizing* some condition.

Historical background[1]

Depression is one of the few psychiatric conditions that have been characterized in a consistent manner from the earliest writing of the Hippocratic physicians through the DSM-5 in 2013. In the 5th century BC, the Hippocratics defined the symptoms of what was then called 'melancholia' in a way that is remarkably similar to the current definitions of depression: 'aversion to food, despondency, sleeplessness, irritability, restlessness' (Hippocrates 1923–1931:185).

Hippocratic physicians recognized two distinct ways in which depressive symptoms could emerge. The first was when depressive symptoms were 'with cause' – that is, normal, proportionate responses to serious losses such as the death of intimates, economic reversals, disappointments in attaining valued life goals, and the like. These contextually appropriate symptoms contrasted with conditions that were 'without cause', which either arose in the absence of situations that would normally produce sadness or were of disproportionate magnitude or duration to their provoking causes. This distinction allowed diagnosticians to distinguish normal sadness that is contextually appropriate from depressive mental disorders. Grief was not a singular condition but one of a family of serious losses.

Well before the Hippocratics, in the *Iliad*, Homer (1986, 24:53–56) provided the example of Achilles' unreasonable grief after the death of his friend Patroclus, which he contrasted to normal grief:

> A sane one may endure
> An even dearer loss: a blood brother
> A son; and yet, by heaven having grieved
> And passed through mourning, he will let it go.

People naturally grieve after the death of intimates, but their suffering typically diminishes with the passage of time. In contrast, Achilles' grief was not natural because it persisted for an unreasonable period and he could not 'let it go'. Hence, it was not his symptoms alone that made his condition disordered. Instead, 'if fear or sadness last for a long time it is melancholia' (Hippocrates 1923–1931:263). Natural fear and sadness persist proportionately to their generating context: only symptoms that 'last for a long time' indicate disorder.

Several centuries later, the renowned Greek physician Aretaeus of Cappadocia (ca AD 150–200) elaborated on the distinction between normal and disordered conditions: '(Melancholic) patients are . . . dejected or unreasonably torpid, without any manifest cause; such is the commencement of melancholy. And they also become peevish, dispirited, sleepless, and start up from a disturbed sleep. Unreasonable fear also seizes them' (Aretaeus 2019). This definition shows the importance of social context in definitions of natural grief and other deep states of sadness. The criterion of 'without any manifest cause' differentiated disorders that are 'unreasonable' from natural sadness, indicating how normal conditions are easily misdiagnosed as disorders when symptoms alone are taken into account.

Such Hippocratic-based definitions prevailed for millennia. The most celebrated work on depression, Robert Burton's *Anatomy of Melancholy* (1621/2001), provided a profound distinction between contextually appropriate sadness, which was a ubiquitous aspect of the human condition, and depressive disorder (both of which were called 'melancholy' at the time):

> Melancholy . . . is either in disposition or habit. In disposition, it is that transitory melancholy which goes and comes upon every small occasion of sorrow, need, sickness, trouble, fear, grief, passion, or perturbation of the mind, any manner of care, discontent, or thought, which causeth anguish, dullness, heaviness, and vexation of spirit. . . . And from these melancholy dispositions, no man living is free. . . . Melancholy, in this sense is the character of mortality.
>
> (Burton 1621/2001:143–144)

In contrast to such natural melancholic feelings that arise after losses such as the death of an intimate, which are the 'character of mortality', melancholic disorders arise 'without any apparent occasion'. Burton also emphasized how the normal response to deaths of intimates need not be mild but often reached intense extremes: 'This is so grievous a torment for the time, that it takes away their appetite, desire of life, extinguisheth all delights, it causeth deep sighs and groans, tears, exclamations . . . howling, roaring, many bitter pangs . . . brave discreet men otherwise oftentimes forget themselves, and weep like children many months together' (Burton 1621/2001:358–359).

William Shakespeare's play *Hamlet*, which was written shortly before Burton's work, comparably notes how grief following the death of a loved one is natural. Hamlet's uncle, now the king, makes a classic Hippocratic distinction between normal and unnatural grief. After Hamlet's father dies his mother marries her dead husband's brother, Claudius, who becomes the new king. Claudius tries to convince Hamlet that grief is normal: 'Tis sweet and commendable in your nature,

Hamlet/To give these mourning duties to your father./But you must know your father lost a father,/That father lost his, and the survivor bound/In filial obligation for some term/To do obsequious sorrow'. Yet, the king also notes how natural grieving can 'go wrong', as in Hamlet's unnatural mourning: 'But to persever/In obstinate condolement is a course/Of impious stubbornness. 'Tis unmanly grief/ It shows a will most incorrect to heaven' (Shakespeare 1601/1988, 1.2:87–95). Hamlet's 'persever[ing]' grief is a sign that his enduring preoccupation with his father's death seems to be unmoored from its context and so is unnatural rather than expectable. Unlike normal grief, prolonged bereavement can indicate the presence of a mental disorder.

Three centuries later, Sigmund Freud (1917/1957:238) made a comparable distinction between normal grief and melancholic disorder:

> Although grief involves grave departures from the normal attitude to life, it never occurs to us to regard it as a morbid condition and hand the mourner over to medical treatment. We rest assured that after a lapse of time it will be overcome, and we look upon any interference with it as inadvisable or even harmful.

While Freud asserted that symptoms associated with mourning are both intense and 'grave departures from the normal', he nevertheless insisted that grief is not a 'morbid' condition and insisted that suffering was a natural part of responding to the death of an intimate. Indeed, he emphasized that it would 'never occur to us' to provide medical treatment to the bereaved. Freud stressed that grief of even the deepest intensity is self-healing, so that with time the mourner returns to a normal psychological state. Medical intervention, he suggested, could actually harm the grieving person through interfering with natural healing processes.

Diagnostic criteria in psychiatric manuals before the DSM-III also separated contextually appropriate grief from depressive disorders. For example, the DSM-II defined depressive neurosis as follows: 'This disorder is manifested by an excessive reaction of depression due to an internal conflict or to an identifiable event such as the loss of a love object or cherished possession' (APA 1968:25). This definition recognized that psychiatrists should not consider as mental disorders reactions such as 'the loss of a love object' that are proportionate and not 'excessive' to their contexts. Thus, an unbroken stream of thought from the Hippocratics through the DSM-II considered grief to be a normal response to loss, not a mental disorder, unless it was particularly severe or prolonged. Evolutionary studies provide good biological reasons for why grief after the death of an intimate is a natural response.

Evolutionary considerations

Most studies of medicalization bracket the question of what is 'really' a disease, instead examining the empirical processes through which a problem becomes defined as such (Conrad 1992). In the case of grief, however, strong justifications exist for why uncomplicated grief is, in fact, natural and not disordered. One reason, noted above, is that medical and literary writings for thousands of years have perennially distinguished proportionate, non-disordered grief from pathological grief that is more severe or persistent than its context warrants. Evolutionary studies provide a second source of validation for treating grief as a natural, non-pathological phenomenon. Three lines of evidence – loss responses among human and nonhuman primates, human infant loss responses that occur developmentally prior to socialization into a culture's emotional scripts, and the cross-cultural universality of loss responses – all indicate that grief is a biologically designed response to the death of intimates.

Nonhuman primates show a clear resemblance to humans in the way they respond to loss. Darwin noted how apes and humans show similar facial expressions in situations that are associated with sadness, including elevated eyebrows, drooping eyelids, horizontal wrinkles across the forehead, and an outward extension and drawing down of the lips (Darwin 1872/1998). In addition, grieving apes, like humans, show decreased locomotor activity, agitation, slouched or fetal-like posture, cessation of play behaviour, and social withdrawal. This indicates that humans inherited a naturally selected response to the death of an intimate from our evolutionary ancestors.

Another source of evidence that grief is biologically designed stems from studies of human infants. The British child psychiatrist John Bowlby conducted the most influential studies, which demonstrated how sadness naturally arises in presocialized infants after the loss of close attachments. Bowlby showed how infants are designed to need strong attachments and that they develop certain types of sadness responses as coping mechanisms when they are separated from their primary caregivers. He observed that healthy infants who are taken from their mothers initially reacted by crying and displaying other expressions of despair. They protested the separation and searched for their mothers. These responses usually evoked sympathy from the mothers, who responded by attending to their infants' needs. When separations were prolonged, however, the infants withdrew and became inactive and apathetic, similar to the symptoms of intense adult loss responses. Prolonged separations resulted in a state of detachment in which young children ceased to respond to parental figures even after they were restored to their lives. Sadness and grief that develops after losses of these relationships thus seem to be aspects of normal, presocialized human nature. When these losses are prolonged and without compensating remedies, however, they can lead to responses that go beyond normal sadness to become depressive disorders (Bowlby 1969/1982).

A third line of evidence showing that grief is not pathological is that the capacity for intense sadness in response to loss appears to be found in all human groups. Darwin was perhaps the first to comment on the universality of sadness responses: 'The expression of grief due to the contraction of the grief-muscles, is by no means confined to Europeans, but appears to be common to all the races of mankind' (Darwin 1872/1998:185). He provided a description of grief among the Australian aborigines that was comparable to the expression of this emotion among Europeans:

> After prolonged suffering the eyes become dull and lack expression, and are often slightly suffused with tears. The eyebrows not rarely are rendered oblique, which is due to their inner ends being raised. This produces peculiarly-formed wrinkles on the forehead which are very different from those of a simple frown; though in some cases a frown alone may be present. The corners of the mouth are drawn downwards, which is so universally recognized as a sign of being out of spirits, that it is almost proverbial.
>
> (Darwin 1872/1998:177)

Considerable subsequent research confirms Darwin's observations that such expressions, especially the contraction of the muscles at the corners of the mouth, are recognized across cultures as representing grief.

The most important studies stem from psychologist Paul Ekman's research on basic human emotions, including sadness. In particular, to test the universality of emotions, Ekman examined facial expressions because they are less susceptible to cultural influences than are verbal reports of emotions. In one type of study, Ekman asked people to show how their faces would look if they felt sad 'because your child died' (Ekman and Friesen 1971). The resulting facial expressions were photographed. Expressions of sadness in these pictures were marked by eyes that are downcast with drooping or tense upper lids, eyebrows that are drawn together, jaws that are closed or slightly open, and lower lips that are drawn down. The photographs were then shown to people in different cultures, and they were asked to select from among several choices of narratives about the situation that triggered the pictured emotion.

Ekman's results indicate overwhelming agreement among persons in different countries about the emotion each photograph expresses. Very high rates of concurrence, ranging from 73% to 90%, existed across five different cultures (Japan, Brazil, Chile, Argentina, and the United States); the concurrence was even higher within each particular culture in ratings of sadness photographs (Ekman 1973). Another study of ten cultures (Estonia, Germany, Greece, Hong Kong, Italy, Japan, Scotland, Sumatra, Turkey, and the United States) indicated between 76% and 92% agreement on facial expressions of sadness (Ekman et al. 1987).

Studies of nonhuman primates, infants, and diverse cultures all point to a universal, biologically grounded basis for treating grief as a natural emotion. Yet, if this is true, grief must have had some sort of survival value that led it to be naturally selected over the course of evolution. Although no consensus exists about the biological function of grief, the most widely accepted explanation, first proposed by Australian psychiatrist Aubrey Lewis (1934), was that depressive reactions such as grief function as a 'cry for help' that calls attention to needy states and elicits social support. The withdrawal, inhibition, and vegetative aspects of depression serve to communicate inner states to other people so that depressed people attract social support after attachment losses. These signs signal others to draw the suffering individual back into the group. Indeed, intense mobilization of ritual expressions of sympathy universally emerges after bereavement and other serious losses (Archer 1999; Turner 2000).

Evolutionary research also shows that normal grieving processes can 'go wrong' and become pathological (Nesse 2000). Dysfunctional bereavement involving severe and sustained states of despondency without a sufficient situational cause tends to alienate or anger other people and diminish social support, leading to isolation and rejection of the afflicted people. Studies of the medicalization of grief, therefore, have a large and varied body of evidence that distinguishes natural from disordered responses to the death of an intimate. This allows them to go beyond descriptions of the medicalizing process and provides grounds to argue against the medicalization of normal grief.

Grief in the DSM-III

The diagnostic tradition that separated normal sadness from depressive disorder that persisted for millennia was abruptly abandoned when the American Psychiatric Association adopted the DSM-III in 1980. At this time, psychiatry profoundly changed the diagnostic criteria for depression. It used overt symptoms themselves instead of the proportionality of symptoms to their context ('excessive') or the cause of symptoms ('due to an internal conflict or to an identifiable event') to define this condition. The new criteria specified that anyone who displayed five symptoms out of the following nine during a two-week period receives a diagnosis of Major Depression (the five must include either depressed mood or diminished interest or pleasure): (1) depressed mood; (2) diminished interest or pleasure in activities; (3) weight gain or loss or change in appetite; (4) insomnia or hypersomnia (excessive sleep); (5) psychomotor agitation or retardation (slowing down); (6) fatigue or loss of energy; (7) feelings of worthlessness or excessive or inappropriate guilt; (8) diminished ability to think or concentrate or indecisiveness; and (9) recurrent thoughts of death or suicidal ideation or suicide attempt (APA 1980:214).

Nonetheless, the criteria contained one attempt to distinguish normal sadness from depressive disorder. It exempted bereaved people from an MDD diagnosis unless their symptoms were still present after two or three months or were especially severe: 'A full depressive syndrome frequently is a normal reaction to [the death of a loved one] with feelings of depression and such associated symptoms as poor appetite, weight loss, and insomnia' (APA 1980:333). This 'bereavement exclusion' (BE) meant that patients would not receive a diagnosis of depression if their symptoms were due to what the DSM defined as a normal period of bereavement after the death of a loved one, lasting no more than two months and not including any especially serious symptom.

The proximate reason for the bereavement exclusion was the empirical research of an influential member of the DSM-III Task Force on Affective Disorders, Paula Clayton (1972), who found that over 40% of bereaved people met criteria similar to MDD one month after the death of an intimate. Further, Clayton found that after three months, only about 15% of her sample remained seriously depressed. Her results reflect the common intuition that people naturally become intensely sad after a loved one dies as well as Freud's contention that ordinary grief is transient and self-healing.

The DSM-III's bereavement exclusion meant that someone who otherwise met the standards for major depression after the death of a loved one was nevertheless not to be diagnosed with a depressive disorder unless the condition involved prolonged or especially severe symptoms. The DSM-III thus associated normal grief with three essential components: it is context-specific, arising after the death of an intimate; its intensity is roughly proportionate to the importance and centrality to one's life of the lost individual; and it gradually subsides over time as people adjust to their new circumstances and return to psychological and social equilibrium. In contrast, complicated or disordered grief must last at least two months (instead of two weeks) and involve at least one especially severe symptom such as morbid preoccupation with worthlessness, prolonged and marked impairment, or psychomotor retardation (APA 1980:333). The BE, however, raised a fundamental issue in how to separate normal sadness from depressive disorder: Is it a unique exception or, alternatively, a model for all loss-related symptoms of sadness?

Extending the bereavement exclusion?[2]

When the DSM-5 Task Force was developing a new edition of the DSM, it had to consider the status of the bereavement exclusion. In our book *The Loss of Sadness*, my coauthor Jerome C. Wakefield and I argued that bereavement should be a model for all kinds of loss situations, not a unique exemption to the depression criteria. There was no reason for the MDD criteria to limit its contextual exclusion to bereavement. The death of an intimate is not a unique loss but exemplifies symptoms that arise in response to many sorts of losses – for example, the unsought end of a love affair, the news that one's spouse has been unfaithful, the dissolution of a romantic relationship, the failure to achieve one's cherished life goals, the loss of financial resources, or the diagnosis of a serious illness in oneself or a loved one. These stressors could result in depressive symptoms that, like bereavement, could be proportionate to their circumstances and not be disordered. The extant DSM-IV's own definition of mental disorder even used the death of a loved one as an 'example' of 'an expectable and culturally sanctioned response to a particular event', not as the single exclusion (APA 1994:xxi). This characterization explicitly considered bereavement to illustrate a much broader category of 'expectable' reactions to events.

Moreover, a substantial body of empirical research showed that the mental health consequences of uncomplicated bereavements were similar to depressions that stemmed from any kind of loss whether the death of a loved one, divorce, unemployment, or the like but were distinct from complicated depressive conditions that were prolonged or featured especially severe symptoms. Wakefield and his collaborators had conducted a number of empirical studies that showed

that other uncomplicated stress-related losses were virtually identical to uncomplicated bereavement-related losses in terms of symptoms, durations, treatment
histories, and degrees of impairment (e.g., Wakefield et al. 2007). Moreover, all
complicated conditions, whether related to bereavement or to other losses, resem-
bled each other and differed from the uncomplicated group. The critical distinction was not between bereavement and other losses but between uncomplicated
conditions following loss and conditions with especially severe symptoms – such
as suicidal thoughts, marked functional impairment, morbid preoccupation with
worthlessness, or psychotic symptoms – or prolonged duration. There was, that
is, no good reason to single out bereavement as the sole exception to the diagnostic criteria. The logical conclusion seemed to be that the bereavement exclusion
should be extended to cover all kind of losses that were not particularly intense
or prolonged.

Researchers connected to the development of the DSM-5 were attentive to these
findings. One member of the DSM-5 Depression Task Force, prominent psychiatric researcher Kenneth Kendler, used his own data set to test the contention that
bereavement was a model for other stressors. His data replicated the finding that
depression that developed after bereavement was identical to that following other
stressful life events (Kendler et al. 2008). 'The DSM-IV position is not logically
defensible. Either the grief exclusion criterion needs to be eliminated or extended
so that no depression that arises in the setting of adversity would be diagnosable',
Kendler concluded (cited in Moran 2011).

The then-president of the American Psychiatric Association, John Oldham,
similarly noted the similarity of bereavement to other losses:

> [The bereavement exclusion is] very limited; it only applies to a death of a
> spouse or a loved one. Why is that different from a very strong reaction after
> you have had your entire home and possessions wiped out by a tsunami, or
> earthquake, or tornado; or what if you are in financial trouble, or laid off from
> work out of the blue? In any of these situations, the exclusion doesn't apply.
> What we know is that any major stress can activate significant depression in
> people who are at risk for it. It doesn't make sense to differentiate the loss of
> a loved one as understandable grief from equally severe stress and sadness
> after other kinds of loss.
>
> (quoted in Brooks 2012)

For Kendler, Oldham, and other psychiatrists, however, the similarity of grief to
other stressors indicated that the BE should be abandoned, not extended. There
was, that is, no reason to single out grief as an unusual type of loss (e.g., Pies
2014).

To address the critique that the equivalence of grief and other stressors showed
that grief was not unique and so there was no justification for the BE, Wakefield
and collaborators went on to conduct studies that showed an even more striking finding: people who developed uncomplicated depressions after all kinds of
losses were more similar to those who were *not depressed* than those who had

complicated depressive conditions (Wakefield and Schmitz 2012, 2013a, 2013b). Using data gathered at two points of time, they found that individuals with uncomplicated cases have similar recurrence rates (3.4%) to people with no history of depression (1.7%); both groups had far lower rates than those with complicated cases (14.6%). Bereaved people were far more comparable to people who had never been depressed than ones with serious or enduring depressive symptoms.

The similarity of all loss-related depressions that were not especially severe or enduring to the conditions of nondepressed people presented a fundamental challenge to the logic of the depression diagnosis. As commentators since antiquity as well as evolutionary studies beginning with Darwin had recognized, symptoms of sadness after loss were often normal, not pathological. If many people who had enough symptoms to meet diagnostic criteria were, in fact, normal, the basic principle of the symptom-based MDD diagnosis would be undermined.

The DSM-5 work group was thus faced with a stark choice. On the one hand, they could expand the BE to cover all uncomplicated responses to loss-related stressors. On the other hand, they could abolish the exclusion and medicalize grief so that all symptoms meeting the two-week MDD criteria were mental disorders. This was an especially consequential decision because for the past thirty years MDD has been the most common psychiatric conditions, accounting for nearly 40% of outpatient diagnoses (Olfson et al. 2002).

The DSM-5's confusion of normal sadness and depressive disorder

The latest edition of the DSM, the DSM-5, was published in 2013. Its criteria for MDD kept the symptom and duration criteria (presented above) that had remained virtually unchanged since the DSM-III. Yet, the DSM-5 eliminated the bereavement exclusion from the textual criteria for MDD. Instead, the DSM-5 added a note to the text that states:

> Responses to a significant loss (e.g. bereavement, financial ruin, losses from a natural disaster, a serious medical illness or disability) may include the feelings of intense sadness, rumination about the loss, insomnia, poor appetite, and weight loss noted in [the symptom criteria], which may resemble a depressive episode. Although such symptoms may be understandable or considered appropriate to the loss, the presence of a major depressive episode in addition to the normal response to a significant loss should also be carefully considered. This decision inevitably requires the exercise of clinical judgment based on the individual's history and the cultural norms for the expression of distress in the context of loss.

(APA 2013:161)

This note does not contain any diagnostic criteria so that the MDD criteria themselves would incorporate normal as well as disordered grief.

The new stipulation modified the earlier definition in two major ways. First, it does not contain any diagnostic criteria so that grieving people are liable to receive a depressive diagnosis after a two-week, rather than a two-month period, which many experts believed was already far too short (e.g., Kleinman 2012). Second, it no longer required the presence of any especially severe symptom to override the MDD standard. Anyone who has suffered the loss of an intimate and has normal symptoms of grief such as sadness, a loss of pleasure, sleeping and eating problems, and fatigue that last for a two-week period following the death would meet the new criteria.

The committee's decision came at the cost of undermining the intellectual coherence of the DSM itself. Consider the DSM-5's *own* definition of mental disorder:

> A mental disorder is a syndrome characterized by clinically significant disturbance in an individual's cognition, emotion regulation, or behavior that reflects a dysfunction in the psychological, biological, or developmental processes underlying mental functioning. Mental disorders are usually associated with significant distress or disability in social, occupational, or other important activities. An expectable or culturally approved response to a common stressor or loss, such as the death of a loved one, is not a mental disorder.
>
> (APA 2013:20)

This basic distinction between expectable distress and mental disorder uses 'the death of a loved one' to illustrate the *difference* between a painful but normal emotion and a pathological condition that should be medicalized. The removal of the BE thus contradicted the manual's explicitly stated criteria for how to define a mental disorder.

Abandoning the BE also undermines the central logic behind psychiatric diagnosis itself. The point of distinguishing one diagnosis from another is to help specify the causes, courses, outcomes, and treatments of various conditions. Yet, combining expectable depressive symptoms that stem from grief, unemployment, divorce, and the like with those that are without cause does the opposite: it blurs conditions that are environmentally caused and sustained with those stemming from individual predispositions; those that are transient and unlikely to recur with ones that are more enduring; and those that are likely to improve without treatment from those that respond to professional interventions. It makes the MDD criteria, which were already far from homogeneous, extraordinarily heterogeneous.

The decision to remove the BE from the MDD criteria also undermines the as-yet-unrealized assumption that mental disorders will ultimately be found to stem from abnormal brain functioning. As diagnosticians for millennia have recognized, two-week periods of uncomplicated grief represent the way that *normal* brains naturally respond to the death of a loved one. Neuroscientific research that relies on the DSM-5 criteria will hopelessly confound brains that are operating naturally with those that are dysfunctional.

Finally, the DSM-5's abandonment of the BE risks an enormous medicalization when MDD encompasses people who grieve for two weeks. Given that about 40% of the bereaved meet these criteria a month after their loss, a majority of the bereaved likely could be diagnosed with MDD after a two-week period (Clayton 1982). Because nearly everyone will suffer the loss of an intimate at some point in their lives, abandoning the bereavement exclusion renders a majority of the population as liable to a diagnosis of depressive disorder.

The DSM-5 also medicalized grief in a second way that is unrelated to the elimination of the bereavement exclusion. It created a new grief disorder, Persistent Complex Bereavement-Related Disorder (PCBD), listed as a category requiring further study. PCBD would medicalize the nondepressive symptoms of grief, such as yearning for the lost person, being pained by or avoiding reminders of the person, or feeling disbelief that the person is gone, which before DSM-5 had never been subject to disorder diagnosis. The proposed diagnostic criteria specify that if several such symptoms continue for over a year after the loss at an intense level, then the grief reaction is to be considered pathological. Although the logic behind this new category differs from the elimination of the bereavement exclusion, PCBD has the potential to medicalize intense normal grief, even when no depressive symptoms are involved.

Why did the DSM-5 medicalize bereavement?

The elimination of the BE in the DSM-5 had no grounding in good conceptual, empirical, or treatment-related reasons. 'There is no scientific basis', two experts in psychiatric diagnosis conclude, 'for removing the bereavement exclusion from the DSM-5' (Wakefield and First 2012). A leading critic of the DSM-5, psychiatrist Allen Frances, asserted: 'This was a stubbornly misguided decision in the face of universal opposition from clinicians, professional associations and journals, the press, and hundreds of thousands of grievers from all around the world' (Frances 2013:186). Moreover, 'without [the bereavement exclusion] the DSM loses its credibility' (Greenberg 2013:114). What led the DSM-5 to alter the MDD diagnosis and to expand the medicalization of distress in the face of such powerful opposition?

Peter Conrad has argued that in the 21st century the three major 'engines of medicalization' are managed care, consumer self-assessments, and biotechnology, which includes the pharmaceutical industry (Conrad 2005). No evidence exists that the first two factors had anything to do with the medicalization of grief in the DSM-5; no consumer group or managed care organization lobbied to remove the bereavement exclusion. There are stronger grounds for asserting that the interests of drug companies were related to the abandonment of the bereavement exclusion.

The drug industry (and mental health professionals) serves to benefit from the removal of the BE, which has the potential to vastly expand the market for its products (Bandini 2015; Granek 2016). The DSM-5 work group itself believed that expanding drug treatments would serve the interests of grieving people. Eight of the eleven members of the APA committee that recommended the new criteria had financial connections to pharmaceutical companies. The chairman of this group, Jan Fawcett, enthusiastically propounds drug treatments for depression: 'I'm still working at 78 because I love to watch patients who have been depressed for years come to life again. You need those medicines to do that' (Fawcett quoted in Whoriskey 2012).

Proponents of removing the bereavement exclusion argued that it could prevent the bereaved from getting treatment that can help them. They urged diagnosis of the bereaved on the grounds that the benefits of treating people who might be at risk of committing suicide or suffering from other severe consequences far outweighed the costs of eliminating the exclusion. The work group cited psychiatrist Sidney Zisook's study of twenty-two bereaved people that claimed over half of the group who were treated with the antidepressant bupropion improved after two months (Zisook et al. 2001). Yet, this study had no placebo arm and its claimed success rate of a little more than half (13 of 22) did not exceed placebo recovery rates in other studies. Zisook stated: 'I'd rather make the mistake of calling someone depressed who may not be depressed than missing the diagnosis of depression, not treating it, and having that person kill themselves' (Wakefield and First 2012:6).

Yet, these arguments were disingenuous: the preexisting DSM-IV bereavement criteria *already* considered grieving persons with especially severe or impairing symptoms such as suicidal risk as not meeting the exclusion criteria. In addition, although the proponents of the new criteria were genuinely interested in alleviating the suffering that accompanies grief, there is no evidence for the vast majority of people suffering from uncomplicated grief that drugs or psychotherapy are more effective than letting the condition run its natural course (Granek 2016).

There was an arguably even more powerful reason than the expansion of drug treatments for the abandonment of the millennia-old recognition that separated normal grieving processes from mental disorders. The DSM-5's decision seems to be related to a fear of *demedicalizing* a large body of loss-related conditions. A high proportion of people receive psychiatric diagnoses after experiencing common losses of relationships, jobs, health, and the like. Expanding the BE to these situations would restrict medical authority over an extremely common and wide-ranging group of distressing conditions. The BE recognized that one common loss was not pathological but extending this logic could have led to a major decline in the number of people who meet MDD diagnostic criteria. Given that MDD is by far the most common psychiatric diagnosis, this could have meant a substantial loss of clients and shrunken psychiatry's range of authority.

Extending the bereavement exclusion, therefore, threatened the client base of mental health treatment as well as the justification for medical authority over distress resulting from common types of losses. The evidence forced the committee to accept that bereavement was equivalent to other losses, but they seemed to have no choice but to abandon the exclusion in order to preserve psychiatry's range of authority. The cost of demedicalization and accompanying loss of legitimacy was too high a price to pay for the greater validity and credibility of psychiatric diagnoses that expanding the BE would have brought about.

Conclusion

The distinction between normal sadness and depressive disorder has been part of Western medicine since the earliest recorded documents. Only in recent times has the distinction been greatly eroded and become in danger of being substantially lost. Even the medicalized DSM manuals before the DSM-5 recognized that humans naturally grieve after the death of a loved one. While such responses often fulfil the criteria for a depressive mental disorder in the short run, normal grief naturally dissipates with the passage of time so that it is unwise to make a depressive diagnosis in the absence of an extended period of watchful waiting. A substantial body of recent evidence showed that grief is a model for, not an exception to, how humans respond to losses of all sorts. Yet, in contrast to the otherwise universal recognition that people naturally become sad after a great variety of losses, the DSM-5 now diagnoses as mental disorders grief that meets its symptomatic criteria after just a two-week period. It ignores the vast amount of research showing that most people who develop symptoms of depression after a loss are not disordered but experiencing contextually appropriate sadness.

The now abandoned bereavement exclusion recognized that, while most grieving – even among people who temporarily meet criteria for MDD – is normal, some grieving processes indicate that something has gone wrong with the loss response. Such dysfunction-caused conditions tend to feature enduring and/ or especially severe symptoms. As the BE recognized, they should be viewed as legitimate mental disorders that fall within the domain of psychiatric treatment.

Although the permanency of the loss associated with grief distinguishes it from most other losses, grief need be no different in principle from intense sadness that arises, for example, after the unsought end of a love affair, the news that one's spouse has been unfaithful, the dissolution of a romantic relationship, the failure to achieve one's cherished life goals, the loss of financial resources, or the diagnosis of a serious illness in oneself or a loved one. Indeed, the DSM's own general definition of mental disorder maintains that 'an expectable or culturally approved response to a common stressor or less, such as the death of a loved one, is not a mental disorder' (APA 2013:20). Yet, emotionally painful responses to other particular loss events such as marital, romantic, health, or financial reversals plainly can be just as 'expectable or culturally approved' as those to bereavement, and should fall under the definition's exclusion as well. Instead of recognizing this, the DSM-5's criteria for MDD eliminated even the narrow exception carved out for bereavement.

In the name of easing distress, psychiatry would medicalize millions of people and arguably interfere with natural healing processes. In medicalizing grief, the DSM-5 might have overreached; time will tell if this affront to science, empirical evidence, and intellectual coherence, not to mention common sense, will help erode the profession's credibility as the official social arbiter of what normality and abnormality are. Yet, at present, medicalization has such great cultural credibility that it is quite possible its range will extend to encompass even such natural phenomena as grief.

Notes

1 This section and the following one are adopted from Horwitz and Wakefield (2007). Used with permission of the publisher.
2 This section and the following one are adopted from Wakefield and Horwitz (2016). Used with permission of the publisher.

References

American Psychiatric Association (1968): *Diagnostic and Statistical Manual of Mental Disorders* (2nd Edition.). Washington, DC: American Psychological Association.

American Psychiatric Association (1980): *Diagnostic and Statistical Manual of Mental Disorders* (3rd Edition.). Washington, DC: American Psychological Association.

American Psychiatric Association (1986): *Diagnostic and Statistical Manual of Mental Disorders* (3rd Revised Edition). Washington, DC: American Psychological Association.

American Psychiatric Association (1994): *Diagnostic and Statistical Manual of Mental Disorders* (4th Edition). Washington, DC: American Psychological Association.

American Psychiatric Association (2013): *Diagnostic and Statistical Manual of Mental Disorders* (5th Edition.). Washington, DC: Author.

Archer, John (1999): *The Nature of Grief: The Evolution and Psychology of Reactions to Loss*. New York: Routledge.

Aretaeus (2019): *Causes and Symptoms of Chronic Diseases*. Available online at: http://perseus.uchicago.edu/perseus-cgi/citequery3.pl?dbname=GreekFeb2011&getid=1&query=Aret.%20SC%201.6.

Bandini, Julia (2015): 'The Medicalisation of Bereavement: (Ab)normal Grief in the DSM-5'. *Death Studies*, 39:347–352.

Bowlby, John (1969/1982): *Attachment and Loss: Volume 1, Attachment*. New York: Basic Books.

Brooks, Megan (2012): 'Lancet Weighs in on DSM-5 Bereavement Exclusion'. *Family Centered Practice*. Available online at: www.scoop.it/t/family-centred-care-practice/p/1228990412/2012/02/17/lancetweighs-in-on-dsm-5-bereavement-exclusion.

Burton, Robert (1621/2001): *The Anatomy of Melancholy*. New York: New York Review of Books.

Clarke, Adele, Janet K. Shim, Laura Mamo, Jennifer R. Fosket and Jennifer R. Fishman (2003): 'Biomedicalisation: Technoscientific Transformations of Health, Illness, and U.S. Biomedicine'. *American Sociological Review*, 68:161–194.

Clayton, Paula J. (1982): 'Bereavement', in Eugene S. Paykel (ed.): *Handbook of Affective Disorders*. London: Churchill Livingstone, pp. 15–46.

Clayton, Paula J., James A. Halikas and William L. Maurice (1972): 'The Depression of Widowhood'. *British Journal of Psychiatry*, 120:71–78.

Conrad, Peter (1992): 'Medicalisation and Social Control'. *Annual Review of Sociology*, 18:209–232.

Conrad, Peter (2005): 'The Shifting Engines of Medicalisation'. *Journal of Health and Social Behavior*, 46:3–14.

Darwin, Charles (1872/1998): *The Expression of the Emotions in Man and Animals*. London: HarperCollins.

Ekman, Paul (1973): *Darwin and Facial Expression: A Century of Research*. San Diego: Academic Press.

Ekman, Paul and Wallace V. Friesen (1971): 'Constants across Cultures in the Face and Emotion'. *Journal of Personality and Social Psychology*, 17:124–129.

Ekman, Paul et al. (1987): 'Universals and Cultural Differences in the Judgments of Facial Expressions of Emotion'. *Journal of Personality and Social Psychology*, 53:712–717.

Frances, Allen (2013): *Normal: An Insider's Revolt Against Out-of-Control Psychiatric Diagnosis*. New York: William Morrow.

Freud, Sigmund (1917/1957): 'Mourning and Melancholia', in James Strachey (ed.): *Standard Edition of the Complete Works of Sigmund Freud* (Volume 14). London: Hogarth Press, pp. 237–258.

Granek, Leeat (2016): 'Medicalizing Grief', in Darcy L. Harris and Tashel C. Bordere (eds.): *Handbook of Social Justice in Loss and Grief*. New York: Routledge, pp. 111–124.

Greenberg, Gary (2013): *The Book of Woe: The DSM and the Unmaking of Psychiatry*. New York: Blue Rider Press.

Hippocrates (1923–1931): *Works of Hippocrates* (Volumes 1–4). Cambridge, MA: Harvard University Press.

Homer (1986): *The Iliad*. New York: Farrar, Straus, Giroux.

Horwitz, Allan V. and Jerome C. Wakefield (2007): *The Loss of Sadness: How Psychiatry Transformed Normal Sorrow into Depressive Disorder*. New York: Oxford University Press.

Kendler, Kenneth S., John Myers and Sidney Zisook (2008): 'Does Bereavement-Related Depression Differ from Major Depression Associated with other Stressful Life Events?'. *American Journal of Psychiatry*, 165:1449–1455.

Kleinman, Arthur (2012): 'Culture, Bereavement and Psychiatry'. *The Lancet*, 379:608–609.

Lewis, Aubrey J. (1934): 'Melancholia: A Clinical Survey of Depressive States'. *Journal of Mental Science*, 80:1–43.

Moran, Mark (2011): 'Bereavement Exclusion may be Gone from New DSM Edition'. *Psychiatric News*, 21, October. Available online at: http://psychnews.psychiatryonline. org/newsArticle.aspx?articleid=180988.

Nesse, Randolph (2000): 'Is Depression an Adaptation?'. *Archives of General Psychiatry*, 57:14–20.

Olfson, Mark, Steven C. Marcus, Benjamin Druss, Lynn Elinson, Terri Tanielian and Harold A. Pincus (2002): 'National Trends in the Outpatient Treatment of Depression'. *Journal of the American Medical Association*, 287:203–209.

Pies, Ronald (2014): 'The Bereavement Exclusion and the DSM-5: An Update and Commentary'. *Innovative Clinical Neuroscience*, 11:19–22.

Shakespeare, William (1601/1988): *Hamlet*. New York: Bantam.

Turner, Jonathan H. (2000): *On the Origins of Human Emotions: A Sociological Inquiry into the Evolution of Human Affect*. Palo Alto, CA: Stanford University Press.

Wakefield, Jerome C. and Michael First (2012): 'Validity of the Bereavement Exclusion to Major Depression: Does the Evidence Support the Proposed Elimination of the Exclusion in DSM-5?'. *World Psychiatry*, 11:3–11.

Wakefield, Jerome C. and Allan V. Horwitz (2016): 'Psychiatry's Continuing Expansion of Depressive Disorder', in Jerome C. Wakefield and Stevens Demazeux (eds.): *Sadness or Depression*. New York: Springer, pp. 173–203.

Wakefield, Jerome C. and Mark F. Schmitz (2012). 'Recurrence of Depression after Bereavement-Related Depression'. *Journal of Nervous and Mental Disease*, 200:480–485.

Wakefield, Jerome C. and Mark F. Schmitz (2013a): 'When Does Depression Become a Disorder? Using Recurrence Rates to Evaluate the Validity of Proposed Changes in Major Depression Diagnostic Thresholds'. *World Psychiatry*, 12:44–452.

Wakefield, Jerome C. and Mark F. Schmitz (2013b). 'Predictive Validation of Single-Episode Uncomplicated Depression as a Benign Subtype of Unipolar Major Depression'. *Acta Psychiatrica Scandanavica*, 128:825–845.

Wakefield Jerome C., Mark F. Schmitz, Michael First and Allan V. Horwitz (2007): 'Extending the bereavement exclusion for major depression to other losses: evidence from the National Comorbidity Survey'. *Archives of General Psychiatry*, 64:433–440.

Whoriskey, Peter (2012): 'Antidepressants to Treat Grief? Psychiatry Panelists with Ties to Drug Industry Say Yes'. *The Washington Post*, 26, December.

Zisook, Sidney, Stephen R. Shuchter, Paola Pedrelli, Jeremy Sable and Simona C. Deaciuc (2001): 'Bupropion Sustained Release for Bereavement: Results of an Open Trial'. *Journal of Clinical Psychiatry*, 62:227–230.

11 Suffocated grief, resilience and survival among African American families

Tashel C. Bordere

Introduction

African American youth and families are disproportionately bereaved by multiple losses across development related to the intersecting forces of individual and institutional discrimination (Jones 1997) and oppression (Bordere 2018; Harris 2009–2010; Rosenblatt and Wallace 2005a; Rosenblatt 2014). In historical and contemporary contexts of pervasive racism and sexual exploitation, where Black lives and deaths do not seem to matter, profound disparities exist in death rates (Umberson et al. 2017), health outcomes (Carter et al. 2017; DeLilly 2012), and grief experiences for African Americans. African American youth and families are uniquely bereaved by disparagingly high rates of premature deaths and nonfatal injuries of male youth (brothers, friends) due to gun violence (Bordere 2014, 2018; Murphy et al. 2002). Homicide loss survivors cope with grief complicated by many external factors (stigma, legal system, media, etc.) and accompanying secondary losses (e.g., loss of safety, control, privacy).

African American families have consistently been confronted with a plethora of tangible and intangible non-death losses and bereavement tied to dehumanization in sexual assault (loss of pre-assault life, loss of trust) and objectification of female youth and young adults (Bryant-Davis et al. 2010; Collins 2000; hooks 1989). Parents and caregivers of African American youth simultaneously contend with loss of peace connected to their challenged ability to protect their children and themselves from loss and injury incurred through prejudice, discrimination (police shootings), and internalized oppression.

In the face of cumulative complex losses connected to racial trauma, African American families across social economic classes have limited options for accessing culturally responsive support. In a study of counsellors who serve individuals coping with race-based trauma, Carrie Hemmings and Amanda M. Evans (2018) found that many counsellors lacked training both in identifying racial trauma and providing services to address this challenge with people of colour. Paralleling the dearth of scholarly literature addressing social justice issues in loss among marginalized groups, many clinicians lack or have limited education and training in this area. It is critical to address this deficit. Researchers studying African American youth and family bereavement have found that meaning-making around loss was rooted in perceived racism and discrimination (Bordere 2018; Holloway 2003; Rosenblatt and Wallace 2005a).

In this chapter, research, theory, and case studies are utilized to critically explore historical and present-day patterns of race-based trauma, unjust loss (Harris and Bordere 2016), 'suffocated grief' (Bordere 2014:169, 2016a:14), and coping among African Americans. Bereavement is situated within social, political, and cultural contexts to examine losses and complications to grief and mourning processes that occur as African American youth and families navigate various institutions (e.g., educational settings, health care systems) (Bronfenbrenner 1977) that serve to oppress and suffocate grief. 'Suffocated grief' or discriminatory penalties disproportionally imposed on marginalized individuals and families (Bordere 2014:169, 2016a:14) are addressed and balanced with patterns of survival and resilience demonstrated amid past and present-day death and non-death loss experiences. The chapter concludes with implications for research and practice.

Disenfranchisement and suffocated grief

Grief around intergenerational and contemporary trauma and loss for African Americans is complex and multifaceted yet largely disenfranchised or unacknowledged (Doka 1989) and suffocated through socially imposed penalties in broader cultural contexts of privilege and systemic oppression (Bordere 2014, 2016a). Privilege is an 'unearned advantage' afforded to majority populations (White, male, able-bodied) (McIntosh 2007:281). It includes the social and political power to create and shape prejudiced beliefs and discriminatory policies and laws, as well as influence societal decisions about the value and legitimacy of Black lives and Black deaths, Black grief and sorrow.

Privilege affords the social power to both disenfranchise and suffocate grief. Disenfranchised or unacknowledged grief (Doka 1989) is influenced by prejudicial beliefs regarding who and what deserves to be mourned. I conceptualize disenfranchised grief as a complementary concept and precursor to suffocated grief (Bordere 2014, 2016a) much like prejudice is a precursor to discrimination. It is one thing to walk by and *not acknowledge* a beautiful street memorial created by a Black adolescent male. However, it is another to arrest and charge him a fine as *penalties* for creating the memorial, hence suffocating grief. These penalties exacerbate and create further losses while attempting to disempower already marginalized individuals. Power hierarchies are maintained through limits and penalties imposed on marginalized groups that challenge scarce resources (emotional, cognitive) and deny access to tools (e.g., voting rights, culturally responsive mental health care) central for upward mobility, optimal health, and day-to-day functioning. The concept of suffocated grief allows for a broadened understanding of the complexities associated with grieving diverse losses (e.g., sexual assault, homicide) in contexts permeated by social injustices (see Bordere 2017).

African American individuals are regularly confronted with socially imposed, reconstructed conceptualizations of their historical and present-day experiences that discount the impact of racial terror and institutionalized slavery (economic losses), and loss and grief on families across generations. That is, *it's not your loss or grief if you were not physically present at the time of slavery. It's not my privilege because I was not physically present to participate in the enslavement of African Americans.* To be underrepresented, existing in the margins of society, is to be questioned and invalidated. It is to have your experiences with loss, your identity, your worth and values, your achievements, your grief, your trauma, your intentions and behaviours regularly interrogated and delegitimized.

Historical perspective

Experiences with dehumanizing losses and suffocated grief can be traced through a brief historical account. Individuals of African ancestry entered the United States through forced migration. Their ability to survive life (Bordere 2014) and show resilience through multiple, complex, cumulative losses (violent death, loss of land) is remarkable, but the legacy of disenfranchisement and grief bred through forced migration and slavery cannot be understated. The transatlantic slave trade and institution of slavery created multiple, sudden, traumatic non-death and death losses for families of African ancestry. It was designed to dismantle and disempower families and communities in an effort to dominate and exploit (economically, sexually) (Gutman 1976). In an effort to disorient and disempower, conditions for domination, family and community ties were severed.

African individuals were seized and separated from individuals who shared similar dialects. They were tightly packed on the floors of ships with no food or shelter in inhumane, unsafe, unsanitary conditions, often bond by chains next to the decaying bodies of deceased individuals who did not survive the horrific journey. Individuals who were captured were intentionally brought to an unfamiliar land with a different language and customs, and forced to participate in gruesome unpaid labour. This institution of forced free labour among individuals of African ancestry would disenfranchise African American populations while benefitting and privileging European American families in ways visible and invisible, conscious and unconscious, for centuries to follow.

Individuals and families of African ancestry endured countless violent deaths (e.g., lynchings), non-death losses, and associated trauma (Eyerman 2004) under the institution of legalized enslavement. For example, females of African ancestry were treated like sexual objects (Gutman 1976), often sexually assaulted in front of male spouses who could not offer physical protection. On any given day, mothers, fathers, daughters, and sons were seized from family units, put on auction blocks, and sold like livestock to the highest bidders. Unless it benefitted slaveholders to keep family members in close proximity, individuals removed from families and sold through slavery would often be relocated to distant or unknown locations never to be reunited with their families of origin or fictive kin (Chatters et al. 1994). The pain of familial separation was further complicated by the ambiguous circumstances surrounding the loss. According to Pauline Boss (1999, 2010), ambiguous losses are those that are unclear, traumatic, and externally driven. In the context of slavery, family members were left to wonder if they would ever see their cared about persons again. Lack of clear information around losses impedes grief and mourning processes. *Do I hold on to the hope that my cared about person is alive and we will be reunited under the institution of slavery? Or, conversely, do I begin grieving our forever physical separation through space or actual death and contemplate reuniting in heaven?*

There are numerous parallels between losses, suffocated grief, and survival in historical and contemporary contexts for African Americans. In this chapter, I argue that two types of losses in particular, the loss of time and loss of energy, intersect with all death and non-death losses related to racism and sexism, as well as other forms of discrimination to further complicate and lessen coping resources paramount to survival and resilience for African American youth and families. Although ongoing disparities in death loss is a major source of grief, non-death losses related to systemic oppression remain an underexplored source of bereavement. Historical non-death losses and systems created to maintain power hierarchies continue to impact and limit opportunity structures for African American populations in contemporary society.

Loss of credit and benefits

Throughout history, from the time of slavery to the present, African American populations across diverse family structures and socioeconomic classes have contended with non-death losses related to improper credit attributions (e.g., inventions) and benefits (financial profit) in discriminatory institutions. In professional environments, for example, it is a common experience for African Americans to present original ideas in group settings (e.g., meetings) in which they are underrepresented and experience a loss of credit and the benefits that would accompany their contributions (job promotion, pay raise). As a researcher and educator, I have participated in meetings in a variety of settings in which my vocalized ideas were taken and repeated verbatim only minutes later by individuals of race and gender privilege and credited to those individuals as if they were being spoken for the first time. This baffling experience can be explained by the perceived invisibility of African Americans, who remain devalued and psychologically absent to individuals of racial, gender, and socioeconomic privilege amid visible physical presence and active engagement.

Managing everyday encounters with racism and loss requires additional time, energy, and risk-taking of marginalized groups. African American individuals are charged with the daily challenge of deciding which losses and microaggressions, or subtle forms of discrimination (Sue et al. 2007), to address and which ones to abandon by playing it 'cool' or seeming unaffected (Smith 2015:6; Majors and Billson 1992). Each option comes at a cost. Self-advocacy around unjust loss and disenfranchisement may be met with spoken or unspoken stereotypes (e.g., 'The Angry Black Woman'), discrimination, and other forms of resistance. Grief is suffocated in environments in which communication of a loss (credit) is reframed, negatively mislabelled (e.g., aggressiveness), and penalized. For example, grief may be suffocated through experiences with 'White Fragility' (DiAngelou 2011;

see Patton and Jordan 2017). Robin DiAngelou (2011) conceptualizes 'White Fragility' as the response of European American individuals when confronted about racism or inequalities. According to DiAngelou:

> White Fragility is a state in which even a minimum amount of racial stress becomes intolerable, triggering a range of defensive moves. These moves include the outward display of emotions such as anger, fear, and guilt, and behaviors such as argumentation, silence, and leaving the stress-inducing situation.
>
> (DiAngelou 2011:54)

Another compelling example of non-death loss related to racism is illustrated in the experiences of African American professionals in academia who are differentially expected to participate in 'invisible labour' or service (mentoring unrepresented students); labour that is culturally significant but not valued or counted for promotion (June 2015). Mentorship of disenfranchised students to improve their chances for matriculation through college is not valued as a source of 'productivity' through the lens of privileged entities who created policies that defined what and who is valuable to universities and the broader society. African American professors underrepresented at predominantly White universities experience the loss of protected time and the ability to be productive free of the additional expectations to provide campus and community service and education, often around issues of diversity and cultural sensitivity, and mentorship of underrepresented students. Their experiences are decontextualized and penalized, as in suffocated grief, at the time of promotion when they are compared to peers of racial privilege who did not bare the extra burdens of unprotected time, racialized stress, isolation, and accompanying losses of emotional, cognitive, and physical energy.

Loss of protection

A loss of protection is a familiar experience for African American youth and families. African American youth are entitled to childhoods in which they are able to engage in developmentally appropriate activities and social interactions. They are entitled to safe environments and protections to prevent and reduce their vulnerability to harm and exposure to violent death scenes and the resulting trauma and grief. Yet, throughout history and in contemporary society, African American youth have not benefitted from protections that should accompany childhood (see King 2011 – 'Stolen Childhood'). In research with college students, Phillip Goff and colleagues (2014) examined whether Black male youth were afforded protections associated with childhood similar to those afforded to same age peers. The researchers found that a label or childhood descriptor (children) was less often applied to Black youth than White peers. Black boys were viewed as older and less innocent than peers from other racial groups. This perception transcends into adulthood for African American men, who despite their actual size and stature, are often labelled by racial majority individuals as 'big' (i.e., big Black guy). Similar descriptors are not utilized in reference to White men. According to Phillip Goff and colleagues (2014), racialized perceptions regarding age and degree of innocence translate to receipt of fewer protections (e.g., less police protection) and other benefits of childhood for Black youth, thereby increasing their risk for harm.

Further, African American youth encounter losses and suffocated grief related to limited protection and support in educational institutions. They are disproportionately impacted by astounding homicide rates, personal vulnerability to death by violence, and losses related to racial, gender, and economic inequities (e.g., low resourced schools). Losses due to homicide are stigmatized and thus students may be less likely to share their loss experiences with teachers or explain their grief around the complexity of their experiences of intersecting losses and trauma. Youth spend a large portion of their weekdays in school, and thus their grief (distractedness, anger, fatigue) and trauma (hypervigilance) are brought into classrooms and school environments. In the absence of information and the presence of stigmatization of African American youth, their normal reactions to loss may be misdiagnosed (misbehaviour, cognitive deficits) and penalized when protections (i.e., bereavement-sensitive policies on attendance, makeup assignments) and supports (schools trained in loss and grief support) are not consistently in place to ensure their academic success and school engagement (Bordere 2014).

In a study of patterns of racial, ethnic, and gender differences in school discipline over time (1995–2005), racial minority students were two to five times more likely to be given suspensions or expulsions than White and Asian American students. John M. Wallace and colleagues (2008) found that despite a decrease in disciplinary actions taken within that time period, there was an increase in disciplinary actions for African American students.

Sense of duty and loss

Recognizing limitations in the extent to which protection can be offered to youth within African American families and communities, multiple socialization forces (families, church) transmit a sense of duty among African American youth to work towards improvement of social conditions that advantage some while disadvantaging other groups. Youth are socialized to understand their responsibility in 'doing the work' or continuing the efforts of ancestors and others who endured great suffering or died in pursuit of basic rights that they would not experience in their lifetime (e.g., Dr./Reverend Martin Luther King Jr., Rosa Parks). However, in this realm of social justice promotion lurks further pain and bereavement.

Loss and trauma related to 'doing the work'/ emotional costs of 'doing the work'

Loss and trauma accompany attempts to uncover social and economic inequalities and advocacy efforts aimed at improving social conditions. These losses are compounded when social justice efforts are met with both disenfranchised grief and suffocated grief in lieu of validation of loss and social change (protective policies) as illustrated in the following case.

Case: resisting oppression: college student protests

In the fall of 2015, student protests at a Midwestern university and other institutions ignited renewed attention to long-standing disparities (racial, ethnic, religious, gender) and inequities in university settings across the nation. Protests (marches, sit-ins, walkouts) around the country designed to highlight concerns for marginalized African American students and allies around unaddressed experiences of racial trauma and loss on college campuses were met with further loss and disenfranchisement. Students participating in the protests experienced myriad losses including loss of time, loss of energy, and loss of relationships, as well as losses related to missed classes and assignments (see Lumpkin and Cole 2018 – 'The Costs of Campus Activism'). African American and other marginalized students experienced suffocated grief when their otherwise normal cognitive, behavioural, and emotional grief expressions were mislabelled and penalized through overtly racist messages of hate, invalidation, and isolation, as well as police presence to restrict and intimidate, and community threats of physical harm, including death. In response to the grief of African American students around race-based trauma (Bryant and Ocampo 2005a; Sanchez-Hucles 1998) and loss, some institutions have implemented policies that restrict the physical spaces and places for protests (i.e., visible grief expressions) on college campuses.

Instrumental or cognitive-behavioural expressions of grief (Doka and Martin 2010) and loss through student protests and activism at other points in history have similarly been criminalized in lieu of validation, enfranchisement, and protection. Sit-ins designed to disrupt institutional oppression have consistently been penalized, in some cases through serious disciplinary actions and arrests of large numbers of protesters (Johnston 2015). Social and institutional resistance to student demands for basic rights to inclusive and safe educational spaces and places on college campuses affirm the continued existence of inequities and oppression of marginalized student populations.

African American individuals and families have resisted oppression and undoubtedly shown cultural resilience, but it has not been without costs. Attempts to disrupt broader systems of oppression have been met with collective grief in the assassinations of prominent civil rights leaders including Dr. Martin Luther King Jr. and Malcolm X, and the more recent 2015 death of 28-year-old Sandra Bland. She was a visible advocate for law enforcement accountability in the shooting deaths of African American youth (Davis and Heilbroner 2018). Bland was arrested following a traffic stop and died by asphyxiation (hanging) in a prison cell; details around her death remain a mystery. Bland's family has vocalized their grief around her death and the ambiguous circumstances, and the secondary losses of time and energy as a function of 'outrage fatigue' (Yang 2018) in the absence of answers (see Rosenblatt 2014). In terms of context, the sheriff charged with investigating Bland's death had previously been fired from his position as police chief following allegations of racism and police brutality and accusations of police mis-conduct (Graham 2015). Thus, there was a loss of ability to have an investigation conducted by someone with limited bias.

Ongoing race-based trauma, loss, and suffocated grief compromise mental, physical, cognitive, and social health outcomes for African American populations across social locations (e.g., social economic class, gender, age), generations, and development (Barrett 1998; Bordere 2017; Rosenblatt and Wallace 2005b; Umberson 2017). The stress and despair of the endless struggle of 'doing the work' is evident in the death of one well-established Black Lives Matter activist who died by suicide on the steps of the state house (see Lowery and Stankiewicz 2016). MarShawn McCarrel's early death (age 23) has brought increased attention to the toll of inequality on marginalized populations, activism, and mental health, with attention to depression.

Cultural values, behaviours, and survival

African American families have long demonstrated the ability to transform con-textual experiences orchestrated for their demise into opportunities to revise cur-rent survival strategies or to develop new ones consonant with cultural values (e.g., dignity). Cultural values among African Americans remain rooted both in African ancestry and adaptations made in contexts of social, educational, and economic inequities, as well as health disparities and disproportionality in pre-ventable death rates. Common values that cut across gender and socioeconomic lines for African American families include spirituality or belief in a higher power (e.g., God), collectivism, interdependence, ancestral pride (racial, ethnic, gender), present-time orientation, self-discipline, education, social support, and social status.

Religious institutions and familial relationships, including extended family (e.g., aunts, uncles) and fictive kin, or individuals perceived as family but are not related by blood or marriage (Chatters et al. 1994), have served as primary sociali-zation agents and protective factors for African American youth and families.

Spiritual coping and the Black church

Without a clear end in sight for the eradication of institutionalized slavery, and the accompanying trauma and loss, African American families persisted in their faith and belief in a higher power (i.e., God). We have seen this same faith and deter-mination serve protective functions for African American families across time as illustrated in the following case.

Case presentation: Jesus take the wheel

Mrs. Linda, an 85-year-old African American female, was hospitalized. Her heart was not pumping effectively, and she was accumulating fluid around her lungs. Her doctors were giving medications to help decrease the fluid. Mrs. Linda and her family informed the medical team that she was being honoured at church the next day (Sunday). The team offered a more aggressive procedure at the bedside to drain the fluid to try to get her to the event. After draining the fluid, the physician asked Mrs. Linda to hum, advising that briefly humming while they remove the catheter makes it less likely to have a complication. She closed her eyes and began humming 'Amazing Grace'.

After a moment, the catheter was out. Mrs. Linda was told she could stop, but she persisted with an even more spirited hum, this time united by the harmonious humming of family members who joined in from the hallway. Mrs. Linda had emerged from the procedure focused on the same faith and source of strength and protection with which she entered it. Her hum/song was her testimony (Griffith et al., 1980) that she went through a trial and made it through the experience. Her family's social support through their collective post-surgery hum was symbolic of the call-and-response characteristic of the Black church wherein the response functions as validation; a bear-witnessing to experience.

In contexts of limited social and political power, African American individuals and families have maintained belief systems rooted in spirituality and the sense of community and support offered through participation in the Black church and mental health support from Black ministers (Taylor et al., 2000) and congregants to aid in coping processes and survival (Kim 2017; McAdoo 2007). Thus, amid the uprising of White Nationalism, hate crimes, and dismantling of human rights policies under the current presidency, many African American individuals have been vigilante but focused on a higher power and religious community support instead of the resurgence of White power. The values that have sustained African American populations are reinforced in the Black church. Faith, hope, patience, endurance, belongingness, interdependence, and self-love are fostered in a variety of ways. The minister/pastor's sermon describes everyday struggles (relationships, economics, racism) balanced with triumphs to promote hope among congregants. The sermon is usually interactive and communal in that it entails a 'call-and-response' (Smitherman 1977; see Pipes 2007) between the minister and congregants. For example, the minister says, 'Can I get an amen?', and congregants respond with affirmations such as 'Amen!' and 'Preach!'.

The music is similarly built around call-and-response communication and is designed to evoke emotional release among individuals who share experiences of social disadvantage and suffocated grief. The notable Bishop Paul S. Morton and The Greater St. Stephen Mass Choir, for example, sing 'Your Tears', which validates emotional expressions of grief in a context free of penalty:

> Your tears are just temporary relief.
> Your tears are just a release of the pain, sorrow, and grief.
> Your tears are expressions that can't be controlled.
> A little crying out is alright,
> But after a while you won't have to cry no more;
> Don't you worry, God's gonna wipe every tear away.

It continues with a reminder of faithfulness ('You've got to hold on') and the promise of better days to come ('A brand new day is dawning!'). The emotionally laden song is a lengthy eight minutes and sixteen seconds intentionally allowing ample time for protective defences (playing it cool, being strong) utilized in the broader society to be lowered so that emotional release is more probable among congregants.

Hymns and other songs promote connectedness ('Never Alone') to offset isolation that comes with disadvantage, racism, and grief. Other songs such as 'I Go to the Rock', 'Hold On, Help Is on the Way', and 'The Battle Is Not Yours, It's the Lord's' reinforce faith and hope and some freedom from the social responsibility to manage and address all social ills and injustices.

Personal power or power over our thoughts and perceptions is also promoted in the church. For example, having a personal relationship with a higher power through prayer. In a broader culture of disenfranchisement and invisibility, a higher power (God) will notice, listen, and value you ('His eye is on the sparrow, so I know he watches over me' – song). This sense of belongingness and community is also fostered through behavior in the form of social support and language in which church members are conceptualized as the church family and titled 'sister' and 'brother' (e.g., Sister Price, Brother West) in keeping with the collectivist nature of African American families.

Within this church family, the opportunity structure is broadened for individuals across development. African American youth have opportunities for mentorship and leadership development that may not be readily accessible in other settings. For example, youth coping with father loss or father absence have access to models and support from adult males within the church. Aging congregants gain social support through the Black church but are bidirectionally valued sources of historical memories and models of resilience. They are often called on to offer testimonies or stories about historical lived experiences with race-related struggles, losses (e.g., health), grief, and triumphs (Griffith et al., 1980) that provide education and promote positive racial identity among younger members. My grandfather gave a testimony about his experience with cancer as he neared the end of his life. He recounted the trials associated with cancer, including his perceived vulnerability in medical systems embedded in individual and institutional racism (see Bordere 2016b; Jones 1997), and his anticipation of a 'better life' and reunion with his siblings in heaven. Providing this testimony in front of the congregation allowed the church family and biological family present to bear witness and offer validation of loss and his anticipated gain in the afterlife.

Funeral rituals are often celebratory in nature (Bordere 2008–2009). Survivors celebrate the life of the deceased and the better life beyond this earth that s/he will experience with God in her/his heavenly home (funeral as 'homegoing'). This 'better life' entails freedom from suffering and oppression. In fact, African American funerals are designed to enfranchise and, in some cases, offer social status that was not achieved in the individual's lifetime due to limited opportunity structures (Bordere 2008–2009; Holloway 2003; Rosenblatt and Wallace 2005a).

Familial socialization

Family and extended kin are highly valued as important sources of socialization and protection for African Americans. With the painful awareness of ongoing sudden losses, African American families prepare themselves and their youth for survival amid these realities and the grief and racial trauma that, for their safety and well-being, cannot be allowed to consume them. For example, enslaved individuals were vulnerable to both disenfranchised grief (Doka 1989) and suffocated grief (Bordere 2014, 2016a) wherein normal grief reactions (e.g., fatigue and distractibility) to losses (e.g., familial separation, death) were not recognized in this dehumanizing context. An especially fatigued enslaved person was misperceived and mislabelled as lazy and less productive and hence penalized (e.g., flogged). This pattern continues today when bereaved African American youth are disengaged from school, in lieu of support, and put in a school-to-prison pipeline through which they are disproportionately incarcerated and imprisoned (see Equal Justice Institute – 'From Slavery to Mass Incarceration', https://eji.org/videos/slavery-to-mass-incarceration). As once stated by Mahatma Ghandi: 'Strength does not come from physical capacity. It comes from an indomitable will' (Gandhi 1920:259).

African American individuals and families were not meant to survive the horrendous experiences and conditions of forced enslavement. Yet, they did. Similarly, in the broader contexts in which African American youth and families are faced with microaggressions (Sue 2010; Sue et al., 2007), they are able to utilize this remarkable feat of ancestral survival and resilience through loss to draw the necessary strength and resolve to function. The institution of slavery produced profound trauma (Eyerman 2004) and losses (e.g., economic, educational, relational) for African American populations, ever-present in their historical memories (Kansteiner 2002) and ongoing disenfranchisement, while facilitating privilege maintenance for members of majority groups. Despite unacknowledged loss, families are able to utilize historical memories to recall and transmit narratives of racism and loss across generations. In research with bereaved African American adults, participants recounted experiences of racism faced by their deceased cared about persons during their lives (Rosenblatt and Wallace 2005a, 2005b).

Familial socialization strategies that provide historical perspectives on disenfranchising losses and suffocated grief are balanced with tools for survival and messages of hope and enfranchisement. Racial and ethnic pride, interdependence, and personal power; self-discipline, self-dignity, spirituality, and educational attainment are emphasized and important in social contexts in which African Americans may be stigmatized by some individuals and institutions. As a young child, I was taught and memorized poems that reinforced these tools for survival. One such poem is William Ernest Henley's (1988) 'Invictus':

> Out of the night that covers me,
> Black as the Pit from pole to pole,
> I thank whatever gods may be
> For my unconquerable soul.

In the fell clutch of circumstance
I have not winced nor cried aloud,
Under the bludgeonings of chance
My head is bloody, but unbowed.

Beyond this place of wrath and tears
Looms but the horror of the shade,
And yet the menace of the years
Finds, and shall find me, unafraid.

It matters not how strait the gate,
How charged with punishments the scroll,
I am the master of my fate:
I am the captain of my soul.
                            (Henley 1988:56)

These messages are transmitted across generations. A poignant example of the intergenerational communication of values promoting survival and resilience is found in the following letter written by my great-grandfather in December 1966 to my mother and her male siblings:

Dear Grand Childrens
You can See By this We have Received you all letter and was
very very Glad to hear from our Grand Childrens
and know that you all Were Well at this time also to know that
our Grandchildrens is *Getting along Good in School*
I am Glad indeed Because *Boy or Girl without Education* have little or
No change [chance] to make or [a] *Good Living for hisself*
or his family the same is for the Grils[Girls] you Can Make or [a]
Good Living for self and For your family *Without So Much Hard Work*
if put Somthing in you all Head and the *Good lord in Heart*
Then you all cant mist the Good Ways this letter leave us
We Will Be Down to See you all and that house
I wont say when I hope it Will be Soon
Give our love to your father and mother.

My great-grandfather, reared in the late 1800s, was not permitted to receive the education that he promoted among his grandchildren in this letter. Yet, his messages are clear. The letter symbolizes remnants of oppression and his survival while his messages were designed to promote resilience (e.g., social mobility) among my mother and her male siblings. It highlights his pride and recognition of their academic achievements and emphasizes the equal importance of education for African American males and females to circumvent struggles related to low educational attainment within already oppressive social contexts. Similarly, the letter reinforces the value of spirituality or belief in a higher power and family cohesiveness as central to successfully navigating life. Finally, the letter begins and ends with attention to personal power and ownership. The letter includes the full names of each grandchild; names intentionally created by their parents. During slavery, African Americans did not have the right to name their children. He concludes the letter with a tone of pride in property ownership as expressed in his anticipation to see 'that house', one of several homes that my grandparents would own. Like my great-grandparents, my grandparents were also limited in their educational opportunities in the contexts of the Deep South. However, they worked and invested in property that would create the economic stability and legacy of prosperity owed but denied to previous generations.

Conclusion and implications

This chapter presented a historical and contemporary examination of death and non-death loss, suffocated grief, and survival for African American youth and families in social and political contexts of systemic oppression. As highlighted in the chapter, the intersection of racism and sexism is central to the grief narratives and lived experiences of African Americans across social locations (e.g., religious affiliation). Safe spaces are needed for this population to be able to express their experiences of racial trauma, loss, and grief free of the additional worry of being stereotyped or revictimized by white fragility.

The issues presented in this chapter have implications for researchers, practitioners, and educators. Each entity has a role in policy development and implementation that could enfranchise grief through both recognition and policy changes. More research is needed that explores the role of discrimination and social disadvantage in the loss (death and non-death) and suffocated grief experiences of African American youth and families in different contexts (school, employment). Further, in socially just practice, it is important for researchers to confirm and share their findings with populations under study and in the communities in which they are served (e.g., churches, youth organizations) (see Bordere 2016a).

In clinical practice, greater training is needed in identifying race-based trauma as well as education around the roles of historical legacies and contemporary patterns of loss and suffocated grief among African American and other marginalized populations for culturally responsive service provision (see Bryant-Davis and Ocampo 2005b). Opportunities to assess awareness of personal privilege and disadvantage and impact on service provision are also central to culturally responsive care. Further, partnerships are needed between trained clinicians and pastors of Black churches. This allows pastors to access resources that support congregants who do not wish to utilize formal support services. It also allows pastors to make referrals to clinicians who offer trustworthy support in which clients can share testimonies of injustices in their loss narratives and explore cultural and personal strengths that promote optimal functioning in their immediate environments and the broader society.

Training opportunities are needed in educational institutions that advance knowledge of racial trauma, student loss, and bereavement and offer concrete support options. It is important for administrators and staff to review school and classroom policies, making necessary adjustments, to ensure that they accommodate the needs of bereaved students, families, and staff in ways that promote academic success and school functioning through both normative and disenfranchising losses. For example, Caregiver-Teacher conferences offer opportunities to check in regarding family transitions or anniversaries that may trigger grief. Loss and survival can be addressed in normal curriculum (social studies – violent losses, power hierarchies) and during holidays (Memorial Day).

References

Barrett, Ronald K. (1998): 'Sociocultural Considerations for Working with Blacks Experiencing Loss and Grief', in Kenneth J. Doka and Joyce D. Davidson (eds.): *Living with Grief: Who We Are, How We Grieve*. New York: Hospice Foundation of America/ Routledge, pp. 83–96.

Bordere, Tashel C. (2008–2009): 'To Look at Death Another Way': Black Teenage Males' Perspectives on Second-Lines and Regular Funerals in New Orleans'. *Omega: Journal of Death and Dying*, 58 (3):213–232.

Bordere, Tashel C. (2014): 'Adolescents and Homicide', in Kenneth J. Doka and Amy Tucci (eds.): *Helping Adolescents Cope with Loss*. Washington, DC: Hospice Foundation of America, pp. 161–181.

Bordere, Tashel C. (2016a): 'Social Justice Conceptualizations in Grief and Loss', in Darcy Harris and Tashel C. Bordere (eds.): *Handbook of Social Justice in Loss and Grief: Exploring Diversity, Equity, and Inclusion*. Amityville, NY: Routledge, pp. 9–20

Bordere, Tashel C. (2016b): "Not Gonna be Laid Out to Dry': Cultural Mistrust in End of Life Care and Strategies for Trust-Building', in Darcy Harris and Tashel. C. Bordere (eds.): *Handbook of Social Justice in Loss and Grief: Exploring Diversity, Equity, and Inclusion*. New York: Routledge, pp. 75–84.

Bordere, Tashel C. (2017): 'Disenfranchisement and Ambiguity in the Face of Loss: The Suffocated Grief of Sexual Assault Survivors'. *Family Relations*, 66 (1):29–45.

Bordere, Tashel C. (2018): 'Grief and Loss among First Nations and African American Youth', in Carrie Arnold (ed.): *Understanding Child and Adolescent Grief: Supporting Loss and Facilitating Growth*. New York: Routledge, pp. 135–146.

Boss, Pauline (1999): 'Insights: Ambiguous Loss: Living with Frozen Grief'. *The Harvard Mental Health Letter/Harvard Medical School*, 16 (5):4–6.

Boss, Pauline (2010): 'The Trauma and Complicated Grief of Ambiguous Loss'. *Pastoral Psychology*, 59 (2):137–145.

Bronfenbrenner, Urie (1977): 'Toward an Experimental Ecology of Human Development'. *American Psychologist*, 32:513–530.

Bryant-Davis, Thema and Carlota Ocampo (2005a): 'Racist Incident-Based Trauma'. *The Counseling Psychologist*, 33 (4):479–500.

Bryant-Davis, Thema and Carlota Ocampo (2005b): 'The Trauma of Racism: Implications for Counseling, Research, and Education'. *The Counseling Psychologist*, 33 (4):574–578.

Bryant-Davis, Thema, Sarah E. Ullman, Yuying Tsong, Shaquita Tillman and Kimberly Smith (2010): "Struggling to Survive': Sexual Assault, Poverty, and Mental Health Outcomes of African American Women'. *American Journal of Orthopsychiatry*, 80 (1):61–70.

Carter, Robert T, Michael Y. Lau, Veronica Johnson, and Katherine Kirkinis (2017): 'Racial Discrimination and Health Outcomes among Racial/Ethnic Minorities: A Meta-Analytic Review'. *Journal of Multicultural Counseling and Development*, 45:232–259.

Chatters, Linda. M., Robert Joseph Taylor and Rukmalie Jayakody (1994): 'Fictive Kinship Relations in Black Extended Families'. *Journal of Comparative Family Studies*, 25 (3):297–312.

Collins, Patricia Hill (2000): *Black Feminist Thought: Knowledge, Consciousness, and the Politics of Empowerment* (2nd Edition). New York: Routledge.

Davis, Kate and David Heilbroner (2018): 'Say Her Name: The Life and Death of Sandra Bland'. *HBO Documentary*, 9, November. HBO and Cozy Post Production, USA. Available online at: www.hbo.com/documentaries/say-her-name-the-life-and-death-of-sandra-bland.

DeLilly, Carol Rose (2012): 'Discrimination and Health Outcomes'. *Issues in Mental Health and Nursing*, 33:801–804.

DiAngelou, Robin (2011): 'White Fragility'. *International Journal of Critical Pedagogy*, 3 (3):54–70.

Doka, Kenneth J. (1989): *Disenfranchised Grief: Recognizing Hidden Sorrow*. Lexington: MA: Lexington Books.

Doka, Kenneth J. and Terry L. Martin (2010): *Grieving Beyond Gender: Understanding the Ways Men and Women Mourn*. New York: Routledge.

Eyerman, Ron (2004): 'The Past in the Present: Culture and the Transmission of Memory'. *Acta Sociologica*, 47 (2):159–169.

Gandhi, Mahatma K. (1924): 'The Doctrine of the Sword' (1920), in *Young India* (1919–1922) (2nd Edition). Madras/Chennai, SE: Triplicane.

Goff, Phillip A., Matthew C. Jackson, A. L. Di Leone Brooke, Carmen M. Cullotta and Natalie A. DiTomasso (2014): 'The Essence of Innocence: Consequences of Dehumanizing Black Children'. *Journal of Personality and Social Psychology*, 106 (4):526–545.

Graham, David A. (2015): 'Sandra Bland and the Long History of Racism in Waller County, Texas'. *The Atlantic, Politics*, 21, July. Available online at: www.theatlantic.com/politics/archive/2015/07/sandra-bland-waller-county-racism/398975/.

Griffith, Ezra H., Thelouizs English and Violet Mayfield (1980): 'Possession, Prayer and Testimony: Therapeutic Aspects of the Wednesday Night Meeting in the Black Church'. *Psychiatry*, 43:120–128.

Gutman, Herbert G. (1976): *The Black Family in Slavery and Freedom, 1750–1925*. New York: Pantheon.

Harris, Darcy (2009–2010): 'Oppression of the Bereaved: A Critical Analysis of Grief in Western Society'. *Omega: Journal of Death and Dying*, 60 (3):241–253.

Harris, Darcy and Tashel C. Bordere (eds.) (2016): *Handbook of Social Injustice in Loss and Grief: Exploring Diversity, Equity, and Inclusion*. New York: Routledge.

Hemmings, Carrie and Amanda M. Evans (2018): 'Identifying and Treating Race-Based Trauma in Counseling'. *Journal of Multicultural Counseling and Development*, 46:20–39.

Henley, William Ernest (1988): *A Book of Versus*. London: D. Nutt.

hooks, bell (1989): *Talking Back: Thinking Feminist, Thinking Black*. Boston, MA: South End Press.

Holloway, Karla F. C. (2003): *Passed On: African American Mourning Stories: A Memorial*. Durham: Duke University Press.

Johnston, Angus (2015): 'Student Protests, Then and Now'. *The Chronicle Review*, 11, December. Available online at: www.chronicle.com/article/Student-Protests-ThenNow/234542.

Jones, James M. (1997): *Prejudice and Racism* (2nd Edition): New York: McGraw-Hill.

June, Audry Williams (2015): 'The Invisible Labor of Minority Professors'. *The Chronicle of Higher Education.* Available online at: www.chronicle.com/article/ The-Invisible-Labor-of/234098.

Kansteiner, Wulf (2002): 'Finding Meaning in Memory: A Methodological Critique of Collective Memory Studies'. *History and Theory*, 41 (2):179–197.

Kim, Paul Y. (2017): 'Religious Support Mediates the Racial Microaggressions-Mental Health Relation among Christian Ethnic Minority Students'. *Psychology of Religion and Spirituality*, 9 (2):148–157.

King, Wilma (2011): *Stolen Childhood: Slave Youth in Nineteenth-Century America* (2nd Edition). Bloomington, IN: Indiana University Press.

Lowery, Wesley and Kevin Stankiewicz (2016): "'My Demons Won Today': Ohio Activist's Suicide Spotlights Depression among Black Lives Matter leaders', *The Washington Post*, 15, February. Available online at: www.washingtonpost.com/news/post-nation/ wp/2016/02/15/my-demons-won-today-ohio-activists-suicide-spotlights-depression- among-black-lives-matter-leaders/?noredirect=on&utm_term=.9cf199ff2406.

Lumpkin, Lauren and Devan Cole (2018): 'The Costs of Campus Activism', *The Nation, Higher Education*, 23, May. Available online at: www.thenation.com/article/ the-costs-of-campus-activism/.

Majors, Richard and Janet M. Billson (1992): *Cool Pose: The Dilemmas of Black Manhood in America.* New York: Lexington Books.

McAdoo, Harriet (2007): *Black Families* (4th Edition): Thousand Oaks, CA: Sage Publications.

McIntosh, Peggy (2007): 'White Privilege: Unpacking the Invisible Knapsack', in Paula S. Rothenberg (ed.): *Race, Class, and Gender in the United States.* New York: Worth.

Murphy, Shirley A., Clark L. Johnson and Janet Lohan (2002): 'The Aftermath of the Violent Death of a Child: An Integration of the Assessments of Parents' Mental Distress and PTSD During the First 5 Years of Bereavement'. *Journal of Loss and Trauma*, 7 (3):203–222.

Patton, Lori D. and Jodi L. Jordan (2017): "'It's Not about 'You', It's about 'Us'": A Black Woman Administrator's Efforts to Disrupt White Fragility in an Urban School'. *Journal of Cases in Educational Leadership*, 20 (1):80–91.

Pipes, William Harrison (2007): 'Old-Time Religion: Benches Can't Say 'Amen'', in Harriet Pipes McAdoo (ed.): *Black Families* (4th Edition). Thousand Oaks: Sage Publications, pp. 101–124.

Rosenblatt, Paul C. (2014): *The Impact of Racism on African American Families: Literature as Social Science.* Burlington, VT: Ashgate Publishing Limited.

Rosenblatt, Paul C. and Beverly Wallace (2005a): *African American Grief.* New York: Routledge.

Rosenblatt, Paul C. and Beverly Wallace (2005b): 'Narratives of Grieving African-Americans about Racism in the Lives of Deceased Family Members'. *Death Studies*, 29:217–235.

Sanchez-Hucles, Janis V. (1998): 'Racism: Emotional Abusiveness and Psychological Trauma for Ethnic Minorities'. *Journal of Emotional Abuse*, 1:69–87.

Smith, Darron T. (2015): 'The Emotional Labor of Playing it Cool: How Black Male Transracial Adoptees Find Ways to Cope within Predominantly White Settings'. *Journal of Social Distress and the Homeless*, 24:93–108.

Smitherman, Geneva (1977): *Talkin and Testifyin: The Language of Black America.* Boston: Houghton.

Sue, Derald W. (ed.) (2010): *Microaggressions and Marginality: Manifestations, Dynamics, and Impact.* Hoboken, NJ: John Wiley and Sons.

Sue, Derald W., Christina M. Capodilupo, Gina C. Torino, Jennifer M. Bucceri, Aisha M. B. Holder, Kevin L. Nadal and Marta Esquilin (2007): 'Racial Microaggressions in Everyday Life: Implications for Practice'. *American Psychologist*, 62 (4):271–286.

Taylor, Robert Joseph, Christopher G. Ellison, Linda M. Chatters, Jeffrey S. Levin and Karen D. Lincoln (2000): 'Mental Health Services in Faith Communities: The Role of Clergy in Black Churches'. *Social Work*, 45 (1):73–87.

Umberson, Debra (2017): 'Black Deaths Matter: Race, Relationship Loss, and Effects on Survivors'. *Journal of Health and Social Behavior*, 58 (4):405–420.

Umberson, Debra, Julie Skalamera Olson, Robert Crosnoe, Hui Liu, Tetyana Purdrovska and Rachel Donnelly (2017): 'Death of Family Members as an Overlooked Source of Racial Disadvantage in the United States'. *Proceedings of the National Academy of Sciences of the United States of America*, 114 (5):915–920.

Wallace John M., Sara Goodkind, Cynthia M. Wallace and Jerald G. Bachman (2008): 'Racial, Ethnic, and Gender Differences in School Discipline among U.S. High School Students: 1991–2005'. *Negro Education Review*, 59 (1–2):47–62.

Yang, Allie (2018): 'Sandra Bland's Sisters Still Demanding Answers, Fighting 'Outrage Fatigue' in 3 Years Since her Death'. *ABC News*, 27, November. Available online at: https://abc news.go.com/US/sandra-blands-sisters-demanding-answers-fighting-outrage-fatigue/ story?id=59442866.

12 Grief in an individualized society

A critical corrective to the advancement of diagnostic culture

Michael Hviid Jacobsen and Anders Petersen

Introduction

We hold it to be neither provocative nor suggestive to claim the following: it is by now a truism that we live in an individualized society in which individuals are held accountable and responsible for seeking answers to a vast array of societal challenges and problems. Although the perspectives vary slightly – and the addressed consequences of the development differ – prominent sociological scholars have pinpointed this situation for some decades now (Giddens 1991; Beck and Beck-Gernsheim 2002; Bauman 2001). The overall rationale of individualization is that individuals, in several historical tempos, have become emancipated from societally sanctioned and supported types of collective life-forms and (traditional) communities in which they were previously embedded. Nowadays, instead, society is supportive of – and even demands – individuals who are responsible for creating and realising their own lives, competences and potentials vis-à-vis institutions such as education, work and family. As Ulrich Beck and Elisabeth Beck-Gernsheim famously formulated it: 'The individual is becoming the basic unit of social reproduction for the first time in history' (Beck and Beck-Gernsheim 2002:xxii).

This does not, however, entail the complete dismantling of societally enforced norms and rules but rather the emergence of a situation in which individualization has become the structurally imposed norm that individuals have to strive for and live by. Individuals living in contemporary society cannot choose individualization; they are forced to choose it. One cannot escape individualization; it has now, for all practical intents and purposes, become a *task*, as Zygmunt Bauman (2000) so poignantly puts it. Perhaps we can clarify this a bit more by pointing to a fundamental concept that captures the central component of individualization – namely, autonomy. In our historical epoch of enhanced individualization, we cannot escape autonomy – rather we are forced to being autonomous. French sociologist Alain Ehrenberg explains this interconnection by claiming the following. The realization of one's personal autonomy in contemporary society has become a specific form of societal discipline (Ehrenberg 1991). That is, individualization is an overall societal demand, formulated as an ideal that each individual ought to follow. Hence, in an individualized society, the autonomous person is heralded as the most precious ideal and value that we should strive for and ultimately be successful in achieving. As this logic operates as the overarching premise of contemporary society, it also encapsulates our most intimate features and feelings in life: identity, love, sexuality and so on. We have to choose to choose our identity – it is not chosen for us. As Anthony Giddens almost programmatically stated: 'We are not what we are, but what we make of ourselves' (Giddens 1991:75), and we cannot avoid (trying) to make something of ourselves. The same applies in relation to love, sexuality, friendship and so on (see, e.g., Bauman 2003).[1]

It is the contention of this chapter that one of our most principal emotions, or what has been referred to as a 'foundational human emotion' (Brinkmann 2018) – namely, grief – is also increasingly permeated by the central tenants of individualization. As we have written elsewhere, we perceive grief as 'an emotion of absence'. That is, grief refers to the human emotion generated by the involuntary loss through death of another human being who is perceived to be of significant importance by the grieving person in question (Petersen and Jacobsen 2018:194). In contemporary society, these emotions are predominantly understood as 'individual' emotions that manifest themselves *inside* those who grieve. In that respect, grief has become – and is increasingly becoming – an individual undertaking and even a privatized pathology that we are individually responsible for and hence individually have to cope with according to specific societal standards and norms. This understanding of grief not only influences lay perceptions and personal manoeuvrings of grief but also resonates well with contemporary research into the phenomenon we call grief and with institutional practices. As we will show in this chapter, this development is partly due to an intensified psychologization and psychitrization of grief that has taken place during the last few decades, meaning that even the more obvious social dimensions of grief seem to become more and more marginalized. This causes, we argue, some serious problems. These problems have been supported, we argue, by the emergence of the diagnosis of 'prolonged grief disorder' that occurs in the diagnostic manual ICD-11 from 2018. In the wake of addressing grief in a diagnostic language – and hence understanding the suffering of grief within the realm of medicine – the individualized perspective of grief is not only supported, but risks of overdiagnosis, pharmacuticalization and overtreatment are also immediate. Thus, we will start this chapter by addressing the increasing psychological and psychiatric colonization of grief, including the coming diagnosis of grief. In the second section, we shall focus on some of the most apparent consequences of this development. In the third section, we will argue in favour of a revitalization of some of the most significant social dimensions and contexts of grief that are – we will show – so important. We conclude this chapter by formulating new pathways and trajectories that we believe research into grief should take.

The psychological and psychiatric colonization of grief

Let us start by making one thing clear: there is not one rather but a lot of answers to the question what grief is or even to what it has been. Historically speaking, the phenomenon of grief, as Peter N. Stearns (2007) has pointed out,[2] is extremely dynamic and interwoven with historically changing socio-structural contexts and societal fluctuations, as well as economic, cultural and normative transformations, and it is interpreted, experienced and enacted within a plethora of religious frameworks and rituals. When it comes to academic research into grief, we often find – even within the same disciplines – discrepancies in how grief should be understood and interpreted. Hence, a uniform definition of grief is a difficult task as is also the charting of its many different faces (Jacobsen and Petersen 2018). This is by no means odd or undesirable. Quite the contrary, we would argue. Academic vigour and 'difference of opinion' is always called for and grief need not be one-dimensionally categorized. In fact, particularly when it comes to the phenomenon of grief, English author C. S. Lewis reminds us all that perhaps we do not need a fleshed-out map but rather an unpredictable narrative when it comes to understanding it. As he poetically wrote:

> Sorrow, however, turns out to be not a state but a process. It needs not a map but a history, and if I don't stop writing that history at some quite arbitrary point, there's no reason why I should ever stop. There is something new to be chronicled every day. Grief is like a long valley, a winding valley where any bend may reveal a totally new landscape.

> (Lewis 1961/1988:50)

However, the logic of the map – to stay within the realm of this metaphor – has colonized the understanding of grief. This map, as we will show, is in modern society largely constructed by relying on psychological and psychiatric theories and clinical insights.

Our usage of the notion of 'colonization' is far from coincidental. We are inspired by Jürgen Habermas, who in his seminal work, *The Theory of Communicative Action*, shows how the lifeworld has been colonized by the logics and rationalities of what he refers to as the system (Habermas 1987). According to Habermas, the lifeworld is to be perceived as the 'background' environment of practices, competences and attitudes representable in terms of people's cognitive horizons. Habermas grounds his social theory in communication and thus focuses on the lifeworld as consisting of socially and culturally sedimented linguistic meanings. The lifeworld is, shortly speaking then, the everyday lives of informal (linguistic) interactions, culturally grounded understandings and mutual accommodations. The system, on the other hand, strictly refers to mutual patterns of strategic action that only serve the interests of institutions and organizations. The main characteristics of strategic actions are, crudely speaking, that they are essentially driven by the means of money and power. The thesis Habermas defends is that the rationality of the system – under the auspice of modern society and late capitalism – forces itself upon the lifeworld, thereby colonizing it. He writes:

> When stripped of their ideological veils, the imperatives of autonomous subsystems make their way into the lifeworld from the outside – like colonial

masters coming into a tribal society – and force a process of assimilation upon it. The diffused perspectives of the local culture cannot be sufficiently coordinated to permit the play of the metropolis and the world market to be grasped from the periphery.

(Habermas 1987:355)

According to Habermas, colonization is largely the same as assimilation. The social logics of the lifeworld are being replaced or pushed aside by those of the system, whereby the lifeworld fully attunes its operational (linguistic, social, cultural, etc.) modus vivendi to that of the system. Now, how can we apply this concept in relation to grief? Well, by showing how the phenomenon of grief has increasingly been colonized – in various tempos – by psychological and psychiatric understandings, we illustrate how other perspectives have lost ground. We are not claiming, however, that we are witnessing a wholesale collapse of other perspectives of grief, but rather that a significant downplaying of these has taken place. This is a development that, as we will show later, has been amplified by the emergence of the diagnosis of grief and the focus on treatment that follows in its wake.

In order to address this process of colonization in a proper manner, we have to divide the following section into two parts. While the first part begins with Sigmund Freud – and thus the psychologization of grief – the second dives into the psychiatrization of the phenomenon in question.

The colonization of grief

It all begins with Freud

Sigmund Freud's groundbreaking essay 'Mourning and Melancholia' (1957) (originally published in 1917) is rightly considered as the first rigorous academic journey into the phenomenon of grief (Archer 1999) and the 'first to introduce the concept of grief into the psychological lexicon' (Granek 2010:49). That is not to say, of course, that prior to Freud, grief was not religiously, anthropologically or philosophically reflected upon (Walter 1999). But Freud's systematic effort to separate mourning from melancholia, the coining of concepts such as 'grief work' and his understanding that grief should not be considered as a pathological condition in need of medical treatment, is to be seen as (one of) the most important foundation upon which academic research into grief rests. Freud, so to speak, set a course for the academic study of grief – a course paved with psychological and psychoanalytical concepts – that is to be perceived as 'a watershed in the history of the conceptualization of grief within the discipline and was crucial to the development of grief as a *psychological kind*' (Granek 2010:52). According to Leeat Granek, Freud not only secured a place for grief in the psychological domain, he also established the foundation for identifying grief as a psychological entity as such.

Although Freud's conceptualization of grief was quickly scrutinized by other psychologists, Granek persuasively argues that the overall perspective of grief as a strictly psychological phenomenon was never really in jeopardy. In fact, its psychological status was only strengthened (Granek 2010:53). The reason why that is the case can be explained in the following manner: as Freud's understanding of grief was the exemplary point of departure, other researchers had to address their critique against his original conceptualization, the primary one being 'grief work'. By 'grief work' Freud expresses his conviction that the grieving person is able to (and ought to) work with, and eventually work herself out of, her grief. Ultimately, the griever should distance herself from her grief, hereby liberating herself from the person she has lost. This is not, and Freud is very clear about this, something one can do instantly. It is a process (Freud 1917/1957:243). The first part of the process is to obey the 'command of reality' – that is, convince oneself that the person lost *really* is dead. The next part is to severing the ties – that is, breaking the bonds – with the deceased. Only by doing so, Freud emphasizes, one is able to emancipate oneself from the grief and thus enable an unrestrained connection with oneself and the social world again. Freud formulates this in the following manner:

> Why this compromise by which the command of reality is carried out piece-meal should be so extraordinarily painful is not at all easy to explain in terms of economics. It is remarkable that this painful unpleasure is taken as a matter of course by us. The fact is, however, that when the work of mourning is completed the ego becomes free and uninhibited again.
>
> (Freud 1917/1957:244)

Now, Freud knew that this emancipation is perhaps never fully accomplished. Although the griever should extricate time and resources to other spheres of life than those associated with the deceased, Freud is painfully aware of the fact that this is a slow and strenuous endeavour that might never come to a full stop (Granek 2010:52).

Freud's many heirs, epigones and successors, explicitly as well as implicitly, incorporated the central premise of the grief work hypothesis – namely, that working with grief is an individual venture that only the grieving individual can embark upon. Amongst some of the most important and influential scholars who followed in the footsteps of Freud – but also diverged significantly from his approach – we find Elisabeth Kübler-Ross (1969). In her five-stage model of grief, the individual component of grief is clearly emphasized. Kübler-Ross stipulates (1) denial and isolation, (2) anger, (3) bargaining, (4) depression and (5) acceptance as the distinct phases grievers have to deal with in order to emotionally manage loss and move on in their personal lives. The same overall logic applies to Collin Murray Parkes' (1972/2001) theory of grieving. In a similar vein to the attachment theory of John Bowlby (1973), Parkes identified four particular phases of bereavement that people go through. These are: (1) shock or numbness, (2) yearning and pining, (3) disorganization and despair and (4) recovery. According to Parkes, grief is best understood as a process of transition of the bereaved individual – a transition that is permeated by a burdensome workload that the grieving individual has to accept in order to steer his/her way through the phases and finally reach the final destination – namely, recovery. Although William Worden's (1991) perspective on grief differs from the others – in terms of vocabulary and by formulating specific tasks people more actively have to work through instead of phases they have to go through – he still perceived these as individual tasks. More specifically, Worden suggested, there are four tasks one should accomplish in order to complete the process of grieving and hence reestablish the lost equilibrium. These are: (1) accept the reality of the loss, (2) work through the pain of grief, (3) adjust to the environment in which the deceased is missing and (4) find an enduring connection with the deceased while embarking on a new life. According to Worden, these phases need not to be approached in a linear fashion[3] and some grievers should even return to the same task many times. For that same reason, Worden acknowledged the fact that it is extremely difficult to settle on a specific timeline for the completion of the different tasks. Grief takes time, so to speak. Finally, Margaret S. Stroebe and Henk Shut's (1999) 'dual process model' of coping with bereavement is worth mentioning. As opposed to the grief work thesis – or to Worden's task-oriented theory for that matter – they focus on two particular stressors (loss and restoration oriented) and the oscillation between them in coping with grief (Stroebe and Shut 1999:197). Thus, they do not concentrate on the emotional management of loss but rather on the process of successfully coping with grief and how that sometimes entails avoiding some of the difficult aspects of grief. Avoidance is not, they argue, negative as such but can actually be seen as part of an extended adaptive coping strategy. Excessive avoidance, however, can be perceived as maladaptive coping and hence detrimental to a positive outcome. Moreover, their model 'emphasizes the equally strenuous tasks of attending to life changes brought about by bereavement, doing new things, managing new roles and identities etc.' (Kofod 2017:34), something which the previously mentioned perspectives did not deal with. Stroebe and Shut make clear that while adaptive coping is necessary in order to achieve restoration – what they refer to as healthy or functional grief – maladaptive coping will lead to the opposite: dysfunctional/ unhealthy grief.

It is evident that these mentioned perspectives and theories have come a long way since Freud. They have challenged some of his central doctrines and clinically shown that some of his pivotal ideas needed correction. Indeed, their perspectives have developed alternatives to the shortcomings of Freud's theory but also to each other. It is equally evident that these perspectives have not moved beyond an individualized focus on grief. The point we wish to establish is that these perspectives pay attention to, and thereby support, an individualized perspective on grief that fits nicely within the confines of an individualized society. That is, to use the vocabulary we presented in the introduction, they – as an overarching premise – perceive grief as a hindrance to realising one's personal autonomy, which is why the final acceptance, recovery, altering roles and identities and so on entails the reorientation of ones possibilities of realising autonomy. Per definition, at least under the auspice of these understandings, this is an individual endeavour, a personal achievement or, in Bauman's words, a *task* to be performed.

What we furthermore want to direct attention to is the fact that theories of grief, within the recent decades, have maintained their individualized foci but altered the grounds on which they do it. The gist of the matter is not that the aforementioned perspectives on grief phases, tasks or processes have withered away and disappeared into oblivion. This is certainly not the case. Both researchers and clinicians working within the field of grief – but also laypeople – are often confronted with them and their specific modelling of grief. Our contention is rather that we have been witnessing a transformation of perspectives. This transformation is not to be understood as a clear-cut paradigmatic shift. In fact, it has been argued that all of the mentioned understandings have 'shaped and informed the recent suggestions to conceptualize grief as a mental disorder' (Kofod 2017:36) and hereby, albeit indirectly and involuntarily, contributed to paving the way for the psychiatric colonization of grief.

The contemporary dominance of psychiatry

Sigmund Freud never made a direct distinction between normal and pathological grief. That is not to say, however, that he thought grief was a normal state to be in. In his account, grief departed greatly form normal undertakings of life as such. But, and this is pivotal, it never occurred to him 'to regard it as a pathological condition and refer it to medical treatment' (Freud 1917/1957:252). Hence, no distinction between normal and pathological grief is needed. However, as historian of psychiatry Edward Shorter has stated, Freud is to be considered as a hiatus in the overall history of psychiatry (Shorter 1997:145). This does not entail, though, that Freud left no mark in psychiatric thinking. He did indeed. It is to say that his psychoanalytical approach within the realm of psychiatry has been replaced by a biomedical understanding. By entitling one of the chapters in his history of psychiatry 'From Freud to Prozac' (Shorter 1997:288), Shorter addresses this development in a clear-cut manner. Perhaps the same is the case when it comes to grief? The complete disregard of Freud's perspective, and the increased focus on the pathological dimensions of grief, has led to a situation in which the victorious implementation of a specific form of psychiatric rationality is taking place.

It is obviously the case that this development did not happen overnight. Without claiming that it took its point of departure in 1961, when George L. Engel asked the famous question, 'Is grief a Disease?' (Engel 1961), it is nonetheless a good place to start. What Engel did in this text was to question the assumption that grief was a normal endeavour when mourning the death of a loved one. Could it be the case, Engel asked, that grief sometimes is to be perceived as a disease? His answer to that question was yes. Some grief reactions were indeed to be perceived as causing illness and hence, under certain circumstances, grief was to be perceived as a disease. Engel's stance has been interpreted as if he stated that grief per se is a disorder and that it hence should be perceived as such (see Wilkinson 2000). In fact, Stephen Wilkinson, whom we are referring to here, uses Engel as a stepping-stone to claim that all grief (even normal grief) is to be understood as a mental disorder (Wilkinson 2000:289). This is, of course, a rather radical claim and something that is not commonplace in grief research. Perhaps Wilkinson is stretching his argument a bit too wide? Or, perhaps he misinterprets Engel in order to substantiate his own argument. Margaret S. Stroebe seems to think so. As she has shown, Engel's text cannot be used for the purpose of pathologising all grief. As she writes, Engel rather

> took grief as an illustrative example to explore the very nature of the concept of disease, his intention was to encourage debate about the categorization of disease, to urge readers to reflect on what constitutes a disease. Engels did not claim that grief is a disease.
>
> (Stroebe 2015:277)

What is of interest here, however, is really not whether specific interpretations of Engel do him justice or not. It is rather the fact that his article paved a significant part of the way in framing normal grief as opposed to grief that could (should?) be perceived as a disease and hence as something pathological. The premise of this discussion differentiates itself from the ones taken by the psychological theories we referred to above by ingraining pathological grief firmly within the realm of psychiatric thinking, thereby also opening the doors wide open for the biomedical approach to disease. As noted by Granek in her convincing article about the increasing psychiatrization (and pathologization) of grief, this development materialized itself in the late 1980s – something which has continued to influence a great deal (if not the majority) of grief research ever since. As she writes:

> By this point, grief theory had become decontextualized from experience and had been psychologized completely. The focus was entirely on symptoms, and the ability to measure, diagnose, and manage grief. . . . By the early 1990s, the focus on grief was almost entirely on its dysfunctional nature.
>
> (Granek 2010:64)

Obviously, the intense focus on complicated grief (e.g., Shear et al., 2011), complicated grief disorder (e.g., Horowitz 2005) and disordered grief (e.g., Prigerson and Maciejewski 2017) that has settled in grief research over the last couple of decades supports Granek's overall claim. Particularly, the implementation of the grief diagnosis 'Prolonged Grief Disorder' in the ICD-11 is a manifestation of the power of psychiatry when it comes to understanding grief as a (potential) pathological disorder. By implementing grief in this diagnostic manual, there is no doubt about the fact that this perspective on grief got its most vital stamp of approval. The description of 'Prolonged Grief Disorder' in the ICD-11 manual is as follows:

> Prolonged grief disorder is a disturbance in which, following the death of a partner, parent, child, or other person close to the bereaved, there is persistent and pervasive grief response characterized by longing for the deceased or persistent preoccupation with the deceased accompanied by intense emotional

pain (e.g. sadness, guilt, anger, denial, blame, difficulty accepting the death, feeling one has lost a part of one's self, an inability to experience positive mood, emotional numbness, difficulty in engaging with social or other activities). The grief response has persisted for an atypically long period of time following the loss (more than 6 months at a minimum) and clearly exceeds expected social, cultural or religious norms for the individual's culture and context. Grief reactions that have persisted for longer periods that are within a normative period of grieving given the person's cultural and religious context are viewed as normal bereavement responses and are not assigned a diagnosis. The disturbance causes significant impairment in personal, family, social, educational, occupational or other important areas of functioning.

(ICD-11, 2018)

It is beyond the scope of this chapter to deal more specifically with the entire content of the diagnosis – all its symptoms, the specific criteria and so on – but we will shortly dwell on the most important arguments of why the diagnosis is perceived to be justifiable. One of the recurring arguments in favour of the diagnosis is that it is the only valid way of distinguishing pathological grief from PTSD, anxiety and depression (e.g., Shear et al. 2011). The main point in this argument is that too many people for too long have received a diagnosis of PTSD, anxiety disorder or especially depression when they in fact were suffering from complicated grief. The mix up of these types of suffering is understandable. The various symptoms of these diseases are quite similar. The treatment, on the contrary, is said to be very different. Lately, a great deal of effort has been put into establishing psychological treatment, where Katherine M. Shear's program, Complicated Grief Treatment – which is scaffolded around Bowlby's (1973) attachment theory, which we referred to earlier – is amongst the most well-known and recognized (Shear 2010). As the name indicates, this treatment program is concerned with targeting 'grief-specific' treatment to those who suffer in a debilitating way from their loss. The program does not cover other mental disorders and neither should it. The focus is solely on grief because, as the argument goes, the 'suffering of bereaved people often confuses clinicians' (Shear 2010:10). This confusion is first and foremost detrimental to the bereaved because it hinders the right treatment of their anguish, often by placing them in the same category as those who are depressed. Second, as Shear states, it is inhumane not to treat people who suffer from their loss (Shear 2010:10), when we in fact have the right tools to do so. So, offering the right and effective kind of treatment is not only the right thing to do practically speaking, it is also the only moral right thing to do. In that respect, Shear's treatment program reminds us of a very important thing that describes the realm of psychiatry – namely, that it is 'a unique medical domain that, unlike other branches of medicine, is necessarily confronted with moral issues. Indeed, without confronting these issues it would never be able to treat those forms of suffering that are themselves moral' (Ehrenberg 1998/2010:23). Suffering from grief is indeed a moral concern as such. Another thing is the severity of the suffering. In order to objectify the scale of the suffering, one relies on the successful endeavour of clearly differentiating between 'normal grief' and 'pathological grief'. In fact, the possibility of this demarcation is another argument in favour of the diagnosis.

Several grief researchers – and practitioners for that matter – conceive the diagnosis as the most concise sharpening tool; it enables the carving out of this distinction (e.g., Prigerson et al. 2009). But what qualifies as 'normal grief' then? In fact, there is no easy way to describe what normal grief consists of because it varies immensely. It is dependent on a vast array of personal, theoretical, cultural and societal dimensions. Some grief researchers, in order to reduce the complexities of normal grief, use vignettes. One of those who does so is Shear, who, together with quite a few colleagues, has used this method to describe what 'normal grief' is. In such a vignette they write a story about Patricia, who lost her husband, Paul, at the age of 50. At the beginning, Patricia was devastated, felt an intense yearning and as if her mind was in a fog that she could not control. Her emotions were running wild; she cried a lot and felt unable to function in her life. But, after seeing a grief counsellor, things started to get better. The counsellor helped, as they explain, Patricia to understand

> that her symptoms were normal. . . . After a few months, Patricia noticed that there were hours, then days, were the fog lifted. She started to laugh again. She accepted an invitation to go out with friends even though she did not really want to, and she had a good time. A vision of her life without Paul began to emerge and the intensity of yearning for him subsided.
>
> (Shear et al. 2011:113)

Three years after the death of her husband, so the vignette ends, Patricia meets another man whom she ends up marrying a couple of years later. Paul is still on her mind, but she has managed to continue her life in a fruitful manner without him.

Now, prior to this vignette Shear and her coauthors have thoroughly described the research and evidence that in their perspective legitimizes a grief diagnosis, and hence the drawing of a distinction between 'normal grief' and 'pathological grief'. Thus, the vignette is a testimony to all that which is not considered pathological grief and thereby does not have the relevant criteria of a disorder. As we saw in the description of prolonged grief disorder, Patricia's story accounts for the exact opposite of the symptoms and the severity of the grief eligible to the label of pathological. This line of research, however, has been scrutinized. Jerome Wakefield, one of the foremost critiques of the label of pathological grief, and hence of implementing prolonged grief disorder in the ICD-11, states very clearly that 'several arguments presented to support the claim that intense grief lasting 6–12 months is more pathological, rather than a severe normal variant' (Wakefield 2013:111) are conceptually flawed and do not hold water in respect to the testing of the research evidence. He thus states that the diagnostic proposals 'are thus scientifically unwarranted' (Wakefield 2013:111). In his perspective, the scientific requirements for the diagnosis of grief are simply not satisfactorily met and thus, no clear-cut distinction between normal and pathological grief can be instated. But it has been, as we have already mentioned above, and this leads us to the third argument in favour of the diagnosis – namely, what one might call the 'argument-by-numbers'.

When taking the diagnostic criteria into consideration, it is often estimated that somewhere between 7% and 10% of grievers are in fact suffering from complicated grief or prolonged grief disorder (Kersting et al., 2011; Lundorff et al., 2017). Some researchers even suggest that as many as 12% of all bereaved individuals meet the criteria of suffering from prolonged grief disorder (Maciejewski and Prigerson 2017). Once a part of this statistic, it goes without saying that treatment is needed. And then we return to the moral issue of psychiatric disorders again: it would be morally wrong not to categorize them rightfully and thereby enable them to be offered the right kind of treatment, the arguments go. By the power of the knowledge that as many as up to 10% of grievers suffer – and hence have the symptoms categorizing the diagnosis – follows a moral obligation to react.

It is, to a large degree, by the force of the arguments presented here that we have witnessed the increasing psychiatrization of grief. For us, it is not a question of the validity of these arguments in themselves – albeit they have been questioned and scrutinized – but it is more the significant impact of this development that is of interest. In that respect we find it obvious that the psychiatrization of grief, in which the diagnosis can be called the crown jewel of the development, has strengthened the individualization of grief. By making grief into a diagnostic and potentially pathological category, psychiatry has not only expanded its territory and hence its area of expertise, a significant narrowing of the phenomenon of grief has simultaneously taken place. That is, a diagnosed grief can only be located inside the head (and to a certain extent the body) of the grieving person. It is he/she who is being labelled mentally ill when receiving the diagnosis. It is hence also he/she who has to take care of the pathological grief, which is where the specific grief treatment comes into the picture. It is his/her functionality that is at stake when diagnosed. All the arrows of grief thereby point in the direction of the person in grief, thereby potentially downplaying the multitude of social dimensions of grief and largely neglecting the negative aspects of this development.

Some consequences of this development

What we have shown in the previous sections of this chapter is but the latest colonization of grief that the profession of psychiatry has brought about. Grief now belongs to a long list of psychiatric phenomena that have become so proliferated in contemporary society – more and more people are being diagnosed with mental disorders – that some commentators have even begun to speak of a necessary softening of the way in which we understand the distinction between normal and pathological. In his latest book, *Our Psychiatric Future*, British sociologist Nicholas Rose plays with words in the title. The psychiatric future is not in the future – the future is already here. One way of addressing this fact is by stating that 'when it comes to the scope of psychiatry today, can we still hold the idea that in some fundamental way, to be diagnosed with a mental disorder is to be classified "pathological"?' (Rose 2018:8). His answer to this question is no, and that this labelling is way too pejorative when it comes to diagnoses of depression anxiety, panic disorders and the like. So many people suffer from these diseases that it has become normal to do so, the argument goes. His idea is thus that we should alter the meaning of normality (and pathological) and think of it as a performative term that is best understood in its uses and in relation to its consequences. If we pause for a minute and begin to think of the diagnosis of grief in this manner, one might say that grief belongs to the same group of sufferings that Rose mentions and hence cannot be considered pathological, especially not if as many as up to 10% of grievers have sufficient symptoms to meet the diagnostic criteria. In this respect, those diagnosed with prolonged grief disorder should not be perceived as pathological.

Although Rose's argumentation is somewhat convincing – and potentially very influential – it nevertheless leaves a great deal of confusion when it comes to grief. First of all, one of the main intentions of the diagnosis is – as we have mentioned – precisely to distinguish between normal and pathological grief in a very substantive way. The protagonists of the diagnosis make this claim again and again: normal grief is not in need of treatment; pathological grief is. Hence, a clear-cut distinction is needed. But what if that distinction is blurred by stating that it is normal to suffer from pathological grief? What is normal grief then? Is normal grief then also pathological because the 'condition' contains distress, suffering, impairment, pain and so on, and hence meets all the necessary criteria of a disorder, as Wilkinson seem to suggest (Wilkinson 2000)? A relativization of normal grief, which seems to be the logical consequence of Rose's argumentation, causes problems.

The same applies to the 'medicalization', to use Peter Conrad's (2007) influential term, of the phenomenon in question. Conrad's analysis of the overall medicalization of society, in which he clearly stipulates how normal human distress, suffering and personal troubles are increasingly being transformed into medicalized objects and mental disorders, is obviously applicable when it comes to grief. And so it has been by Julia Bandini (2015). In her analysis, three potential consequences of the medicalization of grief stand out. First, she directs attention to the potential for overdiagnosis and overtreatment. In some respects, one could make the bold claim that the mere fact that the diagnosis is being introduced will lead to overdiagnosis. A slightly less bold statement is that overdiagnosis will occur because the definition of grief as a disease has been broadened so much that people who just meet the criteria will be given the diagnosis and the offered treatment. Of course, this could potentially open an avenue of overtreatment. Second, Bandini addresses the potential for expanded market shares for pharmaceutical companies. Whereas Bandini is cautious in her conclusions, Granek is more straightforward in her analysis of the medicalization of grief and the possibilities of pharmaceutical intervention. According to her, there is no doubt about the fact that the usage of antidepressant medication in the treatment of complicated grief is widespread already and that the future will witness even more medicinal treatment (Granek

2016:117). This reminds us of John Abraham's (2010) analysis, in which he discusses the possibilities of a regular pharmaceuticalization of society. This entails, according to him, a situation in which an expansion of treatment with pharmaceuticals denotes how society perceives that as the normal way of treating almost any kind of human suffering. Following the line of this argument: Why not a specific pill for grief? Third, Bandini mentions a loss of traditional and cultural methods of adapting to the loss of a loved one (Bandini 2015:351). Perhaps Nancy Berns' (2011) analysis is of help here. The contemporary focus on achieving closure (which of course is a myth) as a way to end the painfulness of grief bypasses the often lengthy and 'difficult' methods of adopting to the loss that are offered by tradition and community or that are ingrained in longstanding cultural practices. Or, we might turn our attention to Danish psychologist Svend Brinkmann, who has argued that this development is not only the case in relation to the suffering of grief. It is also shown in the languages we use to articulate issues of human suffering in general. In his view, alternative understandings of human suffering 'have been somewhat depreciated by the status of the diagnostic language' (Brinkmann 2016:52). Other languages – social, existential, political and so on – have not evaporated from our vocabulary. They have, however, less status today than the diagnostic ditto when it comes to articulating – and thus to organising – our suffering. Would it be that difficult to imagine that the same thing will happen when it comes to grief (for more on this, see Petersen and Jacobsen 2018)?

Addressing the social dimensions of grief in an individualized society

It should be rather obvious by now that the psychiatric colonization of grief has led to an increasing individualization of the phenomenon and to a serious of (potential) consequences that deeply influences the ways in which we handle grief in contemporary society. In that respect, the installing of the grief diagnosis signifies a landmark. This development is, at the same time, easily comprehended and odd. The former, because this development fits so nicely with the overall tendencies of individualization in contemporary society as such. The latter, because the social dimensions of grief are so obvious and important that any element of their neglect seems almost outrageous (see Vera 2003). After all, as Nina R. Jakoby so poignantly has stated, grief *is* a social emotion (Jakoby 2012). It is so, because our emotions of grief are socially shared, shaped (reshaped), distributed and sanctioned. Moreover, only one person seldom grieves the absence of a significant other. Most often, the reality and experience of loss are shared with others who also mourn the loss. As summarized by Liz Stanley and Sue Wise: 'People respond to dying and death, not as decorticated individualized nomads, but as members of networks of interpersonal relationships' (Stanley and Wise 2011:960). In this way, grief is indeed an interpersonal and relational phenomenon existing between the dead and the bereaved as well as among the bereaved. Besides this, grief is deeply interwoven in historically changing socio-structural contexts, rules and norms and (also) takes place – and changes form, content and

218 Michael Hviid Jacobsen and Anders Petersen

structure – in actual face-to-face interactions with other people in everyday life situations (Jacobsen and Petersen 2018).

Of course, it is beyond the scope of this chapter to deal exhaustively with all the many different social dimensions of grief that are in danger of being trivialized if we continue to follow this individualized path. We will, thus, here merely pick out three aspects in order to support and highlight our argumentation. The first concerns the component of identity-formation. Phenomenologist Thomas Fuchs, in a recent article, stated the following:

> This expansion and mutual overlaps of selves may be regarded as the most essential presupposition of grief. For it means that the other is present for me both *as other*, as the real person, and as the 'other-of-myself', as part of my self experience. This renders me totally vulnerable, for in loosing the other, I loose 'half of my self', as it were – the potentialities of experience and self-realization that were bound to the other, and the part of my self and identity that were represented by him.
>
> (Fuchs 2017:50)

We are, also in grief, interconnected with others. When a significant person in our lives dies, this alters our sensation of self and hence the continuation of our identity-formation. Or, as Fuchs writes – echoing George Herbert Mead's (1934) social-psychological truism – parts of our identity are necessarily bound to and dependent on (the recognition of) the significant others. In grief, then, one not only mourns the other as a specific entity – father, friend, husband and so on; one also grieves the loss of the part of the other that was intrinsically connected to one's own further realization in life. In grief, one is thus afflicted by the absence here and now and the absence of some parts of one's future. That goes, of course, for others as well. The loss of future potentialities that were connected with the deceased is a loss most commonly felt by more than just one individual person. In that sense, the deceased has an impact on a wide variety of identities and self-realizations. On a more fundamental level, this implies that identity-formation hardly can be reduced to an individualized endeavour. We cannot just make ourselves up as we wish. As human beings we are entangled in a web of connections with others that influences and in significant ways steers our formation of identity. Not controlling it, but having important impacts on it. In grief, this becomes blatantly obvious.

The second social dimension we wish to direct the attention to is the social stratification of grief. As German-British sociologist Norbert Elias stated many years ago, death is a problem of the living (Elias 1983/2001). Elias is utterly correct, but he also knew that the dead came in many guises. That is, while living, the dead held various social positions that in many ways were transgressed into the way in which people died and into how people were grieved afterwards. All lives matter, but some lives matter more and are more grieveable one could say. How does that show? Well, as many have witnessed when visiting graveyards across the globe, the political, social and economic elite as well as what we nowadays call 'celebrities' have been honoured with more pompous tombstones, mausoleums and luxurious gravesites than the 'common man'. It is only rarely that those at the lower end of the social scale – those with less social status and power – have been offered the same gesture, both due to economic circumstances and because of the fact that their lives were not perceived to be as valuable to the common public or society as such. Hence, in the greater scheme of things, some lives have historically been deemed – in quite an obvious way – to be more grieveable than others. In contemporary society this element is visible in numerous ways. Just think about the millions of immigrants, who, in a desperate attempt to seek living conditions that are worthy of human beings, drown while crossing the Mediterranean in dilapidated boats. Or what about the millions of people on the African continent who die each year from AIDS or other diseases that are in fact treatable? The lack of public grief or mourning over these millions of people is more than thought-provoking, especially when contemplating who else is mourned in the public sphere. In order to describe what it is one grieves about and who is worthy of grief, American philosopher and sociologist Judith Butler (2016) has coined the term 'grievability'. In her account of the phenomenon, what becomes so obvious is the fact that it is the societally differentiated valuation of life that decides what we mourn about and who is worthy of grieving. Some lives are simply so quickly forgotten – or dumped on the historic scrapheap to rot – that there is no incitement to mourn them. Here, however, we need not forget that the social stratification of whom we mourn not only relates to economy and status but also to gender, geography, cause of death, etc., in such a way that we, as a society, almost automatically mourn some much more than others (see also Morse 2018).

As the social stratification of grief is related to *whom* we mourn, it is also linked to *how* we grieve. Although this aspect has not captured a lot of attention within grief research (Allen 2007), it nevertheless deserves more academic interest. Why? Because although we (at least in the Western hemisphere) have witnessed the dismantling of many status hierarchies, the existence of different social classes is still evident and different classes tend to grieve differently. British historian Julie-Marie Strange (2002, 2005) has continuously documented how the care of the dead, the character of the tombstones (private vs. public graves), testaments and so on bear witness to a significant social stratification between the poor and those who were prosperous in the 18th century. What is more, the same differentiation can be made in relation to grief. Whereas the upper classes had the time, social space and economy to mourn their dead, the poor had to develop a much more pragmatic culture of grief that balanced their need to commemorate the deceased and take care of the family's economy at the same time. The simple equation is: if grief keeps you away from work for too long, you don't get food on the table (see also Vincent 1980). The relevant question to ask is whether this is significantly different in contemporary society, not least if we look at it on a global scale.

The third and final social dimension we wish to address here is the stigmatization of grief. Where the social stratification of grief is mainly concerned with status and economy, the stigmatization of grief concerns the acceptability, appropriateness and normative legitimacy of grieving the death of a particular person or even the question of whom is 'allowed' to grieve. The concept of 'stigmatized grief' is indebted to Canadian sociologist Erving Goffman's work on stigma (Goffman 1963). In his work, the concept revolves around how certain identities or actions result in discrediting identities or stigmatization of actions due to their deviance from prevailing societal norms. More specifically, Goffman outlined three types of stigma that were related to behaviour, looks/appearance or affiliation with specific societal groups. It is American gerontologist Kenneth J. Doka (1989) who – by coining the term 'disenfranchised grief' – has most poignantly stipulated the connection between stigma and grief. More specifically Doka defines the concept in the following manner:

> The concept of disenfranchised grief recognizes that societies have sets of norms – in effect 'grieving rules' – that attempt to specify who, when, where, how, how long, and for whom people should grieve. These grieving rules may be codified as personal policies. . . . Such policies reflect the fact that each society defines who has a legitimate right to grieve, and these rights correspond to relationships, primarily familial, that are socially recognised and sanctioned.
>
> (Doka 1999:37)

An important empirical basis, that Doka based his concept of 'disenfranchised grief' on, was the many AIDS-related deaths in the United States in the 1980s. These were, to a large extent, surrounded by widespread cultural homophobia, a fear of getting HIV/AIDS and thus a considerable stigma that was often specifically targeted at homosexuals – something that has been portrayed by Matthew McConaughey in the 2013 movie by Jean-Marc Vallée, *Dallas Buyers Club*. In the movie, McConaughey's real-life character, Ron Woodroof, is not only heavily stigmatized for getting AIDS by his friends and relatives (who think it is a 'gay disease'), but also for helping – and mourning – the people who are dying from AIDS. The legitimacy of mourning the people who by the majority of the population were to blame for their own misfortune due to their 'deviance' was put into question, scrutinized, socially sanctioned and even violently opposed. The grief of 'such' persons is, in itself, deviant and must therefore be combatted. Where do we find disenfranchised grief in contemporary society? Well, there are plenty of examples. One could be the following from our own local community: in 2006, an 18-year-old girl who attended high school in the Northern part of Denmark was brutally killed by her ex-boyfriend at a school dance. Just after the murder, the 23-year-old young man committed suicide. In the Danish media coverage of the events, the tragic loss of the 18-year-old girl was publicly and spontaneously mourned. The grief of her family members was displayed. But there was no mentioning of the grief that affected the parents, friends and relatives of the 23-year-old man. Could this be because the grieving of such a murderer was perceived to be illegitimate? Was it inappropriate to mourn the loss of a brutal killer? Without denigrating the emotional distress of the family of the girl who was killed, one can only speculate about how it must have felt for those who mourned this young man!

Now, one might question whether grief is either disenfranchised or enfranchised, and also problematize that grief 'works' in these binary codes. It nevertheless seems obvious that every society has certain specific 'grief hierarchies' that order which kinds of grief are more legitimate than others (Robson and Walter 2012–2013). These hierarchies are in no way static. They are attuned to the normative structure and development in society, and hence to political, social, cultural and economic currents that alter the overall texture of society.

Conclusion

In this chapter, we have introduced a line of thought that not only shows how grief has become increasingly colonized by psychological and psychiatric thinking, but also a line of thought that criticizes this development. Our aim has not been to go about this in any methodically stringent way, but rather to address some of the social dimensions of grief that are at risk of being trivialized – or be less in focus – in the wake of this development. The individualization of grief is, as we have intended to show, by no means independent of significant currents in contemporary society. That is, we are not able to understand the individualization of grief only by addressing the psychological or psychiatric vernaculars, perspectives and theories that have shaped grief historically. A considerable part of the analysis has to take the societal development into consideration that supports this development. The (continuous) adjustment to an individualized identification with grief is deeply embedded in prevailing norms of continuing individualization – and hence autonomous self-realization – as the overarching societal ideal. Perhaps then, we can highlight this – in a rather provocative manner – by stating that grief, in contemporary society, is best understood as an all-out assault on our happiness (Ariès 1974:94) because grief entails suffering that puts an end to the ongoing realization of one's personal autonomy. Suffering and happy self-realization do not go well hand-in-hand. Therefore, we need to eliminate the suffering as soon as possible by diagnosing and treating its source(s). In order to do that, we need a conceptualization – an ordering – of grief that matches this perspective. In that respect, the diagnosis of complicated or prolonged grief fits like a glove. However, one of our main reservations about the diagnosis is precisely that this ordering runs the risk of neglecting the more obvious social aspects of grief. Our contention is thus that a sociology of sorrow or grief should address these dimensions that we have touched upon here even more, but also that it needs to investigate the wide variety of crucial social dimensions of grief that we have not had the opportunity to focus on in this chapter: the social disciplining of grief, the socially supported and sanctioned scripts of grief, the social struggle for just the right to grieve – just to mention some areas that we believe are in need of thorough sociological investigation.

Notes

1 We are well aware of the fact that this is not the case across nations or continents. Our claims, broadly speaking, cover societies primarily within the Western hemisphere.
2 See, for example, chapters 1–4 in this volume.
3 The same is true with Elisabeth Kübler-Ross's model.

References

Abraham, John (2010): 'Pharmaceuticalization of Society in Context: Theoretical, Empirical and Health Dimensions'. *Sociology*, 44 (4):603–622.

Allen, Chris (2007): 'The Poverty of Death: Social Class, Urban Deprivation and the Criminological Consequences of the Sequestration of Death'. *Mortality*, 12 (1):79–93.

Archer, John (1999): *The Nature of Grief: The Evolution and Psychology Reactions to Loss.* London: Routledge.

Ariès, Philippe (1974): *Western Attitudes Toward Death from the Middle Ages to the Present.* Baltimore: Johns Hopkins University Press.

Bandini, Julia (2015): 'The Medicalization of Bereavement: (Ab)normal Grief in the DSM-5'. *Death Studies*, 39 (6):347–352.

Bauman, Zygmunt (2000): Liquid Modernity. Cambridge: Polity Press.

Bauman, Zygmunt (2001): *The Individualized Society.* Cambridge: Polity Press.

Bauman, Zygmunt (2003): *Liquid Love.* Cambridge: Polity Press.

Beck, Ulrich and Elisabeth Beck-Gernsheim (2002): *Individualisation.* London: Sage Publications.

Berns, Nancy (2011): *Closure: The Rush to End Grief and What It Costs Us.* Philadelphia: Temple University Press.

Bowlby, John (1973): *Attachment and Loss: Separation, Anxiety and Anger* (Volume II). London: Hogarth Press.

Brinkmann, Svend (2016): *Diagnostic Cultures: A Cultural Approach to the Pathologization of Modern Life.* London: Routledge.

Brinkmann, Svend (2018): 'The Grieving Animal: Grief as a Foundational Emotion'. *Theory & Psychology*, 2:193–207.

Butler, Judith (2016): *Frames of War: When is Life Grieveable?* London: Verso.

Conrad, Peter (2007): *The Medicalization of Society.* Baltimore: Johns Hopkins University Press.

Doka, Kenneth J. (1989): *Disenfranchised Grief: Recognizing Hidden Sorrow.* Lexington, MA: Lexington Books/D. C. Heath & Co.

Doka, Kenneth J. (1999): 'Disenfranchised Grief'. *Bereavement Care*, 18 (3):37–39.

Ehrenberg, Alain (1991): *Le Culte de la Performance.* Paris: Hachette-Pluriel.

Ehrenberg, Alain (1998/2010): *The Weariness of the Self.* Montreal: McGill-Queen's University Press.

Elias, Norbert (1983/2001): *The Loneliness of the Dying.* New York: Continuum.

Elisabeth, Kübler-Ross (1969): *On Death and Dying.* London: Routledge.

Engel, George L. (1961): "Is Grief a Disease?' – A Challenge for Medical Research'. *Psychosomatic Medicine*, 23 (1):18–22.

Freud, Sigmund (1917/1957): 'Mourning and Melancholia', in James Strachey (ed.): *The Standard Edition of the Complete Psychological Works of Sigmund Freud* (Volume XIV). London: Hogarth Press, pp. 237–258.

Fuchs, Thomas (2017): 'Presence in Absence: The Ambiguous Phenomenology of Grief'. *Phenomenology and the Cognitive Sciences*, 17:43–63.

Giddens, Anthony (1991): *Modernity and Self-Identity: Self and Society in the Late Modern Age.* Cambridge: Polity Press.

Goffman, Erving (1963): *Stigma: Notes on the Management of Spoiled Identity.* Chicago: Aldine.

Granek, Leeat (2010): 'Grief as Pathology: The Evolution of Grief Theory in Psychology from Freud to the Present'. *History of Psychology*, 13 (1):46–73.

Granek, Leeat (2016): 'Medicalizing Grief', in Darcy L. Harris and Tashel C. Bordere (eds.): *Handbook of Social Justice in Loss and Grief: Exploring Diversity, Equity and Inclusion.* London: Routledge, pp. 111–124.

Habermas, Jürgen (1987): *Theory of Communicative Action, Volume One: Reason and the Rationalization of Society.* Boston, MA.: Beacon Press.

Horowitz, Mardi (2005): 'Mediating on Complicated Grief as a Diagnosis'. *Omega*, 52 (1):87–89.

ICD-11 (2018): 'Prolonged Grief Disorder'. Available online at: https://icd.who.int/browse11/l-m/en#/http://id.who.int/icd/entity/1183832314.

Jacobsen, Michael Hviid and Anders Petersen (2018): 'Sorgens socialitet – en sociologisk kommentar til psykologiseringen og medikaliseringen af menneskelige følelser'. Psyke & Logos, 39 (1):55–73.

Jakoby, Nina R. (2012): 'Grief as a Social Emotion: Theoretical Perspectives'. *Death Studies*, 36 (8):679–711.

Kersting, Anette et al. (2011): 'Prevalence of Complicated Grief in a Representative Population-Based Sample'. *Journal of Affective Disorders*, 131:339–343.

Kofod, Ester Holte (2017): *Parental Grief After Infant Loss: Grief as a Normative Practice.* PhD thesis in Psychology. Aalborg: Aalborg University.

Lewis, C. S. (1961/1988): *A Grief Observed.* New York: Walker & Company.

Lundorff, Marie et al. (2017): 'Prevalence of Prolonged Grief Disorder in Adult Bereavement: A Systematic Review and Meta-Analysis'. *Journal of Affective Disorders*, 212:138–149.

Maciejewski, Paul K. and Holly G. Prigerson (2017): 'Prolonged, but not Complicated, Grief is a Mental Disorder'. *The British Journal of Psychiatry*, 211:1–2.

Mead, George Herbert (1934): *Mind, Self, and Society.* Chicago: University of Chicago Press.

Morse, Tal (2018): 'The Construction of Grievable Death: Toward an Analytical Framework for the Study of Mediatized Death'. *European Journal of Cultural Studies*, 21 (2):242–258.

Parkes, Collin Murray (1972/2001): *Bereavement: Studies of Grief in Adult Life* (3rd Edition). London: Routledge.

Petersen, Anders and Michael Hviid Jacobsen (2018): 'Grief – The Painfulness of Permanent Human Absence', in Michael Hviid Jacobsen (ed.): *Emotions, Everyday Life and Sociology.* London: Routledge. pp. 191–208.

Prigerson, Holly G. and Paul K. Maciejewski (2017): 'Rebuilding Consensus on Valid Criteria for Disordered Grief'. *JAMA Psychiatry*, 74 (5):435–436.

Prigerson, Holly G. et al. (2009): 'Prolonged Grief Disorder: Psychometric Validation for Criteria Proposed for DSM-V and ICD-11'. *PLoS Med*, 6 (8):1–12.

Robson, Patricia and Tony Walter (2012–2013): 'Hierarchies of Loss: A Critique of Disenfranchised Grief'. *Omega*, 66 (2):97–119.

Rose, Nicholas (2018): *The Future of Psychiatry.* Cambridge: Polity Press.

Shear, Katherine M. (2010): 'Complicated Grief Treatment: The Theory, Practice and Outcomes'. *Bereave Care*, 29 (3):10–14.

Shear, Katherine M. et al. (2011): 'Complicated Grief and Related Bereavement Issues for DSM-5'. *Depression and Anxiety*, 28:103–117.

Shorter, Edward (1997): *A History of Psychiatry: From the Era of the Asylum to the Age of Prozac.* New York: John Wiley and Sons.

Stanley, Liz and Sue Wise (2011): 'The Domestication of Death: The Sequestration Thesis and Domestic Figurations'. *Sociology*, 45 (6):947–962.

Stearns, Peter N. (2007): *Revolutions in Sorrow: The American Experience of Death in a Global Perspective*. Boulder, CO: Paradigm Publishers.

Strange, Julie-Marie (2002): 'She Cried Very Little: Death, Grief and Mourning in Working-Class Culture, c. 1880–1914'. *Social History*, 27 (2):143–161.

Strange, Julie-Marie (2005): *Death, Grief and Poverty in Britain, 1870–1914*. Cambridge: Cambridge University Press.

Stroebe, Margaret S. (2015): "Is Grief a Disease?' Why Engel Posed the Question'. *Omega*, 71 (3):272–279.

Stroebe, Margaret S. and Henk Schut (1999): 'The Dual Process Model of Coping with Bereavement: Rational and Description'. *Death Studies*, 23 (3):197–224.

Vera, María I. (2003): 'Social Dimensions of Grief', in Clifton D. Bryant (ed.): *Handbook of Death and Dying* (Volume 2). Thousand Oaks, CA: Sage Publications, p. 838–846.

Vincent, David (1980): 'Love and Death and the Nineteenth Century Working-Class'. *Social History*, 5 (2):223–247.

Wakefield, Jerome (2013): 'Is Complicated/Prolonged Grief a Disorder? – Why the Proposal to Add a Category of Complicated Grief Disorder to the DSM-5 is Conceptually and Empirically Unsound', in Margaret S. Stroebe, Henk Schut and Jan van den Bout (eds.): *Complicated Grief: Scientific Foundations for Health Care Professionals*. London: Routledge, pp. 99–114.

Walter, Tony (1999): *On Bereavement: The Culture of Grief*. Buckingham: Open University Press.

Wilkinson, Stephen (2000): 'Is 'Normal Grief' a Mental Disorder?'. *The Philosophical Quarterly*, 50:289–304.

Worden William J. (1991): *Grief Counseling and Grief Therapy: A Handbook for the Mental Health Practitioner* (2nd Edition). London: Routledge.

Index

Note: page numbers in *italic* indicate a figure on the corresponding page